THIS
TIME
FOR ME

THIS
TIME
FOR ME

A MEMOIR

ALEXANDRA
BILLINGS

WITH JOANNE GORDON

TOPPLE
BOOKS

Little
a

Published by TOPPLE Books/Little A, New York

www.apub.com

Amazon, the Amazon logo, TOPPLE Books, and Little A are trademarks of Amazon.
com, Inc., or its affiliates.

ISBN-13: 9781542029414 (hardcover)
ISBN-10: 1542029414 (hardcover)

ISBN-13: 9781542029407 (paperback)
ISBN-10: 1542029406 (paperback)

Cover design by Rex Bonomelli

Cover photo by Aaron Jay Young

Unless otherwise noted, all interior images are courtesy of the author.

Printed in the United States of America

First edition

This book is dedicated to the three women in my life:
Chrisanne,
Mimi,
and
God.

AUTHOR'S NOTE

This is a memoir—rich in the poetry of memory. Like all memory, it is truth seen through the lens of a very personal experience. Every event in this book happened. Facts are not the core of the work—truth and experience are.

Some names and identifying characteristics have been changed in the interest of protecting privacy.

A NOTE FROM TOPPLE BOOKS

What does it take to be a true trailblazer? Persistence. Creativity. And a sense of humor. Alexandra Billings' life and career are nothing short of astonishing. I know firsthand from our work together on *Transparent* how she has paved the way for Trans actors and created a safer world for young Trans people.

Born in 1962, Alexandra Billings started transitioning in 1980, before the word "Transgender" was commonly used. She forged an identity for herself in a time when she had no openly Trans role models, no path to follow. Alexandra's *This Time for Me* is a bold, witty, and unique look at queer history through the lens of this accomplished actor and activist, whose star keeps rising.

At TOPPLE Books, we are proud to celebrate the work of revolutionaries who have changed the world for the better, like my friend Alexandra Billings.

—Joey Soloway, TOPPLE Books editor-at-large

PROLOGUE

The sound was overwhelming. People chattering, gesturing, munching on lettuce leaves, and guzzling champagne out of fancy flutes. I sat at the table in my black-and-white Carolina Herrera, the first designer gown that I didn't either steal or give a hand job in order to own. Next to me was Jeff Bezos. Across the table were Judith Light and Jeffrey Tambor. I was delightfully sandwiched between Joey Soloway and Amy Landecker, both longtime Chicago theater friends.

It was the end of our first season on the Amazon show *Transparent*. We were being honored by critics and audiences, and the whole thing felt ridiculous. I simply couldn't accept the praise or the celebration. Yet, there I was, all dressed up and plopped in the center of the 2015 Golden Globe Awards in Beverly Hills, wondering how the hell all this had happened.

Ellen DeGeneres waved at us. Two or three fabulously wealthy humans in snappy suits shook Jeff's hand and tried to introduce themselves to us. I sat googly-eyed, plotting a selfie attack on Viola Davis with the precision of a well-trained CIA agent. Commercial breaks at award shows are not for the meek. If you want the Streep pic for your Facebook, you cannot be timid.

And we laughed, and ate, and applauded as the luminaries sailed up to the podium. I missed my wife terribly. Spouses were asked to sit this one out, and dance and sing and watch the awards live next door at the Amazon party. I was texting Chrisanne madly, sending her the backs of famous people's heads, snapping myself eating and giggling with Amy and Joey, and eventually, attempting to pee in a long gown . . . no small feat.

The night went on, the winners beamed, the categories passed, and it never got old; I was never bored. Not once. The fact that I was alive was enough for me. The room spun and I couldn't move. I couldn't mingle. I felt heavy. Undeserving. I was the Brown Trans Hooker in the room, and no matter how much I adorned myself with glitter, that would always be true. My past life was still a part of my present. Despite befriending my shame, I was still a victim of it—always on the outside, guarding my deeply damaged inner life. I missed my wife, and I yearned to *feel* the celebration of that night, rather than simply take pictures of it.

Then they called our name from the stage, and the entire table erupted in a fever of sound. It engulfed me: "And the winner is *Transparent!*" It seemed to echo as we tried to get up from our corner table, stunned and a little lost. Then the room slowed, and in the middle of the screaming crowd, I stopped. As I held the back of a chair, I looked around and remembered. I saw the lights bouncing off the gold banister and streaming across the width of the ballroom, and I saw my first prom with my first real girlfriend, Cassandra. I saw the half-eaten food and the crumbs of bread and the fifty-four packets of empty sugar near my plate. I saw my mother, and Thanksgiving dinner, the first time I came back to our house in Schaumburg, Illinois, in a dress, and the look of horror that swept across her face. I saw my high school gym teacher, I saw my first bully, I saw my high school choir, and then I saw my wife. I saw Chrisanne's face beaming and her eyes dancing in the light of the ballroom, and I ached for her.

Then I saw my father.

I saw my dad's round face and his large hands holding on to his conductor's baton, waving me upward to the stage, where the cast was beginning to gather. Music poured from his fingertips. It engulfed the room as I started toward the white light. I stood on the stage as Joey held the Golden Globe in their hand and I tried to remind myself of what gratitude was—that this had absolutely nothing to do with winning and that the award was not the point. I stood there, praying that somewhere on the planet, another Trans person would see us. That perhaps they were sitting in their room, alone and isolated, thinking they were the only one. And perhaps they had finally decided to leave the planet. They had had enough. But after witnessing our triumph, after sharing our joy, they had decided to stay for a while.

In all fairy tales, there are witches and dragons. There are heroes and magical talismans. There are tornadoes, red shoes, and yellow brick roads. There are close calls and near misses. There are beautiful endings and insidious beginnings. There are births. There are deaths. And for me, there was a princess asleep in the heart space of a presumed prince. And I was lucky enough to marry her.

And so, I'll begin the way all great fairy tales do, with "Once upon a time . . ."

ONE

I Lie

I lie.

I'm not one of those liars who twitches or sweats or panics when they lie. I'm a very, very, very good liar. The problem is not that I lie; the problem is that I have a hard time noticing, admitting, and living in the truth. Even when faced with it, the truth eludes me. I much prefer the world I create to the world I inhabit.

If I don't like the way the story's going, I simply change it.

"You can't always make things up, Scott. That's not the way the world works," my mother would say.

Sure, it does. As long as it's my world.

~

And so . . .

Early one morning, as the sun streaked across the tile of our newly laid kitchen floor, I sat cross-legged in one of Mimi's long, green dresses, barefoot and eating my Frosted Flakes directly from the box, looking out into our backyard. I had only put on lipstick that morning, no

other makeup. I was six and had been dressing up for a while by then. It seemed a part of me. I felt better. I was happy. My feet clicked as I wobbled back and forth on the floor, my long dress covering my knees and my lipstick smearing a bit as the flakes spilled onto my lap and stuck to my cheeks. I began to hum. "We've Only Just Begun" was my theme song. I was humming, playing with a beam of light in the early morning, and picking up random flakes from both my lap and our spotless kitchen floor.

I had found my joy.

Scott

As Mimi turned the corner from the dining room into the kitchen, I felt my heart race. I knew the mess on the floor, and on me, might set her off. I began to clean up as quickly as I could. I was singing a song she loved, and I hoped she might want to join me. She'd never really heard me sing, and I was having such a good time. I thought she might want to come and join me for my Karen Carpenter Frosted Flakes Party.

She stopped as I turned toward her, my back to the sliding glass doors.

Her face dropped and her eyes began to lower. I thought at first she was staring at the crumbs on the floor. Then I realized she was staring at the dress. Her head began to shake. Her mouth turned downward a little, and I felt my insides begin to churn, as if I had eaten bad cheese. She kept staring. She didn't speak or move.

And then in a whisper, she said methodically with great emphasis, "Don't ever. Wear that. Again."

I held my breath.

"Scott? Do you understand me?" she asked. Her eyes flashed black, and her finger pointed at my borrowed gown.

~

If you looked at my life and never asked questions, you'd see a life half planned and mostly dreamed.

My mother spent an extraordinary amount of time making things pretty: dusting them, then making them shine and sparkle. She vacuumed and painted and shellacked and redecorated both our home and herself. I once found her in the living room dusting in between the black and white keys on the piano. When I asked her what she was doing, she answered calmly, "What if someone wants to sit down and play?"

We knew my mother as Mimi, a nickname my brother, Bobby, had given her when he was seven. Mimi was a combination of two complex humans: her stern and occasionally violent father, Emerson Nelson, also known to us as Spike, and her domineering and controlling mother, Dorothy Mueller, known to the family as Dody. As a child of the 1950s, gender roles were clearly defined for her. It took a lifetime of ninja-like skill performed by a gaggle of pathological liars

to learn how to behave, what was acceptable, and how to carefully navigate the neighbors' potential judgment. Mother's given name was Esther (named after Esther Williams, the swimming movie star of the 1940s), but she preferred her middle name, Eloise (after the children's book heroine). Clearly, our family loved to change given names, though it would prove to be a source of great pain to Mimi many years later when I transitioned from Scott to Shanté to Alex.

The little I recall of Dody is not pleasant. She seemed to me to be the great gargoyle atop the faraway steeple, always looking down and illogically constipated. She once yanked me across the dinner table because I made footprints in the living room after she had just finished raking the carpet. Apparently, my feet made the carpet fibers bend in the wrong direction. Mimi's need for perfection was a generation deep. This explained the piano keys . . .

Despite my grandmother's antimaternal demeanor and detached emotional connection, I could see myself best reflected in her side of the family, as the brown part of my lineage was most evident there. When I looked into Dody's eyes, I saw myself. Her brown skin, lean frame, and angular face made me feel like part of a family. But when my dad, Mimi, my brother, and I traveled around together, which wasn't often, I seemed like a sad little orphan straggler, a random brown kid the kindly white people had picked up at a nearby 7-Eleven.

Dad's father, JG, short for Jack George, was Native American. The only way I knew this was because he sported a Western string tie with a large turquoise clasp and he collected arrowheads. He met my grandmother, a flapper, at a 1920s speakeasy. She was a hot dish who was affectionately called Peg Peg.

I was born in 1962 in Inglewood, California. I knew that being white was powerful because it was all I was taught. We had people who helped Mimi mop the floors, but they were not white. We had people

helping with the lawn, or building additions to the house, or babysitting, but they were not white. And our family was white. Without being told, I understood. I saw it. Every day. In every moment. I wanted to fit myself into the frame and make sure the piano was dust-free when the neighbors dropped by. After all, what if someone wanted to sit down and play?

It was decades later that I discovered our entire familial and racial history was one great big fat lie. But that is a whole other book!

And this is one lie I had not invented; this was a lie I inherited.

I learned to do whatever I had to do to remain afloat as the family outcast.

One Halloween, when I was ten, I wanted to be Dorothy from *The Wizard of Oz*, but my mother forced me into a homemade tossed salad costume. When I went out trick-or-treating with my friends, I took the two plastic tomatoes off my collar and strategically placed them on my nipples, telling everyone I was Gypsy Rose Lee. And even at ten, even as Gypsy Rose Lee, as I sang show tunes and took bows when the refrigerator door opened, my clean white life began to show cracks. The man behind the curtain began to shriek and demand attention. Everything was not perfect. Not us, and not me. So we lied . . .

And there was the booze. There were late-night parties at the house, there was Dad and Mimi coming home, crashing into walls, peeing in the underwear drawer. I confronted Mimi only once many years later about her drinking.

"I am *not* an alcoholic!" she proclaimed loudly at the kitchen table, her face red from drinking and her voice rising with defensive rage. "Look at me! Do I *look* like an alcoholic?"

I paused.

"I don't . . . what's an alcoholic supposed to look like, Mimi?"

She sipped.

"You know. Like W. C. Fields or Hedy Lamarr!"

The W. C. Fields reference I got. I never did figure out Hedy Lamarr. My mother was unintentionally hilarious. She and I found enormous joy in each other. I learned my comic timing from Bugs Bunny, Lucille Ball, Carol Burnett . . . and my mother. Mimi's wit was sharp, biting, and instinctive. She wasn't a great thinker or intellectual, but we found each other endlessly entertaining.

And yet, our relationship was fraught. It was complex and complicated and stemmed from both her beginnings and mine. The lies we told and were taught crept up on us and spewed forth like arrows from a tight bow.

And so . . .

As I sat cross-legged and caught, my mouth agape and my shame ignited, it was the first time I was told directly by the human I loved the most that what I was doing was not to be seen. The neighbors knew too much already, and a retreat was paramount.

Mimi went into the kitchen and began to cook breakfast, carefully moving pots and pans and making very little sound. I knew this could never happen again, and if it did, there would be consequences. Mimi's hand appeared, and with quick and furious strokes, she wiped the remaining lipstick from my face with a dry paper towel. She threw it in the garbage, made a hissing sound through her teeth, and went back to the stove.

"Breakfast will be ready soon," she intoned mechanically.

I got up, picked up my dress, left my Frosted Flakes on the floor, and went into the bathroom. I closed the door and sat on the toilet. I knew then that in order to survive, to continue, to keep going, to stay alive, I needed to make a choice. I had to decide right then and there. I had to do what I had to do. Mimi was right. When the story isn't going your way, change the story.

Right.

Absolutely right.

And it was at that moment, sitting on the toilet covered in crumbs of Frosted Flakes and hiking up my mother's floor-length emerald-green silk dress, that I began to lie.

TWO

Marble Estates

Life in Marble Estates was never quite the *Leave It to Beaver* fantasy Mimi had dreamed of. Dad found himself in the arms of too many waitresses, stewardesses, secretaries, and hookers, which inevitably culminated in my parents' divorce. Within a couple of minutes, it seemed, my mother married Bill Kight (as in, "Let's Go Fly a . . ."), and within a few more minutes, Bobby and I were moved into a new house and acquired a new stepbrother and stepsister: Mike and Michelle. Bill had lived across the street from us before he married my mother, and Janet Hay, the woman who gave Mike and Michelle piano lessons every other Thursday, ended up marrying my father.

That's the kind of refined and sturdy stock I come from: Neighbor Swappers.

Questioning who I was never occurred to me. It wasn't a dream, it wasn't a costume, it wasn't an idea, a fad, or political commentary. What I was was a necessity, and for as long as I can remember, I have been trying to find a way to be it without viscerally pissing off the world at large.

Being Transgender requires careful planning, devious escapes, and fabulous costumes. In the 1960s, being me was illegal, both on the streets and in my living room.

Here's what I did in order to avoid jail time in both places . . .

One morning, I slipped on Mimi's white pleather go-go boots, a black bra, and a pair of my black swim trunks and wrapped a sheet around my neck, pretending to be Batgirl. Mimi and Dody were in the kitchen, and I was fighting bad guys in the living room. Our house was a split-level, and the bad guys ran upstairs. I followed them. I was kicking and making *kablam!* and *kerchoff!* sounds as I slid down the banister. I lost my balance and crashed onto the floor, gashing my forehead on the way. I screamed at the top of my lungs, and as blood poured from the open wound near my right eye, my mother picked me up in her arms and rushed me over to the kitchen sink. Dody was panting and yelling at Mother to stick my head under the water while she got a towel. Mimi tried, but was too frightened. There must have been a lot of blood.

"Call an ambulance!" she screamed to my grandmother.

My eyes fluttered. I could see her face through a small sea of red.

"How did this happen, Scott?" she asked, shaking.

"I was playing Batgirl," I answered honestly.

She rolled her eyes.

"Oh dear. You mean . . . Bat*man*."

That was the last thing I remember.

We had a blond-haired, blue-eyed babysitter who was very sweet and very kind. I remember she would play board games with me. I remember her gentleness. I also remember I told her I had a rare blood disease that required me to drink a glass of sugar water at least once a day—a sugar-deficiency thing.

She caught me in our living room one afternoon, dancing in my underwear and wearing a pair of Mimi's pink satin pumps, with a small

bowl of fruit on my head. When she asked what I was doing, I told her I was Carmen Miranda. She said she didn't know who that was.

That was the last time I spoke to her.

In the early sixties, Daniel Boone was a monumental craze, and his raccoon-skin cap (complete with a long, fuzzy tail) became a national fashion statement. Bobby and I each had one and wore them constantly until eventually they started to smell. My parents assumed we were playing wilderness men. In fact, the tail served as my real live ponytail, like Laurie Partridge. I even wore it to bed until all that was left were a couple of strands of fur and a matted ball of sticky goo, and it had to be thrown away. A word of advice: don't ever put your Daniel Boone cap in the washing machine.

My dad was the invisible man when I was a child, and I don't remember much about him. However, when he came back from Vietnam, he brought me a toy poodle, an electronic dog with a control panel. I can still see his sleeve reaching toward me and turning the switch to on. The poodle was jet-black with tiny, floppy ears, and it walked, scooted, and sat down. This was pure magic for me, mainly because it came from my dad. I named the poodle Lady Beautiful.

One night after dinner, I was playing with Lady Beautiful (Lady B for short) in the hallway, giggling and clapping and making her beg for treats. I'd put a cookie on the end of her nose and asked her to sit, lie down, or stand. I had designed a party dress for her—hot pink with blue and red polka dots. It was basically a small kitchen towel held together with safety pins.

"Okay, Lady B. Please stand if you'd like the cookie. Okay?"

I never raised my voice or startled Lady B. After all, she was from a faraway country and had had a very rough childhood.

"What are you doing?" my dad asked, looming over me.

"I'm training Lady B."

"Is that the dog, boy?"

"Yeah. Lady B is her nickname. Her full name is—"

"Don't be a faggot."

He picked Lady Beautiful off the ground and carried her into the kitchen. I followed him. My memory is a little fuzzy, but I can still see my dad clearly in his blue robe and striped pajama bottoms shuffling across the floor. I cannot see his face, but I can hear his tone. It was sharp and pointed. He turned on the garbage disposal and put her paw in the sink and began to grind her up.

I remember screaming.

I was five years old.

G#D T@LKS

Me

Now I lay me down to sleep. I pray the Lord my soul to keep. If I should die before I wake, I pray the Lord my soul to take. Am I going to die before I wake?

XXX

Of course not.

Me

Then why am I asking you to take my soul?

XXX

It's a prayer.

Me

What does that mean?

XXX

It means you're safeguarding.

Me

I don't get it. I don't ask for a cast on my leg before I break it.

(Silence)

Me

I'll ask Mimi in the morning. This is her prayer anyway.

THREE

Fairy Dust

I could barely hear them, but from their tone, I could tell it was becoming heated. I moved closer to the wall that separated the dining room from our bedroom, and pressed my ear against the plaster.

I heard bits and pieces:

"It's disgusting."

"It's not, Eloise. It's just people trying to—"

"They're deviant."

Mimi's voice rose up in a pointed whisper. My dad, sitting inches away from her on the couch, matched it.

"Well . . . . I don't want them around the boys. *That*, I know," she continued.

"Eloise, the fags in his school aren't actors. I teach real—"

"Bob, you're a blind man. You're blind and you're wrong. You're around fags all the time."

I could barely hear them, so I leaned closer to the wall and wrapped my seven-year-old torso around the corner. I could see Mimi, her hands fluttering, her feet tapping, and the ice cubes in her drink clanging

against the sides as she punctuated each line with a slosh and a slight spill.

"They're actors, Eloise."

"And they're fags, Bob."

There was mumbling in between sentences and then, in the middle of a deep silence, everyone took a gulp, and I heard Mimi's voice a half tone lower:

"We need to be careful around Scott. He's starting to lean in that direction."

I caught myself holding my breath, my chest tight and my knuckles cramping from the grip I had on the wall. Don't be a faggot, he had said. That's right. That's what he'd said and that's what the boys say and that's what I was and I needed to fix that because I was already leaning in that direction.

Shortly after the Stonewall riots, as the world around me rumbled and the sixties in America were ending, the fear of queer people was palpable. There was zero information available, and everyone was running. No one knew who or what we were, and no one really cared to find out. So we ran and we ran fast. We were all trying to figure out exactly what it was we were so afraid of. I was turning into something abhorrent. All I knew was that the way I ran, the way I laughed, the way I danced, ate, shook, breathed, wept, sat, stood, read a book, or did the Watusi upset people to no end. There was a container that I didn't fit into, and the world had specific instructions on how I could finagle my way in and pull the lid on tight. Stop squirming, stop making trouble. But I couldn't and didn't, and that made some people run away, and made others want to pummel me.

One of those others was my brother.

When I was about seven, we were playing Marco Polo in our neighbor's pool with three or four of our friends. It was one of the few times Bobby let me hang out with him. He was four years my senior,

and I adored him. It was late at night and summertime. The weather was gorgeous, and there was no school. When I was picked to be "it," I closed my eyes, swam around the pool screaming "Marco!" as the other boys answered back "Polo!" and I attempted to tag them. The voices grew fainter and fainter. I assumed they were moving farther away from me in the pool, going to opposite ends or the deep end, so as not to get tagged. As I would call, I would hear my brother's voice in response. Just hearing his voice, and the fact that we were together, laughing and having fun, made my heart race. I was being very careful not to embarrass him. I tried to lower my voice, to move like the other boys and not sway my hips too much, gesture too extravagantly, or point my toes when I paddled underwater. Anything I could remember that the other boys in school mocked, I wanted to correct. Because Bobby was paying attention to me. He was laughing, and I didn't want to make a mistake.

I didn't want to end up like one of those "fags" Mimi mentioned seeing on TV. I didn't want to be a deviant.

The voices faded and got farther away, and finally I called and called and . . . nothing. There was no answer. I called one more time, and still . . . nothing. I opened my eyes to see they had all left. Including Bobby.

I got out of the pool, walked over to my towel, wrapped it around me, and walked across the street to our house. There was the group of boys with Bobby, standing on our front lawn. When they saw me coming, they laughed and whispered. And then I did what I had been doing in school. What I had mastered. What I knew how to do and what I was beginning to perfect—I laughed along with them. I bound up my pain and my rage and my shame and I laughed.

I saw my brother's freckled face scrunch up and his smile broaden. "You guyyyys . . ." I said, patting one of them on the back.

I was humiliated and I was furious, and I joined them and I laughed.

The fraught relationship with my brother fueled my need to strengthen and hone my survival skills. I had no other choice. I was surrounded by teachers and no one was teaching. I was on my own. Bobby helped me to realize that. The rules of the outside world made absolutely no sense. And I didn't believe in rules.

I believed in a magical being called Glinda. I believed in fairy dust.

FOUR

The Singing and the Drinking

The first time I did it, I didn't second-guess it. I simply did it. Where I live, nobody leaves and no hearts are broken. Where I live, sickness is illegal and all wishes come true. Where I live, there is always a soft place to land. I live and blossom in a place of understanding where anything is possible. I can play with my dolls; I can order a party dress; I can put on makeup and there are no gender barriers. And, no matter what I do, it's never my fault.

It's never my fault when people suddenly disappear. I was sure he would return, but he never did. I waited at the front door night after night after night, but he never, ever came back. Every plane that flew by, every engine starting up, every car that passed our house I assumed was my dad. But it never was. He never came back. He was here, then he wasn't, and suddenly, it seemed as if he had never really been here at all.

It was as if I had made him up.

And so, I *did* make him up.

I didn't second-guess it. I simply did it.

I made him up.

Where I live, people don't go away, and when they do, it's never my fault.

I was nearly seven years old and had been raiding Mimi's closet for as long as I could remember. Jewelry, makeup, shoes, skirts, and wiglets. Anything I could grasp, I wore, pinned on, and smeared. Her closet was like a giant storage space of magical talismans. But even at that age, I knew that all these things hanging neatly in rows, divided by color and season, were forbidden. Her idea of gender was specific and contained. It was 1969, and a revolution of gargantuan size was about to break out around the world. But here, in our little house with our broken family—me; my silent brother, Bobby; Mimi, teaching fifth-grade students she abhorred; and our new stepdad, Bill, a docile, even-tempered man who reminded me of Gig Young—normalcy was the rule. Nothing changed and nothing was shaken. Even the divorce, which seemed to have happened while I was asleep, meant nothing. We never spoke of it, and we never dealt with it. It simply went away. Dad was across town. There was no trauma. Everyone was fine.

Everyone.

Was.

Fine.

My stepfather, Bill, worked for IBM, and in 1972, they transferred him out of California to Schaumburg, Illinois. My brother, Mimi, and I moved into a two-level, two-bedroom house in the whitest neighborhood we could find, in the coldest place on the planet. I was entering the sixth grade in a new place, with new people and new teachers, and hopefully, a new life. Maybe there'd be no more bullies or name-calling, and maybe I could finally stop this "dressing in Mimi's clothes" thing that seemed to destroy everyone.

Maybe.

~

"I think I can play the guitar."

Mimi was driving and only half paying attention to me.

"The what?"

"The guitar. I would like to play the guitar," I repeated.

"Your father will have to pay for it."

And then we turned left.

My dad, who was still in California, got the call from Mimi, and weeks later she took me guitar shopping. Taking lessons bored me. I didn't understand why I needed to continue once I had learned a few chords and how to pick and strum, so I quit shortly thereafter. Because really, it wasn't about the instrument at all. It was about an obsession I unearthed early in my childhood, one that had consumed me ever since I first heard Karen and Judy and Barbra.

I wanted to sing.

I needed to sing.

And I needed accompaniment. And since I wasn't a Mel Tormé, I decided to accompany myself on the guitar.

~

I was sitting in my bedroom and playing "Fire and Rain" by James Taylor. I slowed it down, turning it into a ballad. It had always felt very sad to me. By fourteen, my sadness was very deep and powerful. Although by that time, I had all but mastered the art of the masquerade.

As I began singing, something started to happen to me. I stopped thinking. I didn't worry about the chords or my pitch or how the original song had sounded, or that anyone might be listening. I just sang. Freely. There were a few tears, and I kept singing because the sound made me feel better. But it wasn't just that I felt better. It went deeper than that. It was a spiritual experience that catapulted me into a place of complete abandon, making me unrecognizable to myself. It wasn't

simply an emotional release; it was freedom, and it was frighteningly dangerous.

Then my bedroom door opened.

"Are you singing?" Mimi asked.

Her eyes were wide. Her tone was very odd.

"Yeah."

"What is that?"

"It's 'Fire and Rain,'" I answered.

Her voice was choppy.

"What else can you sing?"

By the end of the day, I had performed a concert for my mother. Sitting in the chair across from me in my bedroom, she clapped and laughed and threw her arms up in the air. Every once in a while, she would tell me how wonderful I was, and the sparkle in her face lit up the room. I wept while strumming, and she said, "Oh, that's my new favorite!" But then I would play another one, and she would say, "Well, that one's much, much better, actually."

That's when I realized that this thing I loved, that I was figuring out how to do, brought my mother into my life in a way I never thought possible. And she finally looked at me the way she looked at Bobby.

And then the parties began.

Mimi and Bill threw many, many parties at which there was lots and lots to drink. Sometimes, after dinner and as the night was speeding up, Mimi would call me into the living room. "Scott! Come on out here and bring your guitar!"

And I would.

Soon, Mimi and I began planning the evenings.

"You'll bring your guitar in about nine thirty and play three or four songs."

"Okay. I'll start with 'Your Song' and then maybe do 'Country Roads' and then . . ."

"I think you should open with 'Country Roads.' I think you want to grab them right from the beginning. And save your big ballad as a closer," she instructed. "That way, you leave them with a little piece of you."

Scott and Mimi

Mimi was my first personal manager.

Her guests were graciously attentive, and the evenings were filled with laughter and drinking and chatting and questions and more drinking. I learned how to redirect a room full of loud drunks and how to hold them at those parties. I was already practiced at making people laugh. This was my escape and my salvation. If you can make a bully giggle, they're less likely to push you down the stairs.

They were gathered downstairs and my cue to enter was approaching. It was a weekend night, and I had recently entered junior high, and it wasn't going well. I was still dressing up at home and occasionally getting caught by Mimi, who pretended it wasn't happening. And I was

now surer than ever that this needed to stop. But how? I couldn't seem to control it. I couldn't seem to slow it down or turn it into acceptable behavior. The shame grew deeper and deeper. And now, it was coupled with anger—a strange, unpredictable anger that would consume me. It caused me to throw things, to break things, to scream at people, and once, I took a knife from the kitchen and jammed it into my brother's bedroom door:

"If you ever come near me again . . ." I yelled.

About an hour later, while my parents were still asleep, Bobby burst open the door and pounded my stomach and my face with his closed fists—over and over and over—as I lay on my bed. His face was beet red as he leaned over me with snot coming from his nose. I curled into the fetal position, moaning and praying for it to stop.

He stopped.

And then he left.

Mimi had had enough of both my language and my attitude and came at me with a ruler as I sat in a chair in my bedroom. I bolted out of the chair, grabbed the ruler with both hands, and smacked her across the face. The impact made a sharp snap, and she rolled back on her heels for a moment. Her face fell and she gasped. She then ran back into her bedroom, slammed the door, and began to weep uncontrollably.

"Stop it!" I screamed. *"Stop it!"*

The violence in the house was running rampant. And it was all my fault.

~

As I tuned my guitar in the living room, noise from the party downstairs grew louder. I stood, waiting for Mimi to seemingly spontaneously call my name. I glanced over at the wet bar that fit snugly in the corner, next to the entrance to our kitchen. On top sat two or three large bottles of

alcohol. Some were gold, some were a reddish-brown, and there was one that was completely clear. I had seen my parents and their friends putting these drinks in small glasses, filling them with ice, and then stirring them with their fingers. It seemed to make them happy—they laughed harder, and the parties really got going once that happened.

So as I waited upstairs, I grabbed a small glass, filled it with ice, and poured in some of the clear stuff. I took a sip. It was awful. Like hot, burning lava melting the back of my throat. It stung, and I coughed and hacked and almost fell to my knees. When I opened my eyes, something had changed. The room got brighter. The sounds from downstairs morphed into music, and the guitar in my hand grew lighter and lighter. I was happier. I was instantly happier than I had been just a minute ago. When I took another sip, the burning decreased, and the happiness engulfed me. My head buzzed and my tongue tingled and every part of me was awake and electric. Mimi called up, and that night, I gave the performance of my life.

The next day was horrific—throwing up, everything spinning in circles. It was difficult, but worth it. I understood what the colored booze was for, and with practice, I discovered how to maintain and control its aftermath. That's really all it was. Control. The people who fell down, crashed into furniture, or said things too loudly had no idea about control.

I kept singing and playing and seeing Mimi look at me with affection and compassion and newness. Her friends complimented me. I began to write my own songs and sing of my loneliness and isolation, but no one really heard me. It seemed to me the only time there was peace, the only time the world slowed down and paid attention, was when I was singing, propped up by the mixture of the clear liquids and the colored ones. The drinking and the singing worked magic. So I kept singing and kept drinking.

I realized that to find my happily-ever-after, I had to keep singing. One winter when I was sixteen, as the snow collected in small mounds outside my window, I understood. The family wasn't going to come together. Not ever. There wasn't going to be an epiphany in this house. There was never going to be a happy ending here. So that winter, as the steam rose from the vent in the floor of my bedroom a year and a half after I took my very first drink, I decided to kill myself.

That was the first time . . .

The winter's cold sliced through my bones, and the sobbing of a hopeless Trans child could be heard for miles.

FIVE

Becoming Judy

I was thirteen, sitting in the theater at Harbor College where my dad worked, leaning forward, watching the back of his hand rise and fall, and rise and fall, again and again. He was graceful and his arms moved with long, broad, gliding gestures. Then he'd jerk his hand backward, slicing the air with knifelike precision, and the orchestra would leap to attention. Music came from the center of him. A large, magical sound emanated from his core and pulled me to the edge of my seat. Finally, I stood up, walked to the aisle, and rocked back and forth, holding my elbow and mumbling to myself (something I do to this day when I'm teaching and the work is changing the atmosphere around me). I was riveted. My dad, whom I didn't know very well at all, was transformed. He was a mythic creature, a mystery. I had resented his disappearances and his recurring need to become an instant father to me, but our devotion to music bound us to each other genetically. When he created, I was transfixed.

He flew in the air and he shot people in the Vietnam War, then he landed and made music with his devoted college students. He had a temper. He was a serial adulterer, a sniper for the CIA, and a violent

drunk who, on occasion, had beaten my mother. He was a lover of Rodgers and Hammerstein and Johann Sebastian Bach. He was a classically trained pianist who loved musical theater and flying planes. He was an adventurer who was completely irresponsible. He was truly one of the funniest people I ever met. His sense of humor was the shield that guarded his insecurities, his deep regret, and his years of shame.

I was absolutely and without question his child.

That night at Harbor College, as I rocked back and forth, was the first time I understood who he was and what he did. He had long been an enigma to me. He was in the middle of recording his college's version of Anthony Newley's 1965 Broadway hit, *The Roar of the Greasepaint—The Smell of the Crowd*. The recording was taking place onstage with a twenty-something-piece orchestra and an eighteen-person cast. Back in the 1970s, when you recorded an album, the musicians and the vocalists stood in the same room and, well . . . musicalized. If there was a mistake, you started again. Everyone started over again. This made for some very long nights. Especially when you add into the mix that most of these artists were college students just learning their craft. But to me, the performers were wonderful and I learned so much from them. Those summers with my dad were where I learned what theater was, how it worked, and what it took to keep it fairy tale–like. I watched sets being built, tickets being printed, posters painted, stages cleaned, and makeup applied. I was fascinated with absolutely everything. But I had never attended an actual recording before.

"Can I watch?" I asked my dad before we went into the theater.

"Yup. But you must keep quiet. You can't make a sound," he said as we walked down the hallway toward the stage.

As the chorus sang "A Wonderful Day Like Today," I found myself bouncing and harmonizing and smiling in the aisle through take after take. I was fascinated. This is what I wanted.

Dad

It was late by the time the final song was put down. The sun was coming up. My dad looked exhausted. His usually jovial expression sagged a bit, and his perky blue eyes drooped, lacking their familiar sparkle.

I, on the other hand, was ready to jump-start the car.

He gathered his music, and he, my stepmother, Janet—the now ex-Marble-Estates-next-door-neighbor's piano teacher—and I walked out of the theater and into the early morning California air.

Dad and Janet were not an affectionate couple, but they were funny. They reminded me a bit of Stiller and Meara, or Abbott and Costello. They played off each other in a way I didn't ever remember happening in our house. Although Mimi and I laughed, it was a rarity

with my brother. And my new stepdad, Bill, although extremely kind and gentle, was not exactly Jim Carrey.

There was a magical twinkle in their new marriage. Janet was an artist as well, and although she wasn't too fond of Bobby and me, she inspired Dad. She fed his soul, and his ego, and his love for spontaneity, and music, and beauty in the world. He didn't speak much about the war or what he did in it. I tried to bring it up a few times, and each time my father would freeze. His entire body would stop, his eyes would deaden, and I could sense the internal battle, relentless and destructive. Whatever it was my father did when he was a pilot, he would take to his grave. Janet saw this and understood it, and although my dad was still drinking to excess, her love for him seemed infinite. They had a shine that attracted people, and this allowed them to behave badly at rehearsals or on opening nights. For me, that shine was addictive. It drew me close to both of them, and the more I spent summers with my dad and Janet, the less I wanted to go back home.

Yet sadly my dad cheated on Janet on multiple occasions, with multiple women. Years later, I came back to visit my dad, and Janet and I went out to lunch. She admitted to me that by the end of the marriage she needed a calculator to keep up with all his affairs. In the divorce, she asked for the moon and got it. She was never one of my favorite people, but if I'm being honest about my feelings . . . Good For Her.

We walked to the car across the parking lot, and Janet and Dad crawled into the front while I made my way into the back seat. My dad was half asleep as we drove home, and Janet was slumped in the seat next to him. But I could barely sit still. My heart was still racing, and this new feeling was almost overwhelming—living in the music with the singers and the musicians, the smell of the sweat, the danger of making a mistake, the triumph of getting it right, and doing it well. There was beauty in the evening, and a great glory in the mess of the morning. It was maddening. It was exhausting. Tempers flew, and at one point my

dad had thrown his music across the floor and an actor almost quit. One member of the orchestra openly wept while she played her flute, and it was true madness. They were not on the verge of discovering a cure for cancer. They were not feeding hordes of starving people. They were simply creating. And I felt as if I were experiencing both a birth and a death. We were at one with the heartbeat of the universe. There was this unmitigated energy and delight and celebration in the room. As with all births, there was jubilation. The best part was, as things got packed up and moved off to the side, and musicians shuffled and actors chattered, my dad announced to the room in his largest voice, "Well, see you all tomorrow!"

That was my favorite part of the night.

"I want to be an actor," I announced to a half-asleep front seat.

"Oh God. Don't do that," Janet slurred.

"You do?" my dad asked.

"Yeah, Daddy. I do. I want to be an actor. And a singer too. And I want to dance. I want to dance too. I want to sing and dance and act and probably write."

"You can't do all of those things, boy. You'll have to pick one. No one really does all of those things."

"Judy Garland did."

"And where is she *today*? Dead!" Janet chimed in.

We laughed. That seemed to wake everyone up.

"You have to get better grades, boy," he said. "Your mother won't even let you think about being in the theater if you don't start getting your grades together. You understand me, boy?"

And there it was.

There was the dichotomy.

My dad had taken to calling my brother and me "boy." I honestly don't remember him using our names. As I approached teenage life, my gender had become a source of rage for many humans on the planet,

especially the ones at school. My dad had grown into a sort of guru for me. He was the source of my budding artistic dream life. But, as he referred to me as "boy," I understood that he did not truly see me. That I did not really exist. I understood that the only real choice I had was to prove to him that not only could I do absolutely everything, but that I was not a boy at all.

That early morning, as I lay in the spare room and the sun began to peek through the curtains, I made a list of how I was going to accomplish my goals. If I could be Judy Garland, that was certain to fix almost everything. I could continue to dress up in secret, and Mimi would hold me tight, and my brother would speak kindly to me, and my dad would fall to his knees and praise me, and see without shame or equivocation that I was his daughter.

Not his boy.

I don't know how, but I never lost hope. I had no actual plan. I lived for my dreams. I knew I needed to create. I needed to be seen.

I would do it for Judy.

SIX

The White Boys

Junior high school in Schaumberg was a reformatory, a house of horrors with no exit. It confined every single horrible human on the planet within one crowded, smelly, hormoned-up, skanky cellblock.

Lunch in the cafeteria at Jane Addams Junior High devolved into lessons in the art of both lying and magic. The magic was smoke and mirrors: disappearing behind the drapes so the bullies could not find you, being so entertaining that when you were sawed in half in front of thirty or forty middle schoolers, you knew how to emerge whole.

The lying was easy. By the time I was thirteen, my imagination and the texture of my lies were richly developed. I boasted that I had a brother who was my protector and who would find my bullies and beat them senseless if they touched me, that I had an uncle who was the assistant principal at the school so they'd better be careful how they treated me, that I could have them expelled, that I had a family connected to the underground mafia, and . . . that I had a father who was an assassin for the CIA and worked across enemy lines in Vietnam.

That last one was true. See, if you mix the truth with the lies, they can't tell the difference. Smoke and mirrors.

But even the magic tricks and the well-performed lies could not always protect me from the bullying and the violence. Sometimes it worked. Mostly it didn't. The abuse accumulated, weighty and cumbersome on my soul. The attacks that occurred at Jane Addams Junior High School between 1973 and 1975 were relentless.

Once, a group of boys found me in front of the art room, which was right across from the cafeteria. Without warning, they dumped a large blue barrel of dead fish over my head. I ran to the principal's office, reeking of fish and stale water, and when the principal finally met with me, he asked what I had done to provoke this kind of violence.

Then there was the boy who tripped me going down the stairs. He would wait every Tuesday and Thursday in the same place, between the threshold and the first stair. If I tried to avoid him and take another route or maybe have someone with me, he would hunt me down. He would find me wherever I was and trip me. Sometimes he threw me down the concrete stairs that trailed off into the back part of the building. Sometimes, surprising me, he pushed me directly into an open classroom while a lesson was in session. As a rule, grace is not one of my attributes. Tripping me has always been easy. And when I fall, I usually land face-first. I've never had much upper-body strength and so bracing myself is always difficult. By the end of the two years at Jane Addams, the bridge of my nose was permanently dented, and my forehead had a black-and-blue mark on it. If you look closely, you can see it still.

The bus was particularly frightening. "Fag," "Scotty-Boy," "Sissy," and any other homophobic slur they could manufacture was shouted by both the girls and the boys as I boarded the bus. I had to make my way to the back because the few times I tried to just get on and sit down as quickly as possible, I'd been shoved to the floor.

On the first day of our final year, everyone was assigned new lockers. I found mine, and scribbled all over it in black marker were the words "FAG" and "Brown Mexico" and "Scotty Homo." Large, dark, dangerously readable letters. As the other students began to fill the hallway, I tried to rub the words off with spit. I wiped and wiped, but nothing happened, and I began to cry. My stomach ached and I started dry heaving. My knees buckled and I fell, unable to catch myself. My head hit the locker, and the loud thud echoed down the hallway. Heads turned. Some people giggled. Some people whispered. One boy came by and, as if I were a football in the first quarter, gave me a running kick in the testicles. With the air knocked out of me, I held my groin and tried to protect my big purple folder. It was brand new, and I didn't want to have to go buy another one. My pal Carmen had drawn Liza Minnelli's face on its cover. He drew her as Sally Bowles, and I had only recently found out she was Judy Garland's daughter. I was completely obsessed and I didn't want to lose it. It was my talisman. Liza sang to the soul of me, and Carmen was my new best buddy. I tried to weep more quietly in the hope that the other boys might just pass me by. Most of them did.

Adults were present every time I was attacked. I would stare at them, blinking, calling out, raising my hand that I might be seen or heard or perhaps rescued. For some reason, the word "help" never seemed to come out of me. I could say "no" or "stop it," but even those phrases seemed to get stuck. Despite no explicit request, couldn't those adults tell I was in trouble? Couldn't they see that I needed them? I was a teenager, and the abuse I suffered was in plain sight.

No one went after the white boys who tormented me. No one stopped them. No one spoke to them. Their behavior extended beyond pranks and bullying and violence, and entered a realm of overweening power. It was during junior high that I began to accept that perhaps I deserved this treatment, that these people probably saw the thing that

I was, this thing that had no name, and I had to be destroyed. To be annihilated. To be silenced and removed. And this condemnation was further emphasized by the grown-ups around me. Not only at home, but now at school as well. There was nowhere for me to go, and there was no one to help me. I was on my own.

So the white boys triumphed.

G#D T@LKS

Me

I like this one girl and her name is Peggy. She has black curly hair and she's really fun. She likes all the things I like too.

XXX

That's amazing. I'm glad. Is there a problem?

Me

You always know when there's a problem. That makes me so happy to know that you always know.

XXX

I always know everything.

Me

I like this one guy. His name is Max. He doesn't know I like him, though.

XXX

Yes, he does.

Me

No. He doesn't.

XXX

Yes. He does.

Me

Does Peggy know I like her?

XXX

No. She doesn't. And she also doesn't know you like boys as much as you like girls.

Me

I want to have sex with everyone.

XXX

Who doesn't?

Me

Christians.

XXX

Who told you that?

Me

Everyone. Mimi.

XXX

I wouldn't just go around having sex with absolutely everyone, but it's fine to *want* to. There's nothing wrong with desire. Most

everyone wants to have sex with everyone else, they just don't go around *doing* it.

Me

I don't know how to have sex with boys . . . cuz I really want to have sex with boys. When I'm with a girl I know what I want to do, and it feels great. I want to be inside her, and I want her inside of me too.

XXX

It's like a fruit salad—everyone gets a little bit of everything.

Me

But when I think about having sex with Max, I only want him inside of me.

XXX

And?

Me

I feel like a girl a lot of the time, but I don't really feel like a *Girl* Girl. I don't feel like Peggy. I don't understand what to do, and I don't understand what I'm *supposed* to do. Also, I know I'm not supposed to want to be with boys.

XXX

Who told you *that*?

Me

Everyone. Mimi.

XXX

You're gonna want to be close to whomever you love. You're gonna want to lie down with the people who see you, who trust you, and who share in the same silliness and laughter and beauty as you. Just be careful and treat the people you sleep with the way you want to be treated.

Me

I think I'm going to ask Peggy out, but I think I'll wait on Max because he's a good friend, and I don't think he likes boys.

XXX

Yes.

Me

Okay.

XXX

Yes.

Me

Are you for real? Like, For Real real?

(Silence)

Me

Okay.

SEVEN

Cin and Sam and the Green Impala

There was Cin.
We were standing in the middle of the garage and holding on to each other. It was the fall. I was thirteen. I could smell the leaves on the ground through the crack in the large, white garage doors. Bill's long, green Impala was parked in its usual spot, which smashed Cin and me against the farthest wall. We were half lit by the cracks of afternoon sun peeking through the one window behind us and through the little slits beneath the two large doors. The TV in the den was blaring, and Cin, with her bright glow and her soft face, stood above me smiling. She was about two inches taller, and so I felt as though she might be holding me up a bit. My knees were weak. I had been kissed before, but none of the kisses felt like this. I was so nervous. My hands were sweaty and my heart was racing and I wanted very badly for this to go well. I kept seeing all my heroes kissing in the movies: Gable, Dietrich, Tracy and Hepburn, and the problem was I couldn't really figure out which was which or who was who.

Do I grab her, like Gable and Crawford? Or do I succumb, like Lana and Kirk?

So, we stood. And chatted. For a while.

Mimi and Bill were upstairs. Mimi had great affection for Cin. She likened her to Dorothy Hamill, who was the reigning queen of adorable in the late seventies. Cin was kind. She treated me softly and gently, and she made me laugh. We liked each other and liked to do the same things. And when things at school got bad, when the bullies got bigger and meaner and crueler, she held me and took care of me and constantly told me there was nothing wrong with not fighting back.

"You don't have to use your fists, Scott. That never solves anything," she comforted in her easy tone. "Peaceful resisting doesn't make you a coward. It makes you kind."

I never forgot her advice.

We kept chatting about the day, about when we'd see each other next, about school, about how much we hated it, about anything except when the kiss was coming. I held on to her and leaned against the green Impala, and we talked about The Boy—the one who had followed me through the halls and down the pathway to my house. I didn't live far from school, so it was easy for my tormentors to prevent me from reaching my safe space.

~

And there was Sam.

Sam was The Boy who followed me.

Stocky, sturdy, and rough. His face was angular, and his hands were like two mitts. He played baseball and football and talked in fragments.

"Hey, you. You're fucked. Me and you. It's gonna happen."

He would follow me home, or highjack me between classes, or wait outside.

I remembered what Cin told me about being kind, and so once after school, I stopped dead while he followed me. He was usually about ten or eleven steps behind, and I turned abruptly and faced him.

"Why are you always hitting me?" I screamed, the tears starting.

His face fell and his eyes got redder and redder. And then, in complete silence, he turned and walked away. I was stunned. I didn't know what had happened or what to do next. I was so used to tricks and lies that I assumed he was off to gather more boys, so I quickly ran toward our house.

That following week Sam disappeared. I would see him in the hallway occasionally, but even a momentary glance caused him to walk in the other direction. Gone. As if he had never been there.

~

"You wanna go drinking tonight?" Carmen asked one summer eve.

Carmen was one of the kindest boys I'd ever met. The first time we spoke was in art class and I was painting at my desk. I wasn't doing very well, and I wasn't very happy. I was going for Jackson Pollock, but it looked as though someone had left the cake out in the rain. Carmen passed by and stood behind me. I could feel him through my back, and I became a little sweaty and a little nervous. My hand shook and I put my brush down. I assumed he was either going to push my head into the desk or call me a name. I waited for it.

Nothing.

"I like it. You have a cool eye," he remarked casually.

And he walked away.

His voice was calm, and it soothed me. He had a dimple on the left side of his face when he smiled, which he did often. And he liked me. He liked what I had to say, and he thought I was funny. He was interested in the great Judy versus Barbra debate I was constantly having

in my head. Carmen was my friend, and he gave me access to a certain club of boys that I would never have been permitted to join without him. He was straight. He was a jock and he was popular. I had no idea why he picked me, but I held him in my heart until the end of the eighth grade, when he went to Conant High School, I went to Schaumburg, and I never saw him again.

But until then, my love for him was unrequited and pure.

By fourteen or fifteen, my drinking could already qualify me for Olympic gold medal status. I was drinking at night mostly and had become an expert at mixing cocktails in our downstairs den.

"Yeah," I answered Carmen gleefully.

"Some other guys are coming with us."

"Okay."

That was unusual, as most of the people I knew and I liked who didn't want me dead were female. But it was Carmen, so I felt safe. And I was excited to be included in anything that remotely smelled of males together, as both my sexual curiosity and my need for acceptance were intense.

We met at the park attached to the school, and joining Carmen and me were a dark-haired boy I'd never met . . . and Sam. I remember my throat tightening, my breath getting short, and my stomach turning upside down. I wanted to run for cover but, because I could see Carmen, I knew I was going to be okay. They walked toward me, three shadows in the dark, crunching playground gravel beneath their sneakers. There was Sam. This time, he was coming straight at me, and it wasn't to attack.

We drank that night.

We drank, and we laughed, and we drank, and we pushed each other on the swings, and we patted each other on the back, and we guzzled wine and beer, and my world grew fuzzier and fuzzier. But I was more of a champ than the other three. It took a lot to get me to a

place where I blacked out, and I knew my limits. So, I stopped drinking somewhere in the middle of the evening and let the others fly off into oblivion.

Eventually, the evening wound down, and we found ourselves trying to either limp home or pass out on the dewy grass. I stumbled and tripped occasionally to show I was just as lost as everyone else. But my head was completely clear, and I knew full well exactly what was happening. I offered my car to take people home. The last to go was Sam.

We sat in the car in front of his house with the motor running.

"What's up?" I asked my new best friend.

"I don't wanna go in wasted. My mom'll kill me. Can I sit here and sober up?"

"Yeah," I said, pretending to be just as drunk. "I'm really, really drunk, though. I'm gonna lie in the back seat."

"'Kay," he answered.

I'm not sure how I knew or when I caught on, but I was absolutely certain Sam was just as sober as I was. His slurring and his teetering seemed like terrible acting. My performance was far more convincing. After all, ever since I was five years old, I had studied with Joan, Bette, Lana, and Kirk. I knew what I was doing.

I closed my eyes, covered myself with a blanket that had been left on the floor of the car, and within minutes I felt Sam's hand on my thigh. I snored for good measure, and in the back seat of my stepdad's green Impala, Sam the Bully became my first male lover. There was never any penetration, but there was plenty of everything else. And it continued that way. I would meet him at his house, and we would sneak off to his bedroom. Or he would come over to mine and we'd do the same. When you're two teenage boys in the suburbs of Chicago in the 1970s, no one thought anything when you closed and locked your bedroom door.

Sam was unfunny.

He was one of those people who couldn't tell a joke, didn't understand a joke, and had no patience with a punch line. But he was smart. Being a jock, he played dumb and tried not to speak up too much around his friends, but he knew things about the universe and God and cars and wind velocity and weather. He even once tried to explain the inner workings of our governmental system to me, but I ended up blowing him before he got to the House of Representatives.

I found smart to be very sexy.

Still do.

When I saw him in the hallway, he would mock me, call me names, walk behind me and swing his hips, and while others laughed, he'd clap and slap his friends' shoulders. Yet, when I saw him later in the evening, he'd look at me as if I were saving him from drowning.

~

And there was Cin.

As I leaned up against the Impala, I stared into Cin's eyes and hoped for the best. I didn't know how to do this, or the best way to approach it, and I wanted it to happen now, so I took the best of everyone I knew on film and put it all into one sweeping gesture. I held her by the small of her back, pulled her gently toward me while simultaneously throwing my head back and tossing my long hair. Ready for my close-up, Mr. DeMille.

And strangely . . . it worked.

We kissed and I felt my heart smile. It was warm and sweet. I never forgot it. It was my first kiss with my first love, and it was everything I'd imagined.

As the garage doors rose, a heavy wave of sunlight sprayed across the floor. The Impala lit up like a Christmas tree tossed on its side. Cin

smiled and told me she'd see me tomorrow at school. I watched her walk down the street as the racket from the white door began to subside.

~

I knew I'd meet Sam sometime that week. I also knew he'd ridicule me. He'd chase me, or he'd walk away if he was alone in the hallway. But later, he'd stare at me, hold me in his arms, talk to me about boats or science. But not once would we kiss.

And there was Cin.
And there was Sam.

EIGHT

It's a Fairy Tale, Dammit

Once upon a time, in a long-ago place with a faraway feeling . . . After all the chaos and madness of moving to Illinois, surviving middle school, hiding my shameful, awful secret, drinking myself into miniblackouts, and never really having many friends, I wanted my entrance into Schaumburg High School to be brand new, as if I could begin again and wipe away my past. So I decided simply to pretend that none of the painful events had ever happened. I had become an expert at convincing myself that everything was fine, great—lying expertly even to myself. And not only was it great now, but it had always been great and would continue to get better. And strangely, even though it took tremendous effort and practice, and despite all I had been through and was still trying to figure out, I was an optimist. I honestly believed that everything was going to turn out all right in the end.

Still do.

~

In order to make a spectacular entrance, I sat underneath a desk. I made this decision prior to walking into the room of twenty-five or so drama students. It was my first week at Schaumburg High, and I knew by this time, age fourteen, that I was going to be an actor. There was nothing else for me. Math and science and geometry and that ridiculous "building walls and fixing cars" class the boys had to take were simply a waste of my time. Did Ann-Margret have any use for fractions? Did Lena Horne dissect frogs and put their innards in long, glass tubes before singing "The Lady Is a Tramp"? And when was the last time Liza fixed a carburetor?

I wanted an acting class. I wanted to know what I was doing and what it meant. I wanted to learn how to do what Hepburn did. I wanted to be free. I wanted to pretend. To dream. To imagine. And here I was, in a small, stuffy classroom after school, milling around with dozens of other oddballs and theater geeks who felt the same way. They were chatting, and gossiping, and gesturing, and pacing, and laughing. All conversation centered on the theater and what it meant to all of us— how it had saved us. We were teenagers in the seventies, sensing the reverberations of the sexual revolution, the newly found women's liberation movement, and a month of gay riots at a bar called Stonewall. We were budding artists anxious to tell our stories.

Our director entered the room, a large, round man with ill-fitting pants and a jovial voice. Everyone took a seat, and I went under the desk at someone's feet, in the first row, where I was sure to be noticed.

I was terrified.

"Hello, everyone," he bellowed, balancing precariously on the edge of his desk and smiling broadly. "My name is Mr. Egan. And if you're here for the fly-fishing club, get out."

We laughed. It was a relief. I don't think I was alone in my terror.

"If you're here for the drama club and you still want to get out, just make sure it's dramatic."

He was funny.

He reminded me of Dad.

I liked Mr. Egan. Very, very much.

He began to talk about art. He spoke about drama and plays and what we'd be doing, and as he spoke I could feel the temperature in the room rise. Collectively all of us inhaled, thrilled and shocked to have found ourselves together and living in the same sacred space. We learned that we had joined a secret club, the Thespians, a sort of Band of Merry Humans, whose mission it was to discover where and how theater had begun. Mr. Egan was a drama guy, but also an educator. He wanted to fill us with hope and promise, but he didn't want us to be stupid.

He finally took a breath and turned out the lights.

"I want to go around the room, and I'd like you to say your full name and where you come from. And don't say your mother."

He pointed to the human on the far right of my row, and one by one people stood and spoke their names. As my turn approached, I began to rehearse. Mimi's parties had been a great training ground. I knew how to work a room. And I had been performing with my dad during the summers, so stage fright wasn't a problem. I just needed to make sure I made it short and succinct. Despite the challenges of my life, my ego was obviously intact.

Finally, my turn came, and with the desk precariously balanced on my back, I rose and made my entrance. I turned to face the rest of the class and saw, far in the back, this black-haired girl with blue-green eyes sitting next to a brunette with clear, pale skin. They were both perched atop a desk.

I couldn't move.

I saw the girl with the black hair first, and there was something in her smile, in her deep blue-green eyes that was unmistakably familiar. The pit of my stomach rumbled, and my hands began to sweat. Then

the brunette girl next to her pulled her long hair over one ear, and my heart beat faster. She was angular. She was sharp and she was tight. She was light and airy and yet there was a weight to her that I could feel from across the room.

My mouth hung open for a moment.

"You'll have to say something, otherwise we're going to start making things up," I heard Mr. Egan say, off in the distance.

"I'm Scott Billings. And I have a mother."

I sat back down, the desk resting on top of me like a tired turtle.

People howled. They giggled and applauded, and I had absolutely no idea why. I didn't know what I had said, or if it had made sense. Nor did I care. I sat at the feet of the stranger who was next and couldn't get the green-eyed girl and the brunette girl out of my head. I couldn't stop thinking about them. As other people spoke, I closed my eyes and drew their faces in my head. More and more voices filled the room, and Mr. Egan was speaking again about our first auditions and how to prepare for them.

The class came to an end, and the room shuffled once again. Crowds frightened me, as I never knew when I was going to be a target, when the violence would come at me, or how it would manifest. So, whenever I found myself in the middle of a large group of people, I used to sing or hum.

And strangely, although my dad and I had overcome our crippled emotions through Rodgers and Hammerstein, it was Mimi's voice that brought me comfort.

Ever since I could remember, the bleakness of being in my room at night with no light and no sound was abjectly terrifying. And every so often, as I screamed and wept and fell apart, she would sit next to me, hold my hand, and sing. Mimi sang. She purred and put her face close to me . . . and sang.

Very, very badly. You see, Mimi was tone deaf.

And although it took some heavy detective work to finally recognize it, her oft-repeated lullaby was from the movie *Mary Poppins*.

"Feed the Birds" became an anthem for me. But despite my singing, there was too much happening, too many people, the brunette girl and the green-eyed girl were somewhere close, and it was all too much. I turned to make my escape, and a hand fell on my shoulder.

A soft voice came from behind me. "Hi."

I turned. It was the brunette girl.

"Oh. Yeah," I mumbled.

"I thought what you said was funny. Bye."

And she was gone.

You can say anything you want about my hands, my ass, my face, my voice, my laugh, my walk, but if you call me funny—I'm toast.

That week I began intense cramming for the auditions for our first play. Studying monologues, reading the play, I began to make friends with a select group of people from our drama club who would eventually become my family. My first, true, beautiful, chosen family. As I saw them and allowed them to see me, and as we went through this teenage journey together, I noticed something . . .

Something had changed.

Something had moved. This wasn't how it was supposed to be in school. I was walking down the hall and people weren't tripping me, or calling me names, or shoving me down the stairs. In fact, it was so strange there was a part of me that almost missed it. I didn't know how to behave. I didn't know what to do with myself, with my hands or my feet. It was as if I had forgotten how to walk at all. I didn't understand what safety felt like. And I had this gang, this strange, weird, hilarious, odd, fabulous, intelligent, curious group where I now belonged, and we'd walk down the halls together. We'd laugh together. We'd eat lunch together. We'd sing for each other. We'd talk about plays and the universe and God and *Star Trek* and Judy and Liza and Barbra.

But it wasn't me that changed.

It was the others.

The ones who had hated me.

I didn't understand what had happened. Had they forgiven me somehow? Perhaps I had done something extraordinary, but I just couldn't figure out what that was. Perhaps I couldn't remember what my actual life had been. Perhaps there was another me walking around, a Scott who was getting kicked, and spat on, and discarded. Yet here I was, living the good life and remembering nothing.

The green-eyed girl and the brunette girl became my bosom buddies. The green-eyed one, whose name was Chrisanne, moved into my life like a five-star general in a war. She didn't need theatrics. She had her intellect. We were cast as brother and sister in our production of *Twelfth Night*. We were supposed to be twins, and although we were both angular, that's really where the similarity ended. I marched us down to the Woodfield Mall and promptly bought us matching shirts and pants. We then came up with a shared gesture to use in the audition and rehearsed matching our voices:

Make me a willow cabin at your gate
And call upon my soul within the house
Write loyal cantons of contemned love
And sing them loud even in the dead of night . . .

Shakespeare seemed to write for her.

The only problem was that I had zero understanding of the text.

"I can teach you," Chrisanne proclaimed flatly.

"You can't teach me in time for the audition, can you?"

"Sure I can. We'll just go over it and it'll make sense to you."

"Well," I began, "we might go over it, but it'll never make sense to me."

We got the roles, and she became my poetry teacher. Chrisanne helped me understand Shakespeare's deep connection to the human

spirit. She helped me tell the story of mistaken identity, disguises, battles and raging anger, false love and true love, unrequited longing and dreamy romance, all mixed in with a generous dose of slapstick and gender swapping. But the truth was, I had absolutely no idea what I was saying.

I saw the brunette girl, Cassandra, even more often. She and I found each other at a time when we were both very broken and needing kindness, and we tumbled into each other's arms. The only problem was that she had a boyfriend, a large jock type with an enormous amount of hair, named David.

"Do you still like him?" I asked one day during lunch.

"No. I want to break up with him, but I'm afraid," Cassandra confided.

"Let's go tell him. This is stupid, right? We want to be together. Let's be together."

She smiled.

I wanted to take care of someone. I had a feeling that he beat her. He radiated violence. I wanted to take her away from him. So, I went with her to see him, and waited in the green Impala for her to come back from his house. She went in and returned about fifteen minutes later.

"Did you tell him?"

"Yup," she said blankly.

"What'd he say?" I asked, a little concerned.

"He was sad."

And right then, as she turned to me, I saw a sort of emptiness, a distancing from what had just happened. Cassandra was seventeen and David was eighteen. They were both older than me and had been together for a few years. This was a large thing, this breakup, and yet Cassandra only seemed bothered by the inconvenience of it, and was thrilled by the newness of us. There was no remorse. Not an ounce.

And although I noticed it, I was filled with such happiness and such relief that I let it go.

There is a great gift in a love that seems all encompassing and a family of artists who receive you without equivocation. It was certainly the respite I had dreamed of. I had a brunette princess, a family from the land of misfit toys, and a newfound safe place. I assumed this was the new normal. I sat with it and danced with it. Nothing could break this spell.

And things were going so well. Things were working out so beautifully. This fairy tale was filled with poetry and brilliance and there wasn't a green witch in sight.

I was protected. Everything was new. I was on my way. Happiness was a willow cabin, and even though the words rang hollow, the truth was laid bare.

Besides, this was a fairy tale, dammit.

All I had to do was rewrite the ending.

And they lived happily ever . . .

And once upon a time under a chair, they all . . .

And they all lived.

NINE

The Very First Time(s)
Chuck

It was freezing cold, something I would never get used to as a California kid. But there I stood, quivering in the Illinois winter, watching him practice.

I come from a football family, so the fact that at sixteen years old I still had absolutely no idea what the game was about says everything about what little value it held for me. But there I was, nose pressed against the iron fence surrounding the practice field, watching intently as teenage boys in white and maroon (which they called red, which drove me nuts) jerseys and matching Lycra pants pushed each other and ran around with an oblong ball like Valjean and the last loaf of bread. Football players reminded me of ballet dancers. They wore the same kind of uniform, but one group leaped over each other, and the other group piled on top of each other. I always thought the second group was far gayer. And even though I had no idea what anyone was doing, watching boys in Lycra jump on top of one another was enough for me.

I'd been watching Chuck for a long time—when he walked down the hall, I stared, and when he talked with his friends, I stared, and

when he came into the cafeteria, I continued to stare. I don't know if he ever saw me or saw me staring. I didn't know and I didn't care. I couldn't stay away from him. I didn't know why, and I didn't know what it was; all I knew was wherever he was, I was going to be there.

It wasn't love. It wasn't like Cassandra. It wasn't like Cin. It wasn't like Carmen. It wasn't like that. It was something else. I couldn't quite figure it out. My insides shook and rattled. It was unnerving and made me a little sick to my stomach. It wasn't pleasant, this feeling.

I hated it.

And I loved it.

I never wanted it to end.

The practice ended, and as soon as the coach blew his whistle, I turned and headed inside. I wanted to make it to the locker room before he did. I would stay after school when I wasn't in rehearsal so I could practice on the gymnastics equipment. I loved being physical and I loved art, so I'd tumble around on the floor and play on the uneven bars and on the balance beam, none of which I was very good at, but all of which made me happy. I would try to time my workouts to the exact moment when Chuck would be changing his clothes.

I ran past the after-school crowd gathering in the hallways and straight into the boys' locker room, where I waited. My heart beating and my brow sweating, I sat at the end of the brown bench that stood between two rows of green, unpolished lockers . . . and I waited.

Cassandra

She was beautiful, a sort of brunette goddess. And she allowed me to be me. At a time when most everyone, apart from the drama group, abused me, she was one of the few who allowed me simply to be. And I

loved her—truly, deeply loved her. We sang together and wrote together and held each other and talked about art, and love, and poetry, and we danced. It was all truly beautiful. And it changed me.

When Cassandra and I were together and alone, I wanted to make love in a gentle, perfect manner. But it never turned out that way. It was usually fast, usually timid, and mostly unsatisfying. I wanted very badly, as I'm sure she did as well, for us to really find ourselves intertwined in artful lovemaking, but it mostly felt like a class in ceramics . . .

Kinda messy and kinda dull.

We had experimented with almost everything we could think of by this time, barring penetration. I think we were both nervous, and certainly fear played a major role in our months of procrastination. I remember, as we lay on her parents' couch in the middle of the day, in the dead of summer, we were holding each other and kissing and touching, and the ceramics class was in full session when, without warning, I felt her press against me in a way that was unfamiliar. Instinctively, I knew what she meant, and I understood what was about to happen. My breathing accelerated as we staggered up the stairs to her room and our clothes came off. She was fierce and gentle. I remember her sound. It was lithe and beautiful, and simultaneously there was an aggression in her that I really loved.

That afternoon, everything we had been doing culminated in my losing my virginity. It felt like everything I had read . . . in the *Penthouse Forum*. I remember we lay on her bed, and I looked out of the window promising myself I would remember this feeling forever. It was a big day for me. I was no longer a virgin, and that meant a great deal. I don't know what endowed the act with such significance. Was it the feeling of masculine power, a learned behavior, or maybe I finally felt some sense of normalcy?

Whatever the reason, I remembered it. I held on to her, hoping it would always, always feel like this.

Chuck

After five or ten minutes, I heard the familiar rumble of male feet and the rattle of voices as they came closer and closer to the locker room. I had now decided to change. I knew where Chuck's locker was, and even though mine was assigned across the room from his, I began taking off my clothes and laying them carefully on the bench. Having no knowledge of seduction or maleness, I decided the best thing to do was emulate the only person I knew who even remotely smelled of Sexy:

Miss Gypsy Rose Lee.

As the boys filed in, slapping each other, cursing, racing toward their respective lockers, there I was, small, brown, and skinny, peeling off my clothes and grinding my hips to an imaginary snare drum. I laid my shirt across the bench and bent over so far that my head tapped the concrete floor. I tried to shimmy out of my pants, but I got caught in the belt buckle, which whacked me in the gonads. I carried on and posed in my white Fruit of the Looms. I began to roll them down à la Gypsy. The boys began to get undressed as quickly as possible and headed for the showers. Some pointed, most guffawed, and some called me "Faggot." I didn't care; this was for Chuck, and somehow, I knew it would work.

I turned around, naked amidst strewn-about Gap clothing. I ended up alone, then began to pick up my underwear and the rest of my things and make my way to my locker. I honestly couldn't believe it hadn't worked. I didn't know what I had done wrong. But . . . it was over and I moved on to plan B.

As I changed and made my way up the stairs in my Saxon gym clothes, I felt a tug at my shirt.

"Hey. Where ya goin'?"

It was Chuck. Dressed in a white pullover sweater and bell-bottomed jeans.

"I . . . um . . . practice."

"Oh," he said calmly.

He smiled.

He walked to the men's restroom across the hall from where we were standing and held the door open. I walked toward him, riddled with fear and bursting with excitement. I shimmied past him, and he closed and locked the door from the inside. He grabbed my crotch and massaged it, and then began to take off my clothes. I could barely breathe. We undressed and he laid me down on the bare, filthy boys' room floor. From his backpack he produced a jar of Vaseline.

Apparently, he'd come prepared.

He lubed himself up and put me on my back. I couldn't say anything. I was excited and truly, deeply frightened. I didn't know what to expect. I had absolutely no frame of reference. He knelt and then stopped.

He saw my face.

"You okay?" he asked.

I couldn't speak. I literally could not form words.

"Scott? You okay?" He leaned back on his haunches, his erection pointing north like a compass. "You scared? There's nothing to fear. Really. It's gonna hurt for a minute and then it's gonna be really fun. I'll go slow, and if you don't like it, we'll stop. Okay?"

I opened my mouth, but still no words.

"Say okay or I won't do it."

I took a breath and closed my eyes . . .

"Okay . . ."

He was half right . . . it hurt like hell. I wasn't sure where the "really fun" part was supposed to come in, unless it was watching Chuck have an orgasm. Otherwise, I could have done without it altogether.

63

Chuck and Cassandra/Cassandra and Chuck

Chuck and I met after Cassandra and the rest of the misfit gang went off to college. They had all been in their final year of high school when I joined the drama club. When they left, I filled the spiritual void with as much anonymous sex as I possibly could.

I fell deeper and deeper in love with Cassandra, even with her away. We saw each other occasionally, broke up a few times, and continued our cookie-cutter lovemaking. In the interim, as the 1970s came to a close, I was visiting restrooms (also known as tearooms) in the local mall, Woodfield, and having sex with other male students between classes, out in the parking lot, and, every once in a while, in the back of the library—which was really the only time I visited the library. Stonewall had ignited a gay revolution that began with the riots in Greenwich Village in 1969 and spread to the halls of Schaumberg High as I, too, cautiously explored my gay emancipation.

My first times gave me a strange glimpse into the ideas of gender and sex. I equated women with romance and men with restrooms. I found that women needed nurturing and time, whereas men needed nothing but a nod and a wink. This would serve me well in the coming years but would also haunt me for the rest of my life. As I blossomed into my teenage years, I was having one hell of a party . . .

And having first times all over the bloody place.

~

The odd thing for me was the more women I had in my life, the more my family ignored any sign of my feminine behavior. As long as I was a ladies' man, everything was fine. What they didn't know was what

else I was doing. I was giving blow jobs under stalls to faceless men in mall restrooms, alleys, and the back rooms of bars and restaurants. They knew nothing of the hand jobs in the smoking areas at my high school, or of the various teachers who seduced me and cajoled me at fourteen and sixteen years old to give them head in the back seat. I was enticed and excited by a male world that seemed purely sexual. It was a world in which these men treated me with disdain and abuse. They jerked me around, threw me on the bed, called me names, and at times, slapped my face and spat in my mouth. It was all part of the lovemaking for me. This was how I judged their desire. The rougher they were, the more desirable I believed I was.

But to my family, mainly my parents, the appearance was enough.

"Scott has more girlfriends than Carter has liver pills," Mimi would boast to her suburban teacher friends.

I wasn't sure exactly how many liver pills Carter was supposed to have, or who exactly Carter was supposed to be, but by her tone and her demeanor, I seemed to be doing just great. So, I kept it up, and hid anything that deviated from her norm.

That was how I stored my shame. And my container was getting bigger.

Things at home were not going well. My mother and stepdad had trouble keeping me honest and keeping me home. I liked to be out, especially when I could lie about my whereabouts and miss school the next day. I was a senior, and by that time my grades were so dismal that any thought of college was laughable. However, at eighteen years old, I was the high school's artist in residence. Although never really the star of any shows, I was cast in almost everything, both plays and musicals. I rarely had lines, and if I did, I was relegated to Guard Number Four, but I made my presence felt. I would juggle carrots in the background while the lead was orating about his dead father. I would race through

the hallways and make siren sounds, even though there were no sirens in the play. Or in the hallways.

So, obviously, I was meant for a higher calling than college. My brother was going to college. That was his responsibility. Not mine. And really, what exactly was a degree supposed to get me? Were there courses in Being a Broadway Star? I never once heard Ethel Merman talk about sorority life.

Max

It was around midnight by the time we got to Max's apartment, and I knew I should get home. He had graduated a year earlier than I did from Schaumburg High, so we knew most of the same people. He was tall and wide and reminded me a bit of a large refrigerator with limbs: big chest, thick arms and legs, and hands that could open two jars at once. We'd met through a mutual friend, and he played the piano. I loved any man who could accompany me. It was a great friendship. His face was kind, and he always spoke in musical terms.

"That movie was a bit too legato for me."

Max gave me a great appreciation of music. His idea of freedom and interpretation fascinated me. He'd play something and I'd sing it, and he'd tell me, "Okay, Scott, let go now. Just sing. Don't worry about hitting any of the notes. Just sing."

We created together, and time would float away. We got lost in the creativity and shared a developing work ethic.

I'd known Max for almost a year. I cannot tell you how it began that night. All I remember is that by the time we arrived at his apartment, with his one long green couch, his scattered piles of laundry, and his

stack of dirty dishes in the sink, it was the witching hour, and I began a small panic . . .

"I gotta get home, Max. My parents . . ."

"I know. It's super late, though. Maybe you should crash here and just call them and let them know where you are," he replied, plopping his music and his bag on the one piece of furniture he owned.

"No. I really should go."

I felt something shift. The room felt different and suddenly I didn't know him at all. I'm sure the evening wore on, but I do not remember what was said, or how we got to the couch. I wanted to go and I told him so. I tried to express my fear, which was growing and taking up more space in me. He tried to calm me. Putting his arm around me. Stroking my head. Smiling in a way I didn't recognize, and then finally, touching my leg and running his hand up my thigh toward my groin.

I sat. I said nothing. I didn't tell him to stop, and I didn't yell or scream or cry for help or hit him or pull away. I sat. I allowed him to grope me and fondle me and undress me and whisper to me and kiss my neck and lay me down on the green couch.

"Okay. Let's do it," he half whispered in my ear.

I wanted to scream. I wanted to tell him to stop, and so I tried to squirm away with him inside me. He laughed and slapped me and hunched down deeper. I screamed one scream and he covered my mouth. And then it was over.

I continued to see Max for the next year. He never touched me like that again and apologized constantly for it. I always accepted his apology and tried to move on. I assumed that if I could shove my agony farther down into my deep well of silence, it would eventually go away.

"It's okay, Max. Let's sing."

TEN

How Do I Get Back to Oz?

I sat down cross-legged with a group of twentysomething-year-old queer men. I was seventeen and spending my final summer in California with my dad at Harbor College. Every year I would spend three months with him, and the rest of the year I would go back to Schaumburg. Back to Mimi. Back and forth. Here and there, to and fro, like a big gay tennis ball. Mimi, Dad, Dad, Mimi. Freedom, Exile, Release, Prison.

Plopped in the middle of a rehearsal, surrounded by queers and show tunes, there was magic. I was free and unbound and filled with wonder. Rehearsing one musical after another, chorus boys would finger snap, and kiss each other, and hold hands, and meet under the black grand piano that was stuffed in the corner of one of the rehearsal rooms and give each other hand jobs. And the women loved them, and held them, and dated them, and complained about them, and asked their advice. And occasionally, there were heterosexuals. Men who would kiss and hold hands and talk sweetly to women, and even at ten, eleven, or twelve years old, I knew that I was not one of them. I do not know

how I knew; all I know is that I knew. And yet, when I joined the gays under the piano, I knew I didn't belong there either.

"Did you have a good time with your dad?" Mimi would ask, eyes wide open.

I would sometimes answer in the affirmative and tell her about the music and the magic and the sparkle.

"It was okay," I would lie. "I like it *here*, though, Mimi. I like it better here. Dad is so weird. His friends are weird too. They're just weird and they make me feel weird."

I was compelled to retreat into the gray world of Schaumburg. I tried to make the best of things.

The boy suit I was forced to put on every single day was getting tighter and tighter. It was getting closer and closer around my neck and my stomach and around my groin. Assuming a face of joy and happiness became a challenge. Mimi said I was happy. Dad said I was happy. Those few who befriended me did so because I appeared to be so happy. So, I pretended to be happy.

But it wasn't enough. I wasn't enough. I needed to be more and I didn't know what. I was drowning, falling deeper into a black pit of endless nothingness. I was being swallowed up. The music stopped. The band had packed up.

What I saw in the mirror disgusted me, and there were no other reflections to borrow or to steal. Everyone was gone. Chrisanne was at college. Cassandra was at college. My posse of theater humans had vanished in a puff of smoke. I had no one in the hallways protecting me, shielding me, or slaying the dragons at the gate. I felt as if I had turned around and the dance floor had emptied. I was alone and I couldn't keep it up anymore—this lie. There was nothing left in my mirror but the truth.

So, one summer day, I decided to kill myself.

I walked into my bathroom. The sun was bright and white hot that day. It was a lazy Friday, just like any other Friday, except that on this particular Friday, I wanted to die. Mimi and Bill were out, and the house was silent. I reached over the sink to the medicine cabinet and emptied a bottle of Tylenol into my hand. I then walked back into my room and turned on the TV. I had left a suicide note in code on my desk, listing the reasons why my life needed to end.

I sat at the edge of my bed, and as the TV blared and the sun streamed into my room, illuminating my bare feet, I started taking the pills. One by one, downing them with water. And as they went down, after a coffee commercial, *The Phil Donahue Show* appeared, already midepisode. There he was, silver haired and quick, stepping up and down the aisle with his microphone as his guide and weapon.

"And down here . . . here, this lady . . . this lady with the red hair. Hello . . . what is it? You look upset," Phil crooned breathlessly. "Are you upset? What has you upset?" He was stabbing her chin with the thick end of the microphone.

"I think she's upset you're trying to make her blow that mic, Phil," I said out loud, taking another pill.

The camera panned from the woman's obviously stern expression to three women onstage. These women, dripping in sequins and beads, hair perfectly coiffed, looking like supermodels, sat in three separate chairs, holding on to one another and settling into their roles as hosts of Phil's party. Two African American women and one white lady with an accent that sounded like Colleen Dewhurst as filtered through Zsa Zsa Gabor. They were all beautiful, elegant, wild, hilarious, witty, intelligent, and very sexy. I realized that the transition from the furious redhead to these magnificent creatures had been carefully planned.

"So . . ." the woman with the red hair began, her voice menacing and her eye squinted, "are you a man or a woman?"

"Dah-ling," the woman with the accent replied with a hand toss, "I am Showgirl."

These were really funny strippers. I liked strippers as a rule, but these three really had it all together. The crowd laughed. The other two women laughed. Phil laughed. I popped more pills and laughed as well. Some audience members applauded. Others booed and shifted in their seats.

And then I stopped. I sat on the edge of my bed, blinked for a moment, and put the pills aside. These women were not strippers. These women were not women, and yet they were. I didn't understand. I tried to get up, woozy from the pills as they began to take effect, and wobbled a little closer to the TV. They were smiling. They were genuine and larger than I could imagine, and most of the audience seemed to like them.

I saw these women, and I stood there by the TV, holding on, and I said out loud, "Oh. My God. There I am."

My head began to swirl. The floor came toward me and punched me in the face as I tasted just the slightest hint of blood. I was so awfully tired. I could really use a long, long sleep.

~

"Tell them you didn't mean to do this," Mimi implored, leaning over me in the hospital bed.

My eyes fluttered. I was lying in a blue paper gown. It was daytime and I was facing one small window. Mimi's eyes were bloodshot, and she was very, very close to me, whispering as if we were sharing state secrets.

"But I *did* mean to do it," I answered in my best stage whisper.

"That doesn't matter. It's against the law doing . . . whatever it is you tried to do. Do you want to go to jail?" she hissed.

"Jail? No. I don't want to go to jail, Mimi."

"Then tell them you didn't mean to do it and that it was an *accident*," she said, moving even closer and breathing on my chin.

"You mean like . . . I was sitting on my bed watching TV and was suddenly attacked by a fistful of Tylenol?"

Just then a very stern, very round man in a white coat walked into my room. My head was heavy and my throat sore from the gigantic tube they shoved down it the previous night. I still had bits of throw-up on my gown; Mimi had spent the entire night holding my head as more and more pills made their way through my system. We had learned that I didn't need a huge number of pills to poison my body.

The round man with the big black clipboard sat down next to me. "So, Scott. What happened?"

His voice was very soothing, but I was absolutely terrified I was going to jail. The poor doctor assumed I was having some sort of psychotic breakdown and ordered me into immediate therapy.

Doctors. Pills. And silence. Neither Mimi nor I nor anyone in our family ever brought up the subject or said the word "suicide." No one really looked at the real me, and so no one could really save me.

Not even me.

As I wept, I would pray, "I just want it to end. I just want it to end . . . so it can start."

~

Sitting cross-legged under the piano trying to make myself fit was futile. Even in the Technicolor world of gays and show tunes, I was an outcast. I simply wasn't one of the shiny gay boys. California living was gorgeous. California living was surreal. But the sheer blinding truth of it made me want to flee.

The dreary, sunken gray and steeliness of Illinois, even as Mimi opened her arms up to me those few times, defeated me. I simply

couldn't take it anymore. I just wanted out. And so I sat cross-legged on the edge of the bed. I sat and took pills and saw the glorious sparkly ladies, glistening in faux diamonds and beckoning me toward them.

But I couldn't get there from here.

I couldn't get there.

How do you get back to Oz? Those shoes only worked one way.

So there I was, trapped and falling fast. Here and there, to and fro, back and forth, spinning fast yet going nowhere.

How do I find my way back to a place everyone told me was a dream?

ELEVEN

Yes . . .

"Let's go to the city tonight," Barb said, flipping her cropped blond curls in my face.

"*Yes!*" I squealed.

Going downtown to me was the zenith of awesomeness and adultness. I had been out of my mother's house for almost a year but was still living in Schaumburg, not very far from where I started. Barb and I met at Thumpers, the local cool restaurant/bar/pickup joint/get-your-pot-for-half-price hangout where we both had gigs.

I would like to go on record as saying that I was a terrible, terrible waiter. I could never really remember much of anything, and people usually gave their orders so quickly that my scribbles looked like some sort of egg dish.

"I need eggs with broccoli-styled eggs on some eggs with a small side of . . . eggs?"

Strangely, I made amazing tips by developing my own sardonic survival technique of caustic comebacks, which suited me well. And weirdly, the customers loved it. Who knew that at the beginning of the 1980s in the Midwestern suburbs, a flaming queeny sissy boy with

too-tight black pants and snappy one-liners could become fashionable and chic?

Customer: "I'd like the fries instead of the baked potato."

Me: "And I'd like a house in the Hamptons."

Customer: "This steak is limp. I ordered it well done, not medium rare."

Me: "That cow is dead. One more degree isn't going to bring it back to life."

And one of my personal favorites:

Customer: "You know, you work for tips and you've got a real attitude. Aren't you afraid people will stop tipping you? What happens if your attitude loses you money?"

Me: "Oh, fuck off."

(That guy left me a hundred dollars wrapped in a used napkin.)

Whatever the reason, my caustic sense of humor worked, and it was finally making me money. Pretty good money, actually. Enough that I could move in with Carlos and Barb, both waiters and both pals, who were renting a condo and needed a roommate. So, by my third month at Thumpers, not only was I the worst waiter in the history of waiters, but I had met new humans, graduated from high school, was making enough money to have my own shared pad, and had restaurant patrons asking to sit in my station, just so they could push their friends to the head of the insult line.

Barb and I were determined to make outings to The City an event. These excursions meant a great deal to me. I had won the battle with my parents about college, insisting that I was going to be incredibly famous one day, and incredibly famous people have no need for long division or the study of the mating habits of the tsetse fly. They railed against me but eventually gave in. I held firm and never really delved any deeper into my fears and inhibitions. My dressing up was now habitual. It was constant, and it was still shameful. Somewhere deep

inside, I knew instinctively that going to another school environment would suffocate or destroy me. Thinking about it tightened my throat. Where would I dress up? I would have roommates. Where would I get my wigs and clothes, and how would I put on my concerts complete with intermissions and autograph signings? How would I find a human who would understand his roommate's obsession with Judy Garland, Liza Minnelli, and Lena Horne, which caused him to lip-synch to their songs at any time, day or night?

Somewhere in me, I knew that if I went to college and was shut up in another atmosphere where I felt stupid, shallow, and ill-equipped to play the part of The Boy, I would die. This time, the pills would take. I didn't know why at the time, I couldn't quite name the panic, but the uneasiness and the bone-scraping fear was enough to dissuade me. My instincts have always been my greatest savior, and they were in high gear. Ultimately, my self-protective carapace actually saved my life. Luckily, my parents gave in with the stipulation that if within the span of one year I was not working steadily as an actor, I would go to school.

So, I made sure I was working within the year.

And I was.

Working.

Steadily.

Within the year.

As an *actor*? Well . . .

It was just beginning to get dark as Barb and I drove through the streets of the North Side of Chicago. Chicago during the fall was busy and beautiful, and we were giggling and singing along with the radio, heading down Broadway on the gayest side of town. Finally, we spotted the large white building with a rooftop café. There was a big, black top hat on the front of it, along with big red lips, half covered by a massive black mustache. It was called Club Victoria. The movie *Victor/Victoria* was brand new, so we knew immediately that we had found the gays.

I had taken to seeking out humans who no longer believed in rules, people who dated and slept with and loved whomever they desired. We felt no sense of gay or straight, and so long as I was still dating both men and women, and sleeping with both men and women, the idea of proclaiming my gender was laughable, not to mention tedious.

I had come out to Mimi a few summers before this in a four-page letter. I took her to the garage and sat next to her as she read it. This letter told her I was gay, that I liked boys. Even at the time, it felt incomplete, untrue. But I had no other language, no other examples, no other way to express my essence besides the language I had been taught about the queer community. Which, at that time, was next to nothing.

Stone-faced and scotch in hand, Mimi sat forward and read.

Afterward, she took a long breath . . .

"Just promise me one thing, Scott," she murmured, taking a sip and looking at me with great sadness and hope. "Promise me you're not going to become a woman."

I smiled.

"That's ridiculous."

~

Riding up to the gay sign, in the gay neighborhood, surrounded by the gays not only made sense to us, it was thrilling and deeply satisfying. It felt natural. There was no fear. There was no hesitation. I understood their speech, and their walk, and their delight, and beauty and rage and power. I understood their sense of style, and flair and humor and wit, and their obsession with all things gorgeous. And I knew that the word "Fabulous" was designed and constructed by my tribe. We owned that word because we had survived by making our world Fabulous by necessity. You see, if we didn't, if we didn't do your hair, or find the right clothes for the function we weren't invited to, or choreograph that

award-winning musical we couldn't bring our same-sex partners to, we were murdered or thrown in jail or ravaged or tossed aside.

I learned that being Fabulous was our key to acceptance.

As Barb and I walked into the bar, the disco music enveloped us, and the tiny club, speckled with colored lights and few humans, pulsated and reverberated. We took a seat at the bar and ordered two drinks. We noticed there were stairs going both up and down. I asked the woman behind the bar how big the place was.

She turned quickly, smiling broadly, her long face amplified by the dirty blond hair that fell around her jaw.

"Downstairs are the dressing rooms. Right up there's the show lounge," she said in a deep alto, cleaning a glass and smiling.

Show lounge?

As that phrase rang in my head, the woman shuffled toward the end of the bar where two men hung their heads in their beers, and as she moved, she revealed a sign hanging from a lone nail right below the shot glasses. It was in green ink, all in caps:

TALENT NIGHT / EVERY THURSDAY / 6:30 P.M.

I poked Barb and pointed to the sign.

"Yeah?" she asked.

"Well! I have Talent!" I half screamed.

I called the bartender over and asked about Talent Night.

"Show up here next Thursday around five-thirty and sign up on the clipboard. It will be at the end of the bar. Don't dress like that!" she instructed.

I was certain this was it. I would perform at a club in downtown Chicago, someone would see me, discover this genius who had somehow slipped through everyone's fingers, and fame would appear on the horizon like the sunlight in the last act of *Who's Afraid of Virginia Woolf?*

The only problem was that I didn't know what I would perform. It was Talent Night and let's face it, I had many talents. Should I sing? Should I tell jokes? How about the one magic trick I knew?

"Why don't you dance?" Barb suggested after we got home.

"That is a great suggestion. After all, I am an excellent dancer. No one knows it, and I am not getting jobs as a dancer, but I have taken six whole lessons at the June Rold Dance Studio in Skokie, Illinois."

"Okay."

Dansation

"But I can't just get up there and dance. That's weird," I argued.

"Wait . . . I know! *Strip!*" Barb announced.

"Really?"

"Sure! That's sexy as hell, and you're still dancing, really," she assured me.

"Yeah. That's right. And I know how to strip . . . I mean . . . how hard can it be . . . I do it every night before bed! *I love it!*" I screamed back.

I decided to do the water number from *Flashdance*. This way, I could strip down to my dance belt, which at that time was a sort of large, triangular, black, polyester-cotton-blend diaper thing that cinched my butt cheeks together and covered my groin like a giant kite. I decided I would re-create the famous moment where Jennifer Beals' dance double sits in the chair, in heels and a G-string, pulls a magical cord connected to nothing, and is splashed with water and stands there with hair wringing wet and buck naked.

Except for my black kite dance belt.

Barb helped me choreograph, and I recruited a stagehand to be up in the flies to douse me on cue. I decided to pantomime the string pull. That would give me a chance to show off my Streep-like Acting Muscle.

The following week, Barb and I arrived at the club an hour early. She stayed upstairs drinking herself calm, and I headed down to the dressing room. As I entered with my blue dance bag and already wearing my white Capezios and leg warmers, I noticed that in the row of seats facing the giant wall-length mirror, there were only women. Every human in this crowded dressing room was female. I felt a little odd, so I asked where the men's changing room was.

"Sit down, girl. You're in the right place," one of the half-dressed women growled, taking a long drag of her cigarette like Gloria Swanson.

"Girl. Girl? *Girl!*"

As the show began, one by one, the girls put on their feathers, sequins, and their long trains of gold and green. They'd giggle, argue, talk about last night's men and the size of their cocks, what they did with them, what they didn't do with them, and what would have happened had they done what they wanted to do with them. There was an enormous amount of cock talk. I readied myself as best I could. As

they disappeared up the rickety, half-painted staircase to the stage, I heard Barbra, Judy, Liza, and Ann-Margret. I couldn't quite figure out what was happening. I couldn't figure out if they were pole dancing to "People," but if that was the case, I was most definitely in the right place.

I turned to the African American woman to my left. With big, brown, saucerlike eyes and long, expressive hands, she seemed to be the captain of the ship. People came to her for advice, for zips, and for extra food. She seemed to have bits of cookies, chips—the kinds of things your mom has in her purse that magically pop out when you even hint you might be hungry.

"Is everyone here a dancer?" I asked.

She brushed out her long black hair and never took her eyes off her reflection in the half-dusted mirror.

"Yeah, girl. We all dance, Miss Thing. Ya got to, really. Ya can't just do one thing. Ya gotta do multiple things. You know what I mean, Miss Two?" She smiled. Her smile was warm and filled me up.

I stood at the threshold of the dressing room. The women lounged in one long row, splashing powder and perfume and tossing long white gloves and pieces of underwear around the room. The thunderous sound of voices echoed through the small space.

"Girl, that man last night. His dick. I mean. Girl. I can't even. Sister."

"Yes, chile, we know how you are. We know that. It ain't nothin' unless it's somethin'."

"Y'all whores kill me. Dick, dick, dick. Don't you have anything else on your minds?"

"Yeah . . . Big Dick."

The entire room guffawed, hands went up in the air, and a woman with flaming red hair stood up and tightened her black girdle.

I couldn't move. I felt obtrusive. I was standing in a half-open door with my mouth open—lost and dazed in a sea of perfume and eye shadow with nothing to add . . . like the Avon lady without her product.

"Close the door, honey," the woman with the flaming red hair said sweetly. "C'mon in and take a seat. You can sit here at the end," she said, pulling out a black chair and guiding me to it.

The other two girls smiled. They continued to dress and apply and fluff and spray, and when they'd glance over at me, they'd occasionally smile.

"I'm Ginger Spice," the woman with the red hair said. "That there is Daphne, and next to her, Diana."

"Hey, girl," Daphne said, her round face exploding in a toothy grin.

Diana moved in closer to the mirror. As she stood up, she leaned in to apply what looked like a false eyelash. Her long, jet-black hair fell down the small of her back as she squinted hard and breathed deeply. She held her finger in place and tilted her head toward me, peering at me through her one open eye.

It was Diana Ross. Same face. Same eyes. Same cheekbones. It was Diana Ross. As she released her finger and batted those magical spiral lashes, I almost burst into hysterical tears. Mahogany. It was Mahogany. Plain and simple, Diana Ross as Mahogany. I was going to get ready next to Stripper Diana Ross as Mahogany.

This was the single greatest night of my life.

"You okay over here, girl?" Ginger asked, her hands placed gently on my shoulders.

Girl.

They kept referring to me as "girl."

"I'm fine. I'm great. Thank you. I'm . . ." I stared at Diana, who was by now on to lash number two. "I'm just really nervous."

"Oh, Miss Two, you ain't gotta be nervous. You just do yo thang, honey. That's it. That's it, Miss Two, you just do the thing you do, and

that's all you have to do." Daphne spoke like a machine gun. Rapid-fire and steady. Her short brown hair bobbing, and her cigarette puffing madly.

I was transfixed.

One bracelet . . . another bracelet. No, not that one, this one. This pair of earrings. Wait. No. Not those . . . those are too much. It's these over here. This pair. She clipped them on her ears and threw her hair back, checking this side of her face, then that side of her face. She shone and glistened as the lights in the dressing room, a little hazy from the face powder in the air, illuminated a legendary performer, sequined, spit polished, and perfect.

I turned my chair to watch the show in the mirror as the conversation continued, and I caught a glimpse of my face. My freshly cut short-cropped hair was tucked neatly behind my ears. I saw my square jaw and my stocky shoulders. I moved in a little closer.

His eyes.

His eyes look so sad, I thought.

"Girl, the rule," Ginger said, seated and painting her face with a large fluffy brush filled with red and pink powder.

I sat back, startled.

"Rule?" I asked, eyes wide.

"Never get too close. You don't wanna see what no one can see."

The other two laughed. Daphne held her hand back, ready to give Diana a high five, and without turning from her reflection, Ms. Ross simply held her hand up as if testing the wind, and Daphne's came crashing down.

"Listen to what she sayin', girl. She's talking right at ya," she said, seeing me in the mirror.

I sat back in my black chair. I swallowed, turned away from the mirror, and began taking things out of my bag. I was done with reflections for now. I had a show to do. I had a number to do. I had a Broadway

career to map out. I didn't have time for all this fortune-cookie stripper bullshit.

I was ready to be seen by the people who would see only what I wanted them to see. I was done looking at myself. It was time to go onstage.

The song began, and the sound pumped through the decrepit speakers, squeaking a bit and causing the thin walls to shake with each downbeat. The stage needed painting badly, and I slipped a few times as various pieces of clothing came off. I twirled a little over here, ran to the other end of the all-too-brief runway, and almost toppled over. Then I centered myself, ready and poised for the splash.

It came.

And when it came, because it came with such force, and because I hadn't really practiced much at all, it knocked me over and onto the barely painted floor. I tried to recover by gyrating my hips and gesturing a few times, but by then, the song had ended, and an empty bucket rolled sadly onto the stage next to my newly scraped right knee. The audience, made up of mostly balding, middle-aged white men, applauded with looks of incredulous horror on their faces. Glancing at one another, some of the men got up with such force that their chairs banged against the too-close cocktail tables.

I slunk back downstairs. Mortified.

I stood in the dressing room, a room full of strippers in a run-down second-rate nightclub, my dance belt dripping wet with stale water, carrying the ice bucket I'd bought at the CVS. The audience thought I was insane, and the performers stood looking at me with great pity.

"Girl. It's okay. This just isn't your thing," one of them comforted me.

She came closer to me, and my chest heaved once before I started to weep. She put her arms around me, and just then, a tall, disheveled blond came rushing down the stairs. "C'mon, bitches! Curtain, whores! Curtain!" she shouted.

Someone threw me a red silk robe, we made our way up the spiral staircase, and we bowed to the twenty-three predominantly obese men in the audience.

As we made our way back downstairs, I moved to the end of the makeup station and began to pack my things. I heard the familiar giggles, the round, robust guffaws as they began to talk about where they'd end up tonight, with whom and with which cock, and then, as I peered into the mirror in front of me, between the streaks of old Windex and fresh face powder, I watched these humans transform. Some took out foam rubber from their chests and hips. Some reached inside their panties and slipped off an apparatus that held their genitals back. Wigs came off. Lashes were peeled. And as I stood there silent, a rapid-fire knock came at the door.

It was Barb.

Her face was white and her voice was quivering.

I opened the door a bit wider than a crack and managed a half-whispered "I . . . huh?"

"Do you know where we are?" she whispered back.

"I . . . huh?"

"We're in a freaking *DRAG BAR!*"

Barb's face widened, and the pure joy that suffused it almost caused me to burst out laughing. I took a breath, turned to her, and with all earnestness whispered, "What's a drag bar?"

She rolled her eyes. She opened the door a crack more and turned my head toward the transformation that was occurring in the middle of the room.

"Those are Transsexuals, Scott. They're not women! This is *AWESOME!*"

Then she disappeared behind the closed door.

I stood in the center of what felt like a fractured piece of glass dropped from a thousand feet. Shards all around me. Danger. I realized

that in order to get to these beautiful humans, I needed to cross the River Jordan. But how? How was I to get from where I stood, all the way over to where they were? It seemed like a forever walk, a walk that would take lifetimes. I couldn't move. I feared I couldn't do it. But I had to get there because it was mine. It was home. It was family. It was Oz.

And as I welled up and began to inhale, Ginger Spice, with her violet eyes and her red wig, held out her hand to me. "Girl, you wanna go upstairs for a cocktail?"

And with that, I pushed through all the shame of hiding, all the repression of what was true for me, and I took my very first breath.

"Yes," I breathed.

After that one yes, along with the openness of my Trans sisters in that crowded dressing room, my life would never be the same. Not ever. They reached over the brokenness of me and brought me with them. And . . .

I had found my tribe. I had found my family.

And that club—where I doused myself with water in 1982, where the birth of me happened and the humans I never thought possible were possible, and where I finally got a taste of my own self and experienced true freedom—hired me.

I didn't have to think about it. I didn't have to ask anyone, and I didn't have to research to see if I might be suffering from some condition. This wasn't an illness. I had spent my life being ill. This was the cure.

So I went back, dressed in one of Barb's white dresses and a pair of old white pumps, and lip-synched to "How Lucky Can You Get" from *Funny Lady*. I worked at Club Victoria off and on for almost two years as a female impersonator, which in the early eighties was what my friends and I called ourselves. I searched the liner notes of my *Flashdance* soundtrack and found the singer named Shanti, the originator of the song "He's a Dream." I loved the name, so I changed the *i* to an *e* and became Shanté. I had found a name. I had found a home.

I had finally found peace.

Introducing Shanté

Drag Language

Miss Thing

A term of endearment as well as an exclamation. It is affectionate and yet can also be a crucial warning.

"You look gorgeous, Miss Thing."

Or . . .

"Miss Thing! That dress! Don't do it!"

Mary

Everyone's called Mary. You. Your husband. Your dog. Your enemy and your best friend. Mary is a bit less familiar than Miss Thing. People closer to you might deserve a Miss Thing, whereas the idiot who stands in the ten-items-or-less aisle at Ralphs with eleven items is definitely "Mary."

Ironically, I don't remember anyone actually named Mary being called "Mary." I have no idea why.

Miss Two

Don't search for Miss One; you'll only waste your time. This is a deeply affectionate version of "Miss Thing." This is for your BFF or your closest relative. "Miss Two" is said with great love and affection for the human in front of you. I loved this phrase. Still do.

Down and Back

These two confused me for the longest time, and I couldn't decipher between them. It's all about aesthetics, really. "Down" and "Back" are for emphasis—if you're in agreement with someone or you want to put an extra emphasis on something.

"That dress is fabulous. Down."

Which means the fabulous is extra fabulous.

Or . . .

"Girl, is this dress fabulous?"

"Back!"

Which means this fabulous is even more fabulous than the previous fabulous.

Okay?!

This really needs to be heard. There is a very specific inflection at the end of this word, as if you're asking a question but do not expect an

answer. This is an agreement. Possibly the strongest affirmation you can give another human. It can also be a cheer of sorts. As if you've done something particularly fantastic and we are truly happy for you.

"That guy fucked the hell out of me last night, girl!"

"OKAY?!"

We are truly happy for you.

Girl

This one took me longest really to understand and implement. "Girl" can be an entire phrase, a single thought, an exclamation, or sometimes an aside. Just like in *Hamlet*.

If your girlfriend is going out on a date, and the man she's seeing is also sleeping with you, as she's getting ready for her date with him, in which you know the two of you will be occupying the same couch in a matter of minutes, and out of the blue she asks if you really like this guy, cuz she does, you might say:

"Girl . . ."

(This is an entire sentence.)

If your girlfriend just bought a fabulous set of Louis Vuitton luggage with her last paycheck instead of paying the three months of back rent she owes, you might say:

"Girl!!!"

(An exclamation.)

When your girlfriend admits her hunky football-playing boyfriend likes to dress up like Mary Tyler Moore and call himself Sylvia, you might say:

"Girrrrrrl . . ."

(An aside.)

~

I was standing on the rooftop of Club Victoria. Daphne stood next to me. It was the summer of 1982, and I had been there for only a few weeks. The vernacular was flying around the dressing room, and I was trying my best to fit in. It seemed even within my own tribe there were rules. Daphne leaned over the concrete railing that surrounded the outdoor patio. We were in rehearsal for the weekend show, and she stood, her half T-shirt revealing her belly button, her hips round and her breasts just buds. And that face. Daphne always reminded me of Diahann Carroll. Her lips were full and her eyes were bright. She drank occasionally, but whatever other drugs she did, they didn't seem to repress her life force. She had a throaty, full laugh, and she was one of the kindest new pals I had. She gave me makeup tips when she could and helped me to form an act that might last beyond a few weeks. I couldn't very well exist on "How Lucky Can You Get" and Betty Buckley's "Memory" from *Cats*.

She also gave me occasional elocution lessons. Daphne was my Henry Higgins.

"Girl, I've got to find Miss Two, down. This is crazy, and Mary . . . I mean, Miss Thing . . . I mean!" she would say, puffing on her cigarette and watching the noonday Chicago summer traffic below us.

"I . . . huh?"

She taught me. And she did it in a way that was about example and not retribution. The first great teachers I had were my drag family. Daphne showed me that teaching can be kind and gentle. It can also be completely ridiculous and super silly. That's what made it that much more joyful for me. We had a language, a musical language that only we knew and only we spoke. And for the very first time in my life, I was not only understood, but I was also heard.

Down.

Back.

Oka*AAYY*?

TWELVE

Christmas and Lana Turner

The phone rang. I was just coming out of the shower and was about ready to do the leg-shaving thing. I realize this should be done in the shower, but when you've had very little practice, you're already in your twenties, you've had no motherly help or sisterly advice, and all the female fam you have are queens, this was the only option.

"Girl. I would suggest stepping out of the shower before you start shaving," Ginger explained to me between shows one night.

"Why?"

"Cuz it's your first couple of times, and you're gonna need balance. Standing like an ostrich under a waterfall is never helpful. Especially when there's a razor involved."

Ginger Spice had become my confidante, my confessor, my surrogate mother when Diana wasn't around, and my best pal. Although Ginger lived in and out of drag, she was always Ginger, and she was always "she." I never used her given name—what we in our community call our "dead name"—even when she did.

"What was your given name?" I asked one night.

"You won't believe it."

"I will."

"After I tell you, it's okay to howl like a monkey, Chauncey."

She always called me Chauncey. I can't remember exactly how it came about, but it was some sort of play on Shanté. My drag name began as "Shanti" with an *i* at the end, but it looked very different in print than it did coming out of one's mouth. I wanted the accent on the final syllable—like "olé" or "matinée" or "I'm gay."

Like that.

But with an *i* at the end, it read as though I was a small house on the far edge of town. It was Ginger who changed the *i* to an *e* and suggested an accent to emphasize the pronunciation.

"And no last name."

"Everybody has a last name, Ging."

"Does Cher?"

Ginger never did characters. She never lip-synched to Liza or Judy or Ethel and never really did impersonations. Back in the early days of drag, especially the late seventies and early eighties, when we were first coming out of the darkness and into the mainstream, female impersonators were just that—they were required to impersonate females. Jim Bailey, arguably one of the most well-known performers at the time, made a living creating the illusion of Peggy Lee, Barbra Streisand, and Phyllis Diller. His Judy Garland was internationally recognized and praised throughout the US and Europe. He was the first of us to appear on nationally syndicated television shows like *The Carol Burnett Show* and *Here's Lucy*. Of course, these shows always used him as the butt of a joke, the revelation that Jim wasn't Phyllis, or Peggy, or Barbra, that he was in fact a man in a dress.

Bailey himself constantly reiterated that he was "an actor," and not a female impersonator. This was during the early eighties when drag queens and female impersonation were underground fetishes. We grew

accustomed to being entrapped outside of our clubs and nightspots. So, Bailey was always very careful. In a now infamous *Here's Lucy* episode, Lucy promises to get Phyllis Diller to appear at a benefit and, of course, is unable to deliver her. Lucy sees Bailey and hires him for the show, which turns out to be a huge success. A scene in this episode shows Jim in his dressing room, half in drag, and for absolutely no reason at all, we get a glimpse of him lighting up a long, brown cigar and smoking it. His shape changes so radically, it's as if he becomes John Wayne. He swaggers, shoulders back, head cocked, swaying back and forth as if the horse he rode in on were seasick. Even in my early teens, before I found my tribe on Phil's talk show, I was mortified. I didn't understand why people were laughing. And although I don't know this for a fact, I don't think Jim ever smoked a cigar in his life. It was a prop designed to draw attention to and underscore his maleness. This was a Man who did Manly Things. This was not a faggot in a wig. The only terminology available at the time for our community was clinical, the only other categories we had were pre- and post-op Transsexuals. And had Jim been one of those, it would have meant the end of his career.

This remains the only *Lucy* episode I cannot watch.

Ginger was a revolutionary performer. The only other female impersonator I knew at that time who was simply herself and no one else onstage was the infamous Chili Pepper, a legend at the Baton in downtown Chicago. But the Baton was unattainable. It had been featured on talk shows and written about in the *Los Angeles Times* and the *New York Times*, and Chili herself was good friends with Oprah Winfrey, who seemed to be the Phil Donahue of the early eighties. No one at Club Victoria entertained the idea that any of us would ever set foot on that stage. It was too far away. Too much of a dream.

"But Chauncey . . . I think if anyone can get there—you can," Ginger would cajole.

Ginger's expressive face and deep golden eyes looked right through me. To be honest, I was never sure why she liked me so much, or why our friendship happened so fast. It never made much sense. She was so kind to me. Doing my makeup, picking out clothes, helping me practice lip-synching. Being with Ginger Spice was among the few occasions that my rage and my bone-rattling fear of any close human relationship seemed to be at rest. There was rarely peace in my life, but Ginger gave me respites of calm. Her hands soothed my forehead, her laughter rang through the soul of me, and her advice was golden.

But Ginger had a temper.

That was one of the many things we shared. There was this bubbling, cellular anger that seemed to permeate almost everything we did and everyone we met. We were mistrustful and suspicious, sometimes of each other. I stole from Ginger: booze, dresses, jewelry, and sometimes money from her purse while she was onstage. She always knew and always forgave me, but I got a few slaps and was pushed into a few walls. I once saw Ginger take a bottle of beer and crack it over a man's head after a show. His head gushed blood as he grabbed at his face with both hands. The two other men at his table screamed. Ginger stood there, the half-cracked bottle in her hand pointing directly at the bloody victim's chest.

"Call an ambulance!" the men at the table yelled, backing away from Ginger.

"Holy shit, girl. Stop!" I screamed.

"Shut the fuck up, Chauncey!"

She moved closer to the bloody, quivering man, whose white tank top was streaked dark brown, small spatters on his neck and shoulders.

"Go ahead and say it again, bitch," she murmured.

The man screamed in pain and headed for the door, closely followed by his two pals. Jennifer, the owner of Club Victoria, stood behind the door, calmly wiping glasses and smiling.

I never found out what happened, or what he said to her, and I knew enough not to ask. Ging was not exactly an open book. But I admired the way she handled herself. Especially with men.

~

The answering machine in my apartment picked up as I stood, dripping wet, razor in hand.

"Scott? It's Mimi. Hello? Oh. That's right . . . I'm having a party next month. I would like you to be there. I know you have to . . . I know that you have to be . . . don't bring any presents. I know you can't afford presents, so please do not bring anything. How are your teeth? Have you quit smoking yet? I hope you have a car. Do you have a car? You have to drive from the city all the way to Schaumburg. I don't know how you're going to do that if you don't have a car. (Pause. Clink, clink, clink go the ice cubes in her cocktail.) Okay. It'll be the week before Christmas, and wouldn't it be nice if you brought your guitar? I think people would enjoy that. You're still singing, aren't you? (Clink.) All right. Monday the eighteenth at six, and please don't bring any presents. I know you can't afford any presents. Wear something muted. Bye. (Clink.)"

The razor slipped out of my hand and landed on the fuzzy purple bath mat.

It had been almost two years since Mimi and I had spoken. After I moved out, every now and then I'd borrow a friend's car, usually Ginger's, and trot out to the suburbs to sit in our old kitchen and chat and gossip and giggle and be with my mother for about an hour. The visits were usually pleasant, as Mimi would start drinking around noon, and by the time I arrived, she was just sauced enough to ignore all the lies I was feeding her.

"Where are you working now?" she'd ask.

"I'm singing downtown in a nightclub. I have a trio and a brilliant musical director."

"I'd love to come one night. When are you performing?"

"Oh, we closed last week, Mimi. Next time."

I was living in Ginger's old studio two stories above a gay bar called Christopher Street in the heart of Gaytown. I was still working at Club Victoria as Shanté, and my life was rich with friends, rife with anger and street fights, and my love affair with booze and cocaine was just beginning.

I'd sit with Mimi, wearing a baseball cap, puffy sweatshirt to hide my budding breasts started by the female hormones I was buying illegally and ingesting, big, baggy jeans, and sneakers. My face was usually stained from the previous night's drag makeup, with small traces of red liner and blobs of mascara still stuck in the corners of each eye. My nail polish was wiped off, and pale pink rouge dusted my cheeks. It was ridiculous, and I don't know who I thought I was fooling, except perhaps Mimi. I had told her when I left home at eighteen that I was performing as a female impersonator, but she wasn't aware of the kind of club I was working in or of my new chosen family, who had taken me in and adopted me, and she certainly didn't know who I was. If I didn't know, how could she?

As happy as I was, I was also that unhappy. I thought I had found the place I belonged, but the deeper I looked, the more out of place I felt. This idea of impersonating a female was insanity. I wasn't impersonating anyone, with the possible exception of myself. The real performance I was giving was offstage, and the falseness of my existence was starting to wear me down. I knew I wasn't a drag queen. I hated taking off my identity and shoving Shanté into a closet with my coats and boots. I hated the falsies and the padded hips. I wanted my body to reflect my spirit. And I wanted a family who lifted me up instead of throwing me aside. I wasn't Scott, and I wasn't Ginger, and I wasn't Shanté, and I wasn't Jim Bailey, and I wasn't a son or a daughter, and I

was lost. I was tumbling and I was seething, and I honestly didn't know why. I had tried several times to burn Shanté, to take the foam rubber and the hormones and put them in the trash and the fireplace and set them all ablaze. But that only lasted until the weekend. And then there was the rebirth. The inevitable, awful rebirth of Shanté.

So, I told Mimi that I was a female impersonator and a singer. I worked in clubs and I sang.

"Then when you come here you have to dress down."

"Dress down?" I asked.

"I don't want to see any of that. I cannot see any of what you're talking about. You're my Scott. And that's it. If you want to be here, you have to dress down."

So, I would visit and lie and dress down.

But one day, I had had enough.

"I'm not doing this anymore, Mimi. I can't," I confessed one afternoon at the kitchen table.

"Do what?"

"Visit you like this. I come into the house dressed like Foster Brooks, and you hide me in the kitchen and shuffle me out the back door at seven. I'm a dirty secret and I can't do this anymore."

Silence.

Mimi sat back in her chair and looked out the kitchen window, and without turning her head away, she said quietly, "Okay. I guess that's the way it'll have to be, then."

"What do you mean?"

"I guess we can't see each other."

And we didn't. Until the phone rang two years later, and she invited me to her Christmas party with my guitar and ordered me to wear something muted.

~

The night I drove down, the Chicago winter was in full swing. Ginger lent me her brown station wagon, and I was attempting to navigate the forty-five-minute drive from downtown to Schaumburg by way of the icy interstate—in six-inch heels. I hadn't chosen something muted. Shanté dressed. Shanté entered a room. Shanté came through the doorway with large, teased, Aqua-Netted hair, with something that sparkled, with tan hose that came in eggs, and bejeweled and bangled and necklaced and perfumed. Shanté was my outlet, and she was my savior. She allowed me to experiment and dream. I never had an adolescence as a young girl, so I was making up for lost time. I forced myself into playing a role so that my gender was less of an identity and more of a statement. Shanté demanded attention and respect, though she rarely earned it. I was learning that all those years of silence, when I was beaten or pushed or spat on, all those times being raped or handled or shoved against lockers and having my groin grabbed, of trying to hide what little I had left of myself in the nearest closet, and all those adults who blamed me, were over. I had had enough. It was my turn. So I got loud. I got loud in what I wore, what I said, and how I moved.

And now Mimi was going to see *Me*. Well . . . a cartoon version of me. And so were her friends.

This wasn't a costume. This was who I was and who I always dreamed of being . . . or so I thought.

I was Shanté.

Free. Large. And ready.

As I pulled up to the house, I saw rows of cars parked by the curb. Snow continued to fall, covering the windshields. I pulled up as close as I could to the house. I had decided on an electric-green, skintight cocktail dress, peppered with sequins at the hem and a slit running up the back right below my ass. The front plunged enough to where my hormone breasts, with help from a push-up bra from Diana and falsies, folded twice, showed ample cleavage. I had on a pair of white opera

gloves, and for a reason only explained by my need to make an entrance, I wore a white-blond wig that swept over my right eye. My hair was packed with so much spray and littered with white flakes, clinging on for dear life and gathering at the crown of my head like a yarmulke. My secondhand beige coat with the tattered right sleeve fell just below my knees, and my black pumps smooshed into the slush at the doorstep of the house. I had on bright-red lipstick, and there were sparkles on my false eyelashes—just at the tips. I didn't want to be too much.

I rang the bell.

The sounds of the party emanated from inside, and the glow of the lights in the top-story living room landed on the manicured rosebushes lining the walkway.

Mimi opened the door dressed in a red-velvet pantsuit and sporting dozens of light gold necklaces. She looked radiant and drunk. Her face was flushed, and her alabaster skin was lined with blush and too much mascara.

We stood at the threshold, staring at each other—the snow collecting in my Aqua Net.

"My God," she spat out, frozen in terror. "You look like Lana Turner."

I took that as a compliment and swept past her.

The evening consisted of me tossing one-liners left and right to my mother's suburban teacher friends—never really answering their questions and believing I was the hit of the party.

"Where are you working now?"

"Did you say *where*, or *who*?"

Silence.

"I love your outfit. It's really beautiful."

"Thanks. I sucked a lot of dick for this dress!"

Silence . . . and horror . . .

"I'm wondering . . . your hair . . . is it yours?"

"It better be mine, fer fuck's sake . . . I *paid* enough for it!"

Mimi would scamper into the living room and then scamper out. People would ask me questions, and I'd scream the answers. I didn't bring my guitar, and Mimi's friends had all been promised a concert. I hadn't told Mother that I had recently sold the guitar to buy drugs and that the last time I sang was with Dad during one of his summer musicals when I was a teenager. My voice rang far too masculine in me for it to be released in song. There is a truth and a power in singing, and I was nowhere near ready to begin to excavate.

The evening wore on, with Mimi drinking and serving sandwiches and dips, playing a few albums to couples dancing in the living room, and me bouncing between the couch and the bathroom doing line after line on Mother's new marble counter. As midnight approached, I began to say my goodbyes, with people enthusiastically shaking my hand. But I couldn't find Mimi. I assumed I had been the hit of the party, and she was busy going up and down the stairs taking bows for me.

"Your daughter is delightful."

"She's so charming."

"What a wit! What an intellect!"

"She reminds me of Auntie Mame. So adorably outrageous."

I met up with her best friend, Frieda, in the kitchen. Frieda and Mimi had befriended each other when Frieda's husband, Jim, and Bill met at IBM, where they were both employed. Frieda was German and always hinted she was, as a very young girl, a Holocaust survivor. She reminded me of Tina Turner: a lion's mane of hair and piercing brown eyes. She had great legs and a fantastic sense of humor. She was always on my side, yet always treated Mimi with great care and compassion. I had a wonderful photograph of the two of them: They were at some party, sitting at a white table, their arms around each other. Mother's face was lit from the inside. There are very few times Mimi was genuinely and openly happy. This was one of them. Her smile beamed, and

Frieda's arms seemed to latch on to her as if Mimi was falling and Frieda had caught her midair. They were both filled with joy. Frieda loved my mother, and the feeling was obvious and beautiful.

"Where's Mimi? I wanted to say goodbye," I asked Frieda as she leaned against the door.

"She's not downstairs?"

"Nope."

Frieda stared at my wig. She took a breath and smiled.

"Well . . . maybe she's in the bathroom. Want me to go find her?"

"No. I gotta go. I gotta get back. Will you tell her bye for me?" I hugged her. "Will you say goodbye?"

Frieda held on to me. For a while. I was quivering because my body was craving more coke. I wanted to get to the car to grab the extra package and do it before I started to come down.

"I really gotta go, girl," I said, pulling away.

"I'll tell her." She put her drink on the table and walked to the front door with me. "And merry Christmas, Scott."

"Merry Christmas."

I walked back to the station wagon and snorted the last of my stash from the glove compartment. I drove along the highway, eventually taking off the blond wig, which had fallen so far it looked as though I was wearing a melted vanilla ice cream cone. As I sped along, the snow falling more and more, I heard rattling behind me. I ignored it, but it continued and sounded close, as if it might be coming from the back seat.

"Great," I mumbled.

I pulled off the road, put the car in park, and peered into the back. Sitting on the passenger side, wrapped in gold-and-red paper and tied with a huge blood-red bow, was a package with a small card. I sat dumbfounded.

I pulled the card open: "Merry Christmas. I love you. Mimi."

My eyes filled up and my hands started to shake. I unwrapped the rectangular box, took off the lid, and lifted the sheet of tissue paper. I pulled out a white crewneck sweater with long sleeves covered in small, white pearls. The sleeves had tiny ruffles, and the bottom of the sweater flared just a bit.

It was a woman's sweater.

It was a woman's sweater meant for a woman and given to me by my mother. There was no word for what I was. I wasn't a drag queen, and I wasn't a son. There were no examples on TV or in film or in theater, and so my mother couldn't point to anyone and see me, and I couldn't take her by the hand, and lead her toward anyone, and say, "There I am. See? That's me right there." We were drowning in prejudice and misinformation. All we knew of each other was what we had told one another. And that wasn't very much. My pain was masked by drugs, her grief was masked by booze, and yet there it was, staring at me—under the tissue and tucked away in the back seat.

I curled up, holding the pearl sweater to my foam chest. I slowly rocked back and forth and closed my eyes. I wished she were there so I could throw my arms around her and really thank her.

I lifted the card one last time and read it out loud.

"Merry Christmas. I love you. Mimi."

No name.

She simply said she loved me.

That was all.

That Christmas I spent alone in my apartment with a small fake tree that fit on my desk and lit up when you clapped your hands. I watched movies all day, ate frozen fried chicken, and got high. And from the time I woke up until I went to bed that night, I never took off the sweater.

And I felt just like Lana Fucking Turner.

THIRTEEN

Hooker Stories

Every Saturday afternoon at the club, there'd be a get-together. The bar would open at 9:00 a.m., and drunks from far and wide would congregate. Occasionally, Ginger and I and some of the other girls would arrive and drink for free, dressed in our finest Saturday-afternoon drag, and chat with men while knuckling it at the bar. Sex was easy. Sex was never a problem. Even though almost everything I possessed either popped off or came unglued, the men who wanted sex had their own idea of what we were, and who they were when they were with us. They identified as straight and yet never had a problem with my penis. In fact, that was the first thing they asked, eyes wide.

"Do you still have it?"

"Sure. Do you?"

Very few of them got that joke.

One afternoon, as the men trickled in, I caught the attention of a middle-aged man sitting alone at the end of the bar. He was sipping his beer, eyes darting back and forth like he was watching a tennis match. I

grabbed my 7 and 7 (the only alcoholic drink I really liked) and walked up to him.

"You okay?" I asked.

His face was a little sad. He was an average-looking guy, dressed in an oversized, flowered Hawaiian shirt and white shorts. It was toward the end of summer but still hot enough for the shorts. The shirt defied explanation.

"Yeah. I'm okay."

I sipped my drink, and his eyes kept moving from left to right.

"Nice shirt."

He smiled. And suddenly his eyes stopped darting and he looked up at me.

"How much?" he asked pointedly.

"How much what? For the shirt? Is this a game-show thing?"

He smiled again. "For a hand job in the back."

"You wanna give me a hand job in the back?"

"I'll give you a hand job, but how much for me? For everything?"

I still wasn't quite there yet. I thought by "everything" he was still referring to his Hawaiian vacation outfit.

"For the whole ensemble? I'd say . . . thirty bucks. And that's being generous. I mean, no offense, but you look a little like a gay ice-cream man. Do I win something now?"

He laughed . . . this time out loud.

"You're fuckin' funny. How's fifty?"

He put a fifty-dollar bill on the counter next to my 7 and 7. I stared at it for about a minute. When you've spent months and months eating mac and cheese and stealing soup cans from the supermarket down the street, fifty dollars is a fortune. I don't think I had actually ever seen a fifty-dollar bill at that time.

Why was he laying down fifty dollars? Was this the prize for guessing how much his gay ice-cream man outfit cost? Maybe he was really

that drunk. I didn't think I could take his money. Seemed unfair. I mean, he just asked how much, and I . . .

And as I sat there ruminating, I heard a clarion clang. Like a bell, except with irony.

I grabbed the fifty and we sauntered into the back.

I really couldn't believe how easy it was, how easily these men could throw money at me like this, and all I had to do was lie down, use my mouth or my hand, and within minutes, they'd be finished. They were so excited and ready—it never took much time. And for some strange reason, the more sarcastic or sardonic I was, the more money they'd throw at me.

Dude grabbing his crotch: "Hey, baby. You wanna guy with a big dick?"

Me: "Love one, baby. Is that where you keep his number?"

In sex work, I had strangely found something I was very, very good at. I don't mean I was a good lover. You actually don't have to be a good lover to be a good prostitute. Being a lover requires vulnerability and kindness, compassion and compromise. You need to be attentive and open. Being a good lover is about the spiritual dialogue you and your partner create in order that you understand and speak a language founded not only in sexual attraction, but mutual respect and honor. Your lover is your friend and your guide.

To be a good prostitute, you don't have to be any of those things, you only have to *act* them.

None of it is real. So, when he's fucking you, he isn't. When he's going down on you or kissing you or holding you or sticking his fingers inside you, he isn't at all. Because you aren't there. You aren't present. You cannot be. If you find yourself there, if you catch yourself in the mirror, you must immediately disappear.

I know. I've done it.

So, don't.

Don't show up.

You might lose yourself for good.

~

I was a sex worker in the 1980s off and on for almost four years. And in that time, I cannot begin to tell you the variety of humans I encountered. And before it all fell apart and became an awful, degrading, and insidious nightmare, it was actually kind of funny.

There was a guy who used to dress up as a clown. He wore a red nose, baggy striped pants, and big purple shoes. I'd go to his condo in Lake Point Tower, fancy, high-priced condos stacked on top of each other and overlooking Lake Michigan. He spoke in a very high-pitched, squeaky voice. If you can imagine a beloved cartoon rodent on pounds of helium begging you to fuck him in the ass, that gives you an idea of my challenges. He also had a horn that he'd beep when he was climaxing. It was like making Harpo Marx come. He paid me five hundred dollars, and I swear to this day, it was mainly to keep me from laughing.

A handsome, strapping young blond guy was a friend of a girlfriend of mine. I worked on the streets when I first started to hook, but eventually I built up a clientele, and my tricks were usually recommendations. At that time, in the eighties, right before the AIDS plague hit us, Transsexual prostitutes were like the golden ticket. We were a commodity. We were sought after, and the more I figured that out, the higher my price rose. Plus, I was funny. I was a good conversationalist, and I was an actor. I could go anywhere, and you could take me anywhere. One week I'd be at the leather bar on Halsted Street, and the next I'd be at the Playboy Club in the ritziest part of Chicago. I was fast becoming well known, as well as high priced.

This man was guaranteed to be good money, and I didn't have to spend all night with him. All night could cost you up to a thousand

dollars if I knew you had it. And I could smell rich guys at five hundred paces.

Still can.

He arrived dressed impeccably. A wave of blond hair swept over his face, and he boasted a chiseled jawline and a statuesque, square-shouldered physique. He reminded me of Hubbell in *The Way We Were*. In fact, as I greeted him at the door, I gave his stray hairs a gentle push with my index finger. The reference went unappreciated, but it wasn't the first time I'd felt like Barbra Streisand.

He took me to an expensive steak dinner, and we laughed and drank and did a few lines of coke at the table, and he surprisingly volunteered information about himself. I had learned early on not to ask questions—only to comment on what's been said at the table. Everything else was off limits. I didn't ask what anyone did, what their marital status was, or even how they were doing. I listened. I'd nod and surreptitiously take copious notes, which always came in handy.

We arrived at my apartment, and he took off his overcoat and laid it on the foot of my bed. It was all very romantic old-movie stuff, and the role came easily to me. I knew Audrey Hepburn and Shirley MacLaine, and so I knew how to inhabit these imaginary personae. We were playing a scene together, and I was really loving it. He was very handsome.

"I'll be right back," he said, kissing my nose.

He actually kissed my nose.

I got halfway undressed, because they love to take things off you, and perched myself in a half light created by the streetlamps outside. I sat on the bed. Perched and half lit.

And, from out of my bathroom walked the tallest, blondest, most contoured drag queen I'd ever seen. His square jaw was shaded by some tacky Revlon brown usually reserved for clowns or bruises. His suit had been replaced with a long off-white slip, and on his feet, a pair of

marabou-lined bright-purple bedroom slippers. He wore a dollar-nine-ty-nine bleached-blond wig, cocked to the side, teetering off one ear.

Then he opened his blood-red-lipsticked mouth, and in his best Bea Arthur contralto he warbled, "Call me Helga."

He was a United States senator.

Still is, I think.

~

I was standing on the streets praying for the wind to die down. But in Chicago, when it's winter, begging for anything does absolutely nothing. And because I needed rent and food, I needed tricks and I needed them fast. So, I stood there in my short, almost groin-high black mini-skirt and a tube top in January, smiling and slinging my fake fur over my shoulder.

I had only been hooking for a few months, but as meeting men in the club didn't always make ends meet when you needed booze and cocaine, you did what you had to do. The police loved to drive by and point and laugh and throw drinks at us, arrest us and chase us, and rape us in alleys.

They always got a fight from me.

"Fuck you and fuck your mother, you dirty shit fuck!" I'd scream as they drove past. If the car turned around, I was always close enough to an alley or a storefront to hide. And if they passed, my rage would take over and I'd end up kicking in a window or pushing my fist through the glass door of an unsuspecting corner store.

I walked up and back, to the corner and then to the store across the street, to the stop sign, and then to the abandoned building, over and over. The wind whipped between my legs, and every time a car passed, I'd stop, smile, and pretend I dropped something so I could bend over.

And then a car stopped.

I looked up, my legs purple from the cold. I smiled and sauntered over to the passenger window.

Three young boys, dressed in sweatshirts and jeans and ripped tees, giggled and leered at my breasts.

"Hey. Get in, babe," the driver said.

I peered into the car. One boy was driving, the other was closest to me, and in the back seat was the one who actually looked the youngest.

"Why?" I asked.

I knew they weren't cops so I didn't have to play the "I need directions" game, but I wanted to make sure they understood what was happening.

"We wanna hang out," the driver continued, batting his big, sparkling baby blues.

"I don't hang out."

I walked away. They followed.

"Naw . . . he means, ya know . . . like . . . *hang out*. Like with your tits out."

"Yeah!" the one in the back chirped. "*All* the way out!"

They squealed like they were at Coney Island.

I stopped.

"What the fuck, boys? How old are you? I don't fuck kids," I admonished sternly.

I was all of twentysomething myself, and they were most likely only four or five years younger, but by this time in my life, I considered myself sophisticated and mature. I knew things. Things had happened to me. And I took no shit.

"Babe. We just wanna have fun. Seriously," the driver pleaded, leaning toward me.

I walked to the window.

"Okay. Fifty dollars. Each," I said carefully.

"Totally," he replied as the door to the back seat swung open.

I slammed it shut.

"Lemme see the money."

They hesitated and looked at each other, and then finally, the driver took out his wallet and produced $150 in twenties, tens, and fives. It took him a while to count it all out, but as he did, I collected it in the palm of my hand and slipped the wads into my shoes.

It happened very quickly. There was no real buildup. No crescendo. I was in the back, and then my legs were spread, and the car was speeding, and there was yelling. At one point, there were so many hands on me, grabbing and clutching and ripping, I couldn't tell whether I was crying out or they were. I was turned over. I was whipped and slapped. I had fingers and dildoes and penises stuffed inside me. And then, as I was rolled over, covered in spit and cum, red faced from being slapped and punched, I felt a long, smooth blade near my penis. A hand held the tip, and a voice whispered menacingly in my ear, "You wanna be a fucking chick? You don't need this fucking thing. Do you?"

"Fucking faggot!" another voice yelled.

My eyes fluttered and I couldn't see very well. There was a small veil of red blurring my vision. The blade moved up and down the shaft of my penis, and just as it began to saw and pinch, a voice from the front screamed, "DUCK!"

The car suddenly stopped. I reached for the door, flung it open, and escaped, bleeding and naked.

I wept on the way home, and when I finally crumpled at the foot of my locked front door, I checked my penis and my shoes.

Thank God.

Both intact.

There was a guy who used to pay me a thousand dollars to clean my house with a toothbrush. All I had to do was curse at him and occasionally call him names. He did this dressed as a "baby horse." I don't mean as a pony; I mean a full-grown man in a horse head wearing a diaper.

I told my girlfriends this story over and over, and to this day, they call me a liar.

I do not blame them.

As the years went by and I moved up in my financial bracket, the drugs got better, and the money piled higher. I most likely would have been quite wealthy had it not been for those nasty drugs.

One night, I met a trick at the club, and we spent the evening doing blow from bar to bar. It was sometime in the spring. I remember the smell of the air as we wandered outside, getting higher and higher. He was tall, with long legs like a basketball player. Beautiful skin, but his face had been beaten up. He had a great sense of humor, and we laughed a lot. That goes a long way with me. He hired me for the entire night, including his place and a sleepover . . . an arrangement I would always escape from in the middle of the night.

We took a cab to the South Side of Chicago. This was in the 1980s, when Cabrini-Green, a public housing project, was fully operational. I had only heard of the South Side and had never been there. My own race was a bit of mystery. I knew in my heart I was not a white person. But I had learned well—lies were an essential part of my foundation. As my chosen family were mostly Trans, mostly women, and mostly Trans women of color, I had no problem with race . . . well . . . almost no problem.

"What would you do if I ever fell in love with a Black girl, Mimi?"

"Well, I wouldn't care. I mean, you couldn't bring her inside the house, but I wouldn't care."

As we walked up the stairs and through two or three rickety gates barely held in place by a couple of rusty screws, I heard crying, laughing, scolding, slapping, and everything else. It was almost 2:00 a.m. on a weekend, and the building was alive and awake.

We came up to a brown door, he knocked three times, and we entered. The room was filled with only men. Men lying on the filthy,

broken couch near the open window, slouched in the corner in twos and threes, and some giving each other hand jobs in the bathroom. He took my hand, smiled, and we walked into the kitchen. It was lit by one hanging bulb over a small round table. Three men sat, woozy and rocking slowly from side to side. They had the stupidest grins on their faces. Honestly. They looked like idiots.

"Wanna?" he asked as he reached for a small syringe in the middle of the table.

I stared at it. My mind started playing back every single scene from *Lady Sings the Blues*, and I couldn't focus very well.

I wanted it.

And I really had no idea why.

But I wanted it more than I had ever wanted anything in my life.

As the needle goes in, there's a small prick. It's not like someone taking blood, as a trained nurse or medical professional would. The person shooting you up could be . . . a plumber. There is a moment of pain and then a complete and idyllic euphoria that starts at your toes and flies like a speeding train toward the top of your head. You aren't lightheaded. You feel clearer than you think. Hyperaware of the fact of it all. And then there's an ease, and everything that you thought was going badly suddenly isn't. It's fine. It's all going to be fine. My mother will love me. My dad will find me. I will have a boyfriend who doesn't pay me by the hour. Everything's fine.

And I so wanted everything to be fine.

My rage was consuming my heart space. I was experiencing moments filled with anger and a lack of power that made it difficult to breathe. And the smack stopped it dead in its tracks. From that moment on, I swore, for the rest of my life, I was never going to be without this. Not ever.

I woke up the next morning, and there were a few men left in the room, passed out, just as I had been. I was naked and shivering,

and through the bars on the windows, the morning sun peeked over the buildings across the park. I was sore. I had been fucked. A lot. By many people. My purse was gone, my keys, my shoes, and my clothes. I walked into the bedroom, turned on a blazing overhead light, and searched for sweats and a top. I found some men's flip-flops, and I grabbed a wad of money that lay on the dresser. I then staggered half eyed into the kitchen where a man was bleeding from his mouth and twitching. I grabbed the rest of the stash on the table, two or three used syringes, stuffed everything in my pocket, and left.

I was already in need of another fix.

The eighties were the time of the woman. Those shoulder pads took up most of the space we weren't allowed into. But you see, I was never a woman. Not that kind. I wasn't Melanie Griffith in a power suit, and I'd never get a job behind the makeup counter at Marshall Field's. There was no place for us. It was still illegal to be a Transsexual, and walking across the street dressed in what the law deemed "female attire without the presence of two articles of male clothing" was punishable by a short stay in jail. Ginger Spice and I both spent time there. As I hooked, she pointed me in the right direction and taught me how to go from working the streets to my own apartment near Lake Shore Drive.

"I wish you wouldn't do this, Chauncey, but since you're going to, let's do it right," she'd say.

We didn't have any public role models or elders making speeches and standing up in front of Congress. And those who did were categorized as angry, righteous drag queens. They were influential and powerful, but that's not what I was. I was a Transsexual Woman. I knew that now. And as I began to travel in more mainstream circles, I started to understand what it meant to assimilate and how these humans felt about us. Consequently, I knew exactly what *not* to do.

I never hooked because I was forced to. I wanted to hook. I liked it. I liked the power and the control I had, especially over men. I had

accumulated so much resentment that keeping them at bay was a pleasure. I never enjoyed the sex. Not once. Not with any one of them. It was automatic, like turning on an appliance. But I did it. No one made me do it. It was mine and it helped me hone my survival skills. I had learned how to survive.

And these skills picked up in my twenties were about to serve me better than anything I had experienced in my life so far. Because things were cascading rapidly into a very deep well.

FOURTEEN

Crashing Through the Looking Glass
Donny

I woke up with crust in my eyes. They were glued shut with the kind of glue you cannot remove unless you have something special from Walgreens. I bumped and crashed into the hallway and around the corner to the shared bathroom. My stomach ached and I threw up a little. I opened the door, and some kind of greasy substance stuck to my fingers. I turned on the hot water and splashed a little on my face. The crust began to melt away.

The glass was foggy where the hot water made a small line of steam. It cut my face in half. Right down the middle. I was split. I looked and looked but I couldn't seem to find me. Hidden behind last night's dripping mascara was a gaunt ghost of a person. I peered at myself, trying to smile. I had always had such a nice smile. But I couldn't remember how to lift the corners of my mouth.

Smile.

Try and smile.

Oh. Think happy thoughts. Think happy thoughts and remember . . .

I threw up in the sink.

I wiped my mouth on a used brown towel someone in the building had left behind, and I walked back to our room. It wasn't until I closed the door behind me that I realized I was naked—naked except for the two large bandages underneath my newly formed breasts. I wiped away a few drops of leaking silicone and sat on the edge of the bed. I remember lying down in the hotel while Michelle, a lithe, angelic creature of around thirty, jammed a large needle filled with illegal silicone into my male chest and pushed and pounded and massaged the silicone into me as she began to mold my female breasts. I could still feel the shots of novocaine that had never really worked, like a half moon around the bandages. My breasts were beginning to form from the hormones I was taking, but not nearly fast enough. The rest of the girls were all getting these injections because implants were far too expensive. The procedure was illegal, but Michelle was a former registered nurse, so I felt a little safer.

I searched the table next to the bed for more pain pills. I found three. Not nearly enough, so I swallowed them with a swig of whatever booze was still in the bottom of the shot glass next to the black lamp.

I think it was night. I couldn't really tell.

Donny snored. His pink body rose as a huge sound blasted from his nostrils. I saw the top of his carrot-colored hair and his funny pointed ears peeking over the thin blue blanket that covered us. We fought last night about something, and he had punched me in the jaw. I had flown into a table and then stabbed him in the right arm with a steak knife.

We were sore but had sex afterward, and he always snored after sex, which is why I thought it was night.

We had been evicted from our apartment on the North Side of Chicago and were living in the Motel Carlos on the iffy side of town. I was hooking and so was he. We had met in a drag club, slept together, moved in together, got high together, and beat each other up—a lot. Our street fights were legendary.

"Girl. Donny's beating the fuck out of you," Diana would say.

"It's only because I can't outrun him. Once I can outrun him, things will change."

We lived in one room next to a couple with a huge dog that rarely stopped barking and below a couple who rarely stopped fucking. Oddly enough, you couldn't really tell them apart.

I lumbered over to the drawn curtains and opened them.

The night air blew in through the baseball-sized hole in the lower left corner of the window, and darkness flooded the room, making it even darker than before. I stared outside, wavering a bit from both the pain and the pills I had swallowed. When Donny and I met, I had wanted a man. I had wanted a man so that I could be a woman. I wanted all the things I had read about and all the things I had seen in movies—someone to open my door, put on my coat, carry me, lift me, get things for me, make sure I was okay and beautiful and alive on the planet and that I mattered. I wanted a man to hear me and walk like a man with me, so that other people would see that I was not the man.

I was never the man.

I didn't know what it meant to be the man.

My head started to get fuzzier. I looked at the street below. I heard Madonna blaring from someone's apartment across the street. I never got her. She sounded like she was in constant pain. I looked down at the eight floors below us as a few hookers and drug dealers passed by. Someone snuck behind a little gay boy in drag and snatched his bag. He started screaming as the guy ran guffawing down the street and disappeared into the alley.

Stupid Homo in Drag. You don't carry your damn bag by your side.

"Idiot. Take off your damn heels if you're gonna catch that Muther-Fucker!"

Idiot.

Donny stirred. He rolled over. The blanket fell below his chest. He was beautiful. His white skin shone in the dark like a polished alabaster pearl. He was thin, but not too thin, and just a bit taller than me. He had a crooked smile and a silly, goofy laugh. His hands were big, and his legs were thick and round. He was the second love of my life, and I would have done anything for him. And I did. While he slept with almost all my girlfriends, and a few boyfriends as well, I sucked dick and gave hand jobs in the back of drag bars to keep us afloat. We were six months behind on the rent and were repeatedly evicted because Donny couldn't stay sober. We always had cocaine, and that, usually, was all we had.

I opened the window all the way and breathed in. It was Monday night, and I was working at La Cage in downtown Chicago. We didn't have shows until the weekend—only Friday, Saturday, and Sunday—so to survive we had to have side jobs. The only things I knew how to do were lip-synch and fuck. As a Transsexual in the eighties, those seemed to be the only choices for me.

So, I did them . . .

Really well.

I stood on top of the ledge, crouched to get my head through the window, and took an even larger breath. The air felt wonderful. It filled me up, and as droplets of silicone continued to seep through the loosely wrapped bandages, I felt the breeze lift my unwashed hair and caress my naked body.

"Babe?" I heard from behind.

I turned and saw Donny's face, his eyes droopy and silly.

My head spun a bit.

I pretend air-kissed him, half smiled, turned toward Madonna's squeal, and jumped.

And crash. Crash. Crash went the glass . . .

FIFTEEN

Just Keep Walking

It was his voice, I think. The first time he said hello to me there was a feeling in my chest, as if he had thumped me like a watermelon. I vibrated with the sound of his voice. And that never went away. I would crumble every time he told me he loved me. My insides would melt, and he would take my hand and look at me, all the way in, and breathe with me. And he talked to me. He looked me in the eyes, told me about the world, what he thought about it, how it might be changing, what we were like in it, and how it moved and angered him.

And occasionally, he even asked me what I thought.

I had had affairs with women in this way, emotional and kind and loving, but the men I'd been with had been all about sex. As I grew into my idea of the feminine construct, which I knew only from what I had witnessed and what I had been taught, the idea of being with men should have made more sense to me. It didn't.

Paul was different, though. He didn't reflect other people's expectations. He filled a space in me in a way I'd longed for but had never really known. When Paul asked me to marry him, I said yes and yes and yes. I wanted to be with Paul, and I wanted to leave behind all the

other humans in my life: the men and the women and the friends and the family. I wanted desperately to start over. I was growing into this new life, away from suburbia, but also away from what I knew to be my truth. We were living together in his apartment on the North Side of Chicago, and it was blissful. I was twenty-three years old, and the gay revolution was in its infancy. Paul preferred me to stay a boy and dress up only for work, and since I wanted him, and I wanted to be married, and I wanted to live in an apartment with nice things and have a job and be with a human who seemed to be in love with me, I said yes.

Yes, Paul. I will marry you and stay a boy for you.

I said nothing about what was true for me and had been true since I could remember . . . I simply said, "Yes."

But there was Chrisanne to consider.

Her presence in my life was getting larger and larger. She and I had developed a relationship that was familial and deep. There were very few days that we didn't speak to each other. We explained this feeling not only to each other, but to others, by stating that we were related. Sisters.

Well, brother and sister at that point.

Scott and Chrisanne—last year of high school

When Chrisanne and I met for the first time at my first drama club meeting in high school, it was like a whisper. There was no great sign from the heavens. There was no flash of lightning, no split in the sky. There had been no warning—I had always heard that miracles came with a warning. Like Moses. You had to be available and ready. I was neither of those things. I thought it was just a meeting. But almost immediately I knew there was something. I could feel it. It was different from meeting Cassandra, although she was the one I initially loved. I truly believe to this very day that it needed to happen in that order. Cassandra and I needed to have a love affair, and that love affair would lead me to Chrisanne.

Chrisanne has always been the first person I think of when things go well. She has always been the first person I turn to when bad things happen. When I have been in trouble—deep, emotional, spiritual trouble—she has always been present. She gives me strength. Seeing her is healing. Even when we have disagreed, which we often have, she provides a foundation under my feet.

~

I sat on the couch in her living room, the black night speckled with stars. I had been performing at Club Victoria for a few years, living onstage as Shanté and living my life offstage as Scott. Chrisanne was one of the few women I knew who seemed in charge of her life and of her power. She worked in an office with big doors, corner offices, and health insurance. I was lip-synching to Dorothy Loudon and sucking dick in back alleys while selling cocaine out of my one-room apartment above a gay bar. We had very different lives.

Only a few weeks before this, Ginger had given me an ultimatum:

"You have to make up your mind, Chauncey. You can't keep going back and forth like this. It's a waste of time," she lectured.

"It is?"

I knew exactly what she meant, but I didn't know how to solve it. Changing from Shanté to Scott was dizzying. Maddening. It was a lie and it made me physically ill. I wasn't Ginger.

"Either make a decision or stop whining," she rebuked me in the car after work one night.

"What do you mean? I don't whine," I whined.

"You want to live like this, then do it. But stop pretending you're not. That's all I'm saying. The only one you're lying to . . . is You."

Her blue eyes flashed, and she put her hand gently on my knee.

"Try this. Tomorrow, get dressed. Put on something you'd walk around in in the daytime, and if people notice, if they throw things or chase you down the street, you'll know what's what."

"What is this . . . like a drag test?" I asked, grabbing my purse.

"It's either that or you keep living a damn lie," she reiterated.

I knew what she meant and I knew she was right. The next day I woke up and said out loud, to the universe, "Okay. I'm going out. If one thing happens to me, if one person says anything to me, I'll know it's a sign and I'm not meant to live this way. So . . . that's it. One person. One thing. And that's it."

It was more of a threat than anything else. I wasn't sure who I was threatening or what exactly was supposed to happen if things didn't work out, but I chose my favorite cotton dress, put on a pair of red slingbacks, did my hair as best I could, and put on minimal makeup. I walked around the block two or three times, my legs shaking, my knees buckling, and my insides trembling. I had never gone out during the day. Shanté breathed at night. I wasn't used to the sun. This was the first time I would walk around the streets of Chicago dressed as myself and certainly the first time at high noon on a weekday. I lived a block away from the train. People were coming in and out on their way to lunch or meetings, and the chance of running into a crowd was high.

I was also aware that walking around this way could get me killed. If they thought I was trying to fool them, trick them, make them believe I was something other than I was, I was dead. I had to assimilate, had to look like a Woman.

I have huge shoulders, so I needed to wear something that was cut on a bias to make them appear smaller. I had no hips or curves whatsoever, so I chose to wear a dress that flared out at the sides to give the illusion of a figure. My hair was boyish and short. I curled it, sprayed it, teased it . . . gave it height and weight and depth. Women have long hair; men do not.

Allure. This was about a definite and specific set of rules passed down to me at a very early age. This was about fitting into a gender container marked in large red letters and blessed by the ideal of "American beauty." I was there to be caressed by the male gaze. It had nothing to do with my comfort or my desires. I was now moving into another realm of possibility, and all of it was for them, for the men. I was there to attract them, to entice them, to seduce them. And I loved it. I relished it. I wanted to do it well and I wanted to do it often. As I dressed, I found myself humming. Happy. Excited to go out in the middle of the day and fool all those women and strut by all those men.

I walked outside and around the block and walked to a 7-Eleven and walked toward the trains and walked and walked and walked and . . . nothing happened. No rocks, no name-calling, no pushing or shoving. There were a few whistles, and a few men stopped and looked me up and down slowly and smirked.

I loved it. I embraced it.

I had found my power.

Or so I thought.

~

Chrisanne cooks like other people work out—with a zeal and a flair and great aplomb and attention. There we sat, just the two of us, as we had so many times, talking, having a few drinks, and talking. Like high school. Just as I remembered.

She made me laugh. Chrisanne is one of those humans who know how to tickle me. She wasn't silly; I was the silly one. She wasn't outrageous; that was my role. She was witty. She was smart. She was learned, an intellectual. She was a voracious reader and had a hunger for knowledge. Her humor came from her truth. She is one of the most truthful people in my life, which came in handy, as lying is practically part of my genetic makeup.

Chrisanne also drank. A lot.

She drank and she drank to get drunk. And when she got drunk, something happened. Something took over. The beauty and the grace in her being and in her eyes were replaced by a deep, black rage. She got mean. Vindictive. She wanted revenge, and I was never quite sure on whom. She once slapped me so hard across the face during one of her drunken blackouts that I fell across the bathroom and hit the wall. There are times I can still feel that slap. As we grew up and my own addictions grew, so did hers. When we were together, and she began to drink, I would watch very carefully. I could tell by her stance, her ability to put things together, and mostly by her humor, how far gone she was. Her voice would lower, her eyes would narrow, and she would stop being joyful. She stopped being playful.

She simply wasn't funny anymore. She was drunk.

I watched as she leaned back in her favorite chair in her beautifully decorated apartment with the starlight streaming in and the fire stoked. As I sipped my wine, I stared hard into those green, green eyes.

"What?" she said in her knowing Yoda tone.

"Nothing. Well . . . I have something to tell you."

"Okay."

She put her drink down and came over to the couch.

She took my hand and, for one brief moment, sobered up completely, as if she'd been awakened from a dream.

"You're going to live like this, aren't you?"

I sat across from her, in a dark-purple turtleneck sweater I had borrowed from Ginger, a black skirt, and black patent leather pumps. I had told her I was coming right from work and that I didn't have time to change, but, like most of what came out of my face back then, this was a lie. I wanted to explain to her what had happened, what I discovered on my walk, that I had found myself, and that I was becoming a woman.

My eyes widened, although not really in shock. Chrisanne and I had known for some time that we shared a very similar space—whatever one was going through, the other experienced as well.

"Yes," I answered quietly. "I am."

She moved closer to me, and her face changed. She went away for a moment. A far-off, distant look came over her, and yet she felt closer and closer to me. I had to leave. I wasn't quite sure what was happening, either to me or to Chrisanne, but it was starting to make my stomach upset, and an overwhelming feeling of dread and sadness roared through me. It lifted me off the couch and toward the door.

"I have to go," I announced.

Chrisanne got up slowly and walked toward me. As we stood on the threshold of her doorway, half in and half out of the night air, she put her hand gently on my chest. She left it there for a moment, and then released me. And as I walked out, I heard the door close behind me.

Had I known it would be two years before we saw each other again, I might have stayed a little longer.

But for a while, I got angry.

Very, very angry.

At Absolutely Everything.

Chrisanne and Paul never met. She came over to the apartment once and I showed her around, but he was held up at work. Waiting tables can be treacherous and unpredictable. I wanted to get them together. It was important to me that whomever I married would be someone Chrisanne liked and who liked her. Our relationship was part of who I was becoming, and I knew it needed care and time. I wanted badly for Paul to love her just the way I did. After the tour of the house, we arranged another time for her to come back, hopefully for dinner, so the two of them could meet. But it never happened.

Paul loved me. I know he did. And I loved him. But sometimes obsession fills a space even love cannot reach. One night after work, I came home at 3:00 a.m. on a Friday, after my third show, and found Paul and a waiter with very blond hair on the floor of our living room, passed out and naked.

I said nothing.

I did nothing.

I felt a large, cavernous hole open up in me. I felt my skin crawl and my breath leave my body. I slammed the front door so that the sound might startle them into opening their eyes, but all it did was lull them into a more restful sleep.

I went downstairs without saying a word, tiptoeing so as not to wake either one of them, and found a small gray suitcase. I packed it with things I needed to make it through the night. I crept back upstairs, walking softly, barely breathing, and into the hallway, grabbing my coat, as it was just the very beginning of winter in Chicago. And I walked out of the door.

I do not remember much about the next few days, except for calling some friends to come and help me move my things out of the apartment and holding on to that little gray suitcase. I remember quitting my job at Club Victoria and throwing away my breast pads and my hip pads and my bras and underwear and stockings and pumps and sequined headdresses

and hundreds of dollars' worth of makeup and lashes. I remember looking at them in the garbage and seeing a parade of all the humans who had ridiculed me, raped me, loved me, heard me, and . . . left me.

No more. They couldn't touch me anymore. I was normal. I was just a normal faggot with normal desires. That was it. My mother was right. It was just a phase.

I stayed at a friend's house. Later that week I grabbed my gray suitcase, got my coat, and went out into the cold. I walked around the block and buttoned my coat. I walked past a bus station, a train station, a taxi stand, an exit from the El, a silent theater box office, a restaurant I'd never seen before, and some midtown traffic. The sun was coming up, and I had no idea where I was.

So, I kept walking.

I walked and I walked and I walked and I walked and I walked . . . for a year, living on the streets of Chicago.

And no one was able to hurt me.

I just kept walking.

SIXTEEN

Alex Doesn't Live Here Anymore

You can't be here. Hey. Hey." Something poked me in the rib. "Hey. Get up or I'll put you in the back of the car."

I opened my eyes. There was a bright light burning the inside of my brain, but I couldn't quite make out where I was. How had I ended up on this patch of grass? My ass was soaked, and my jeans were dripping. I was lying on my side, very comfortable and curled up with my head on an old pillow that I carried with me in my gray suitcase. I had placed the pillow on a rock and put my head down. I remembered doing that.

"Get! Up!" the male voice repeated roughly.

"Can I just sleep for a minute?" I asked, eyes closed to avoid the beam of light.

I felt an arm grab me and pull me to my feet, my T-shirt tangling in his blue uniform. It was night. Or late afternoon. I stood as straight as I could. My armpits stuck shut. My groin was itchy, and I could smell the stench from my feet. I picked up my sneakers and grabbed my gray suitcase.

"You can't stay here. This is somebody's front lawn. C'mon," he commanded, moving me off the wet grass.

"What's the name of this day?" I asked, stumbling onto the sidewalk.

He laughed and walked toward the police car, where the lights were flashing red and white and blue and red and white and blue and red . . .

"It's like a disco!" I muttered.

I put my pillow back inside the suitcase. And then, as I had done day after day after day after day, I began to walk. When you're homeless, that's how you spend the day. You walk. You walk to pass the time, and you walk to keep from screaming, and you walk and you walk and you walk until your stomach aches so badly that throwing up relieves nothing. You keep walking, and when you can't walk anymore, you stop, and you try to catch your breath.

But you can't do that on someone's lawn, or sidewalk, or in front of their building, or in the back of their building, or on the side of their building, and you can't lean or lie down or take a break or ask for help. If your hand is outstretched when you ask for help, people keep walking. Their eyes see you, but their hearts do not. They walk as if they're reminding themselves of whatever it is they forgot. So you learn to make signs or sing songs or dance or smile. You learn to smile when you ask, "May I . . ."

And you always say "Excuse me." You're not going to get anywhere unless you say "Excuse me."

It was daytime, and my feet were bleeding. The bottoms bled, and it was hot. I was sweating, and I couldn't find a place to wash off. There were so many shelters, but I was raped once, and robbed once, and kicked out once because I slapped a woman in the face, and I was doused with hot water once. So shelters frightened me. All I wanted was to pee and shower, but when I went to those places, they would put me in with the men. With boys. I had breasts and hips and I was curvy

because of what I had bought for my body, and they put me in cots next to boys. There was no place for us. And we were so many. I was brown. I was a Transsexual. I was homeless, and I didn't exist. There were so many of us walking and walking, and during the eighties, when there were rumblings of death and a virus and something awful happening to the gay boys, there was nothing for girls like me. I was a chick with a dick, and there was certainly no room in my country for me.

And there were so very many of us.

I was walking and I hadn't eaten, and I think it was breakfast time, so I walked to the Burger King down the street from the 7-Eleven. I went to the blue dumpster. Every morning at a certain time, they emptied day- or week-old bread into the dumpsters. If I could get to it in time, I'd put it in my suitcase for later. And if I walked fast enough, before anyone reported me, I could dig people's trash out of the garbage cans in the front by the entrance to the store.

I couldn't remember Mimi or my house, and I couldn't remember the address of the club where I had worked, or where Donny or Paul were. I could no longer see Chrisanne's face or hear her voice, and I couldn't figure out how to work the pay phones. If I did have money to call, who would I call? Smack and meth were cheaper than lovers, and they helped me to forget.

Nothing made sense or was familiar or was the way I remembered it. The streets curved, and sometimes voices came at me. Once I heard an MC announce my name, and Mimi called me for dinner, and an audience chuckled or giggled or wept into their hands. I could hear faint noises, and sometimes I'd travel down a road and bump into humans I thought I knew from way, way back, and so I'd speak to them, but then when I'd hear them cry for help, I realized I didn't know who they were. I met a hookah-smoking caterpillar, and I think I once ate a cake that made me far too tall for the rest of the world.

I walked with my gray suitcase in my hand, and it turned cold, as if I were walking into the next chapter. It just got cold, but I was still walking. I didn't remember lying down or eating or finding another front lawn. I just walked and the road curved, and sometimes I heard honking through a thick cloud of dust and guts and blood and fear and a red, red sheet of body parts littering a long, grassy field. Off, off, off with their heads, I'd say.

It just got odder.

Bigger.

Louder.

Curiouser and curiouser . . .

The sun peeked out, and it was very hot. I was sweating. I switched arms because the gray suitcase got heavy. And this fuzzy group, like an out-of-focus picture, appeared in front of me. A smiling cat under a large, pink umbrella. Smiling and waving. And coming closer. It frightened me, so I backed up and started to scream. The cat had a long chiffon scarf and a smile with teeth gleaming, and I couldn't catch my breath, and I screamed . . .

"Chauncey!" the voice screeched back. "Stop! Stop! What the . . . where've you been? Where the fuck have you been?"

She grabbed me as I lay on the ground, eyes closed and seeing through shards of brokenness, and Ginger, with her favorite yellow scarf falling to my neck, smiled and wept.

I breathed. I barely took in a breath, and my head ached and I couldn't swallow. I touched her face because I had seen so many other things that vanished, I wanted to hold on to this for as long as I could.

"Ging?" I asked.

She held me, and my body hurt so bad I froze solid. Every small bone broke into pieces. My insides turned to dust, and I began to fly away.

"You're fucking back," she sobbed.

I was back. It had taken me a while to find my way. I lay on the ground in front of La Cage, and the restaurant next door to it and the outside café where we had all sat having lunch came slowly into focus.

It had taken me almost one full year, but when I climbed back among the living, I ended up exactly where I had left off.

The same, only different.

SEVENTEEN

The Green-Eyed Girl Sitting on the Desk

My name is Scott Billings. And I have a mother."

I sat back down and crossed my fingers.

Chrisanne put me in my place. She never let me get away with much of anything. Her voice had a lilt. It moved. It rang around me like a bell. I didn't think it was love, but I wasn't sure what love was, so even if it was some kind of love, I wouldn't have known it then. Her no-nonsense approach to me was bizarre, and I didn't like it much. I didn't care for the way she was able to see me. I wasn't used to being seen. Growing up invisible, when someone spots you from across the room while they're sitting on top of a desk as you rise from underneath one, being seen is unsettling.

And yet, she really only saw what I made sure the rest of the world saw.

Or so I thought.

Back in 1976, we had a theater posse. Filled with humans who sang and danced and quoted Tennessee Williams:

"Hey, Becky. You dropped your pencil. Here ya go."

"Oh . . . thank you. I've always depended on the kindness of strangers."

We were fourteen years old, and I had found my humans.

~

Her parents called her Chrissy, and her friends called her Chris, and I called her Chrisanne. Her jet-black hair framed her white face, and through a peek of bangs and a cherublike smile were those eyes. They were bright and beloved and shocking. When she was angry, they'd light up and flare and shoot star stuff at you. And when she was happy, when she was really, really happy, they'd sparkle as she let out a sigh that was centuries old.

"I can see the rest of time in the center of your eyes," I'd say.

And she'd smile.

And when she'd smile, everything shifted. There was a peace I had never felt before. This wasn't love. It couldn't be love, because I wasn't really sure what love was, but it was necessary, and so I kept it close and held it dear and tried to make sure my life was devoted to helping it blossom. And she was damn funny. She made me laugh so hard that once I fell off a bed. She was a protector and guide. When we skipped at the zoo, or devoured bowls of ice cream at Farrell's in Chicago, or when we sat around in Cassandra's living room and talked about God and faith and justice, and sometimes *1776*, if she was leading the conversation, I would take her face in my hands and say, "You know everything."

Scott and Chrisanne post–high school

She would smile.

"No, I don't," she would lie.

When she got angry, her anger persisted, and it spread out. It erupted in spurts, like mine did. It was a rage I didn't understand and couldn't handle for very long. So, I did what I knew how to do. I made her laugh. I made everyone laugh, but most importantly, I made Chrisanne laugh. And sometimes, that would stop the emotional madness. Sometimes it would work, and sometimes it wouldn't. On the days that it didn't, her voice would rise and slam against the walls. Things might go flying, and she'd end up saying things that cut deep.

"Well, that was stupid!"

"You deserved it. What did you expect?"

"There's a reason people don't love you."

Sometimes there wouldn't be rage behind the awfulness; there would be cruelty instead. It would come at me slowly and with malice and intentionality. It would sneak up on me. I was the prey. Chrisanne would look me up and down, walk toward me, and seethe. With her eyes lowered to slits, her fists would clench, and then out would come something horrible. Then I would rage back, white hot, and throw

things, smash bottles, create complete and utter chaos in the world around me. As a queer teen who had no idea what queer was, I did not know what loving and being loved was supposed to feel like. I needed to take charge of the world around me, and so I crushed it. I wanted things to be as damaged as I was.

~

Chrisanne could drink anyone under the table, and as they climbed out from under it, she would toast them with a few more drinks. Her life in the 1980s was corporate. It was full of large brick buildings in downtown St. Louis and then later in Chicago. No matter how much she drank, she wasn't sloppy, and she wasn't loud, and she didn't dance around and put a lampshade on her head. She conducted business. She would suit up, as she called it.

"Time to put on the armor," she would say.

Makeup. Curling irons. Skirts and heels and hose and lipstick and perfume. She hated it. It smothered her. But it was learned and expected. As one of the few women still in her twenties working in a position of power as a vice president, or a head of things, or champion salesperson, she played the game. And mostly, she hated it. So, she drank, sometimes responsibly, but sometimes not.

"I have to check the paper," she said one morning.

"Huh? What are you checking?" I asked.

"The obits. The hospitals."

"Why?"

"I wanna make sure I didn't kill anybody last night."

She was a traveler. She moved. She went from place to place and from job to job—losing this one, getting fired from that one, quitting the next one. She became well versed in most everything. Perhaps changing jobs damaged her ego, although in my opinion, many times

she was fired simply because she was female and had opinions. The eighties male didn't really know what to do with a tough, intelligent, opinionated woman.

When Donny and I were kicked out of our apartment the first time, she took us in. We slept in the back of her two-bedroom apartment. Chrisanne had a bank account and a car and furniture and suits and food in her cupboard, and when you went for cereal in the morning, you didn't open a cabinet to cockroaches falling onto the counter. Chrisanne cleaned and ate and paid her bills and bought nice things and took trips.

We sat on her couch around midnight. She was drinking, and I was inhaling lines of cocaine in her bathroom every hour or so.

"I miss him," she whispered, looking into her glass.

"Who?"

"Scott."

Silence.

"You don't have to," I murmured. "He's right here."

She looked up, and the pain and loss in her eyes broke me in two. I don't think I'll ever forget that evening. She saw right through me. Was this right? Was I doing the right thing? I am a Transsexual. I know I am. I have always felt this way, and I have found my family, and Diana and Daphne and Ginger have all surrounded me with familial love. I was doing the right thing; I knew I was. But Chrisanne hated it, and that tore my insides out.

"No," she declared, sipping her drink and looking down. "You killed him."

~

I once left her in a strange man's apartment hyped up on one single line of cocaine and some pot.

"I can't breathe," she spluttered, clutching her chest.

"You can too. If you couldn't breathe, you wouldn't be talking. You'd be dead."

"I can't feel my feet."

"I can't help you with that."

I guided her to the strange man's bed, as the strange man lay face-down on his living room rug and the sun peeked through the half-closed window shades.

"Lie here," I stammered, shaking from the need for more coke.

"I can't."

"Why not?"

"I can't see my eyes."

Silence.

"You don't have to *see* your eyes to lie down. Just close them and I'll be back."

"I can't close my eyes."

"You can if I knock you out with an ashtray."

She closed her eyes, and I left her there.

I never came back.

We split up once. We left each other. I didn't want to be near her, and she didn't want to be near me. I was transitioning and she hated it, and I hated her for hating it. After Club Victoria, Ginger found me the job at La Cage. Chrisanne and I hadn't seen each other in almost a year. We hadn't spoken, and I was glad.

"Chauncey, someone left this for you." Ginger handed me a small, neatly folded note.

"What do you mean someone left it for me? Who?"

"I'm not the fucking postmaster general. Someone left it at the box office downstairs, girl."

The note read, "I love you."

And stuffed in it was ten dollars.

I ran down the stairs, trying to close my robe as I poured out onto the street. In the darkness, dotted by the Chicago streetlamps, I saw her.

We met and remet. We fought and came back together. My anger and drug use were completely out of control, and so were hers. We held each other up and let each other fall. Somewhere down the road in our thirties, through our breakups and reconciliations, we decided to move in together. I had found a fantastic apartment that I couldn't afford, and Chrisanne reluctantly agreed to move in for a few months simply to help me with the rent. The plan was after I got an actual roommate, she would move out.

That was the plan. And she was always such a good planner . . .

~

"My name is Scott Billings. And I have a mother."

Everyone laughed. I looked around that room filled with teenage angst, and every single one of them was laughing. And then, next to the brunette was this green-eyed girl sitting on a desk. She looked at me. Her lips pulled back into a smile, and she kept looking. Everyone was laughing.

Everyone in the room.

Except her.

Because she knew exactly what I was doing.

G#D T@LKS

Me

(Silence)

XXX
Hey.

Me

(Silence)

XXX
Hey . . .

Me

(Silence)

XXX
Wait.

Me

Fuck you.

XXX

Wait . . . I have to tell you something . . .

EIGHTEEN

The Plague

It was gorgeous out. I was standing with my hand on the piano, leaning into it just a bit and feeling the night air go through me like a whisper. I was only halfway through my set, and I still had all night to sing. The crowd was fair. Not too crowded, not too light. The Gentry was such a small club that seventy-five people felt packed, and even a group of twenty scattered among the cocktail tables and along the bar seemed full.

There were two Gentrys back then: one on Rush Street, which we called "playing uptown," and one on Halsted, right in the center of Boystown. They were two of the most successful nightclubs in Chicago in the 1990s and were owned and operated by the lithe, squirrelly, and mostly tipsy David Edwards. I was fortunate to have played both, and later in my career I sang at the third club he built, on State Street.

My gigs lasted four hours. I usually sang right after Honey West, who was the sole proprietor and owner of early Sunday nights. Before Honey, the club was empty; after Honey, you could barely get in the front door.

The club was long, like a bowling alley. The piano was smack in the middle of the room, so the audience was split to my right and left. To see everyone, my head had to spin like a lighthouse. Attempting to keep the crowds at bay while they drank, fainted, threw up, gave each other hand jobs in corners, and stuffed dollar bills into the glass bowl in the center of the piano was a full-time job. Like many small rooms, chatter came with the territory. But if you could get them, if you could grab them and sing through to them, reach them in some spiritual way that shook them, they'd be there for you. They could be raucous, but they were the funniest, most joyful, easygoing, delightful, and kind group I'd ever played for. Chicago audiences were truly magnificent.

When they wanted to be.

~

"I'm so hot," my friend Dan complained, sweating.

"I can see that. You're like a stuck pig," I responded.

He laughed.

Dan had one of those really big, awful, cover-your-ears-here-it-comes kinds of laughs.

No matter the joke, it was Jo Anne Worley Hilarious. He'd had this flu now for almost a week, and he wasn't getting any better.

"I think we should go to the doctor," I said.

"I can't do that. I don't have any fucking money. Do you have fucking money?"

"I don't have fucking money."

Actually . . . I had been hooking that week, so I did have actual money from actual fucking, but I was saving that for frivolous stuff. Like food.

"Well, we have to do something. You can't live on saltines and NyQuil."

"Who says?"

Dan wasn't the most attractive guy I'd ever met, and he wasn't the smartest, but there was a kindness and a sweet sensitivity about him, and our friendship held a deep place in my heart. He was insanely funny, and most of our conversations sounded like dialogue from a 1920s movie. We'd met at La Cage. The club was sandwiched between upscale stores and a leather bar where two-for-one mai tais and fisting were the norm. He was a waiter, and I was one of the entertainers.

Dan had this damn flu. This damn flu was getting in the way of us doing coke and watching Bette Davis. I hated this damn flu.

I remembered a few weeks back, we were at a party, and some boys sitting cross-legged on the couch across from us were talking about a gay cancer that was sweeping our community. I wondered if Dan might have gay cancer and asked again about the doctor we couldn't afford.

"I can't, Alex. We'd have to sneak into the ER or something."

And just like that . . . a plot was born.

We decided that for Dan to get into the ER we needed to create an actual emergency. He had to be bleeding, or showing his spleen or something. I lived in a small, cockroach-infested hovel on Dakin and was conveniently between men. I was alone and available to hatch these half-baked ideas. The hospital was literally down one block.

"You have to be bleeding," I instructed as I began to dress his soaking-wet body.

"I do?"

"You do if it's an emergency."

I grabbed some ketchup, sprinkled it on his T-shirt, and we hobbled out into the frosty night air. As we approached the hospital, I told him to limp.

"Limp, dammit."

"But I thought I was shot," he argued, still sweating.

"Who said you were shot?"

"Well, nobody, but . . . isn't this a bullet hole? This is bullet-hole blood."

"How the fuck would you know bullet-hole blood from any other kind of fucking blood? Are you nuts? You can't be shot!"

"Why not?" he asked, out of breath as we walked up to the ER entrance.

"If you were shot, you'd have a fucking bullet in your chest! Where's the fucking BULLET?"

"I LEFT IT AT HOME, OKAY!"

We were screaming in the cold Chicago air as we passed a parked ambulance and made our way into the lobby and the semiclean hallway leading to admissions. I don't remember how we got in to see a doctor, but I do know they didn't buy any of our idiocy. It was the moment when they saw Dan that I remember—the look of horror on the nurse's face. I wasn't sure why she was so stunned. I knew he didn't look great, but I really didn't see the need for the Eddie Cantor take. Looking back, I realize that I had become accustomed to him—his smell, his crusty, chapped lips, the flecks falling from his tear ducts, his red, blotchy complexion, his rail-thin frame, and the fact that his sweat was like a faucet you couldn't shut off. He was so frail that the bones in his hands stuck out.

But you see, I was still so very involved with myself—what I was feeling, and whatever I was going through. I was hooking and snorting piles of cocaine, and had recently discovered my newest lover, heroin. Sticking needles in my arm didn't leave me with a whole lot of disposable time.

They put Dan in a small room partially covered by a thin, white curtain. The nurse, a sweet-voiced young woman, took care of him tenderly. She sat next to him, asked questions, and wrote down what he said, her eyes never leaving his. She was really seeing him. She would write, but her eyes never left his gaze. From across the room, I saw

Dan begin to shrink. He was talking but getting progressively smaller. I wanted her to stop asking questions. It seemed to me her questions were making him sicker.

"Okay. I think that's enough, probably," I heard myself command. "Can we get some pills and go home now?"

"He's not going anywhere," she replied calmly.

Dan's eyes were closed, and he seemed to be sleeping in a way I didn't recognize.

"No, we have to go home now," I said, shaking. "Right now."

I was frightened, and I had no idea why.

"He can't go anywhere. He has a fever of a hundred and three."

Dan stayed in the hospital for almost a week, and I lost my drug buddy, which I hated. One night at the club after a show, I was standing at the bar, and one of the bartenders asked about him.

"Hey, Shanté. Where's Dan, anyway?"

"Oh . . . he's . . . he's still got the flu. He's at my apartment," I lied.

"Fuck. I hope he doesn't have that thing."

"That Thing" echoed in my head. I knew a couple other boys who had That Thing, and they both seemed to have the same kind of symptoms Dan had. But people either said nothing and called it a really bad flu, or they spoke about That Thing in a mystical, almost lethal whisper. I didn't want to talk about That Thing and, at 4:00 a.m. after doing two shows for fourteen people, I didn't want to delve any deeper into Dan.

"I'm going home."

On my way out, the bartender asked me to tell Dan he hoped he felt better. I pretended not to hear him.

I arrived at the hospital sometime around 8:00 or 9:00 a.m. the next day. I checked Dan's bed, but even from a distance I could tell they had moved him.

"Where's Dan?" I asked the nurse at the front desk.

She looked him up in her register and stated coldly, "He's in his room."

"No, he's not. I was just there, and that's someone else in his bed. You've moved him. Where is he?"

"Ma'am. Are you a relation?"

"I'm his sister. His only surviving sister. Our other two sisters died in a freak elevator accident."

She rolled her eyes and came out from behind the desk. She led me down the hallway and back to the room I had just come from.

"There he is," she said, pointing to the half-bald stick figure lying twisted in the bedsheets.

She motioned me in.

"He's sleeping, so don't stay too long."

I stood in the doorway, and the door closed slowly behind me. The morning sun peered through the window. Dan's face was twisted and a strange yellow color. His eyes were sunken so far in that I thought they had given him black glasses. He was tangled in the sheets as if he had been struggling. His torso was wrapped around the blanket, and his left leg hung over the bed, revealing brown blotches and broken, jagged toenails. His mouth hung open, and I could see he was still sweating. He was still there, part of him, anyway. I wanted to throw my arms around him. I wanted to hold him and tell him everything was going to be okay, but I didn't know how to do it. I had no training in empathy.

His naked chest rose up and down . . . up and down. He tried to open his eyes. I could smell his breath from across the room. And then, like an arrow being shot at close range . . . I ran. I ran out the door and down the hall and out the front of the hospital and then stopped dead and took out a cigarette.

I smoked standing in front of the hospital. I didn't look back. I stood there until I finished my cigarette.

I think Dan died sometime later. Alone, half naked, thin and breaking, and without me. I really don't know what happened to him.

I left.

After all, I had a show that night.

~

I kept singing.

I remember being in a short, beaded, black cocktail dress that night. I remember this only because the crowd was a bit larger than usual, and consequently, the background noise got thicker. The talking overpowered my singing. So, I tried my usual trick in a last-ditch effort to be seen by the entire room. I climbed on top of the baby grand in the center of the room, and as I did, the sound of the beads clanging against the black polished wood woke everyone from their respective comas. I also playfully stuck the microphone in several not-too-discreet places to emphasize each ridiculous moment.

"You're with me *now*, aren't ya?" I teased.

I began another song, and as I did, I watched a small group fill in the empty spots toward the open glass doors. They were a bit solemn. They were holding on to one another, clutching each other and moving in tandem. All five of them, all men past fifty, were relying on each other to help them to their seats. Something had happened, and I had been in the club business long enough to know when not to ask.

This was one of those times.

They came to get away, and my job was to make sure that happened. I wanted to help them escape.

As I hoisted myself into a sitting position on the piano, the crowd calmed. The wide-open doors blew a cool breeze into the room. I began to sing, and the men in the back looked up. Their eyes were misty and desperate. I didn't know what else to do, so I kept singing.

It was the only thing I could do.

The only choice I had. It was my only recourse.

~

"You busy, Miss Thing?" Diana asked in her brusque alto.

"No. Why?"

"We have to go visit Daphne."

I knew the tone. By the end of the eighties, the gay cancer had turned from GRID (gay-related immune deficiency) into something called AIDS (acquired immune deficiency syndrome), which was caused by the human immunodeficiency virus (HIV).

But to us, to all of us on the ground, we simply said "it."

"Does she have it?"

"Did you hear . . . Michael's got it?"

"I think I may have it. I'm not sure."

By now, my closet was crammed with more and more black dresses. Because, you see, all the queers were dying—much to the relief of many in our country.

Especially the president, Ronald Reagan, and his administration. At numerous press conferences, Larry Speakes, Reagan's press secretary, was asked about the president's plans to address the AIDS crisis. In each exchange, his derogatory tone and dismissive remarks were underscored by the snickers and laughter of the press corps, the vast majority of whom were cisgender white men.

But the straight, white, cis men were the only ones laughing.

We were not laughing.

We were busy burying each other.

I met Diana at her house, and we took a cab to Daphne. Diana was my chosen mom. My birth mother hadn't spoken to me for five years.

"Mimi. What if I got that gay cancer? I could come back home and stay here. Right? At least I'd have a place to go."

In the late eighties, when the cancer was in its infancy, I was still visiting Mimi "dressed down." I was Scott. Burying friends left and right, discovering lesions, and thinking up new ways to get our tribe into ERs became the norm. I didn't want to end up a stick figure staring out the window in a borrowed bed while my family searched the obits for my whereabouts. The cancer in the eighties was turning birth families into every Ingmar Bergman scene ever created. And scenes of my own personal fate continued . . .

"Well, Scott . . ." She took a long breath and then walked to the other side of the kitchen to grab her drink. "I don't think so."

She took a sip and looked out the window.

That was the last conversation we had.

~

As we walked up the stairs to Daphne's one-bedroom, a stench hit us that I assumed was coming from some open trash cans below. As we got to her front door, the smell intensified. Diana had a key, and we walked in. The apartment, draped in purple and lavender scarves, oversized throw pillows, and ornate lamps, was dwarfed by a large bed that had been wheeled in front of the bay windows and took up much of the living room.

The last time I saw Daphne, she'd been suffering from that nasty Chicago cold everyone seemed to be getting. I didn't know if she had "it" or not, and neither did anyone else. I suspect Daphne knew but kept the knowledge to herself. This was during the time when the stigma was lethal, and people were so frightened and had so little information that even telling someone with whom you worked that you were ill could get you fired. Legally fired. This illness was coming after us. Only

us—the Gays . . . and Trans women. We thought we were safe. We were not. I was losing sisters like spare socks.

Daphne was gorgeous. Her lip-synching was incredible. Dionne Warwick thrived in her soul, and every time she sang "I'll Never Love This Way Again," something in my heart cracked open. Her gestures were perfection. Watching her hold that final note as she sank lower and lower into the earth, red faced and veins bulging, the entire audience was enthralled and leaning forward. She was the epitome of grace. Her laugh was throaty, and her wit razor sharp.

"Miss Thing, Miss Thing, uh, uh, Miss Thing Shanté!" she would repeat. "Shanté, girl . . . you see, you see that man in the front row, girl? You see that man with hair and the bangs?"

"Yeah, girl. I saw him. Why?" I asked, smiling.

"Don't uh, uh, run your fingers through his hair, girl. Don't you do it, bitch."

"Huh? Why?"

"Because I did, and his motherfucking hair fell into his motherfucking lap!"

Diana and I held on to each other as we approached the bed. Daphne was sleeping. Her chest rose slowly up and back down again. The smell of dirty clothes and unwashed body assaulted our nostrils. I walked over to her:

"Daph? Girl?" I whispered.

She turned her head.

"Shanté, girl . . ." Her voice was barely audible. The repetition was gone.

Diana was on the other side of the bed. She put her hand on Daphne's hip. I stayed at least a foot away. As my friends began to die, and I spent time with them, hearing about their deaths, witnessing their deaths, or dreaming about their deaths, I began to step farther and farther away. My feelings and my heart grew smaller. I was surrounded by

an invisible monster, arms outstretched and screaming, and I couldn't make a sound. I couldn't tell them I loved them, that I was sorry, that I wanted to be there every time someone left, or that I hated what was happening, or that it was unfair and stupid.

I hated this damn disease.

But I couldn't speak, and I couldn't run.

I simply backed away.

"How you feeling, girl?" Diana asked, sitting down next to Daphne. "You need something?"

"No. I . . . hungry?" she whispered back.

Diana went into the kitchen, where food was piled on paper plates stacked in various corners, and rummaged her way through the cupboards. She found a can of soup and put it on the stove. That was Mama. Making her way through the storm with ease.

I still couldn't move . . . or speak.

Diana heated up the soup, put it in a small bowl with a plastic spoon, and fed Daphne, propping her head up in her lap. I watched. Silent and ashamed.

After her meal, Diana laid Daphne's sweat-soaked head on the pillow and whispered we should come back soon to clean up, change her clothes and her sheets. I said I would. I did not.

I remember Daphne's funeral. Diana went, as did many of my girlfriends from Club Victoria. Diana showed me the announcement from the church where services were held for her. Her family removed her wig, wiped off her makeup, and put her in a three-piece suit.

"They buried her out of drag, girl," Diana said, tears in her voice. "They buried her out of goddamn drag."

And at the top of the announcement, I read her given name and "beloved son" . . .

Beloved son.

They raped her.

~

The president was silent. There were ritual congratulatory marches and public announcements on talk shows. Our leaders were apparently thrilled that the plague was killing all the right people. We were surrounded by nothing and everything all at the same time. We were drowning, and the only lifeboats were manned by us.

"I could come here, right? If something happened to me. If I got it, I could come here."

"Well, Scott. I don't know."

~

It was sometime in winter, and I was walking somewhere, and there was that crusty, crunchy Midwestern snow on the ground. It lined the streets and had been shoveled off to the side in rows and rows of brown and white goo. My feet crackled as I walked. Halsted Street in Chicago was quiet. There were sheets smeared with blood hanging out of windows. Occasionally, I would pass by an open door, and the smell of shit and dried death would waft up my nose. I was used to the smell by now. I recognized it. So did everyone else. I passed a bar where I had once scored coke, and sold my ass and got fucked behind the bar, and laughed and drank with girlfriends, and the bar's windows were painted black and scarred with the fingerprints of the dead.

I turned a corner and across from me was a small, frail man wearing a white robe. It was freezing out. What was he doing? Was he crazy? He had a walker and wore big, heavy snow shoes, but no coat. The light changed and he hobbled toward me. His knees were scabby and his face was sunken. I backed up. I backed away as he came toward me, sick with disease and smothered in memories. I backed up into a corner

and pretended to window-shop. He passed by me. As he did, I saw his brown bowl-cut hair. It was Ben.

Where was he going? I knew Ben. I knew Ben and did coke with Ben, and Ben was one of those muscle gays who always had a tan no matter what time of year. But Ben was off to die, to lie back down in his bed and wither away. Or maybe he was off to get more coke, or maybe he was off to buy too many pills or throw himself off his rooftop and land on someone's VW. Like Manny had.

I had buried Sam, and that guy, and those women, and Pearl, and CJ, and some other Trans girlfriends. There was that time we had to drop off a friend's body at the Cook County Hospital ER because no funeral home would put us in the ground. It was a plague, you see, and no one knew how you got it. And even when they did understand its transmission, it didn't matter, because it was the fags who were dying, and that was just fine. You didn't get well. You never got well. No one, not one single human I knew, heard of, or read about got well. Because there was nothing. There were no vaccines and no information. And no one survived it.

When you got it, you died from it.

Sometimes within days.

And I walked past a bar that had a piano in it, and I thought it would be amazing to hear music again. I couldn't remember music very well. My friends were emaciated and throwing up and losing their hair and dying at twenty-three. They were being thrown out of their homes and left in the streets. They were discarded, and I was weeping and screaming and running toward them with arms outstretched, begging them not to go. Only I wasn't. I was silent and crawling into my coke, and heroin, and booze, in an endless maze of humiliation. The planet had become a war zone. I walked down the middle of the street, and the light changed. There were cars beeping, and people screaming, and the

sun was gone, and a streetlight sparkled off the snow islands on either side of me. I saw a bus and I stopped, praying it would keep coming.

Then I heard a piercing scream. It happened again, and I turned my head and there was a dead body of a young man lying facedown on one of the snow mounds. A woman in a fur coat carrying two bags was standing over him, screaming. There was a small trickle of blood coming from his sunken eyes. His face was blotchy, and his hands were bony and jagged.

I looked at him hard.

"Good for you," I thought. "Good for fucking you."

~

I hopped off the piano, finished my song, and, speaking casually to the audience, found my way to the table of men. They sat right in front of the open doors that brought in that nice cool breeze from Halsted Street. They were still looking up at me, eyes wide and chins soft. I stood at the threshold of the open doors, and off in the distance was the flickering light I had seen at the beginning of the evening.

"'Just in Time.'" I nodded to the accompanist over my shoulder.

It was time to put a smile on these boys' faces and do a standard in the middle of the street, dodging traffic. Perhaps I would time it right and that little flicker of light miles away down the road might catch up to me. I could do the Patti LuPone sidestep out of the way, just in the nick of time.

But that's the trouble with those little flickering lights: You have to be careful. Sometimes the light at the end of the tunnel is a runaway train . . .

~

She was taking longer than usual to get up the stairs. Ginger had bound-less energy. I've seen her impersonate Tina Turner at 3:00 a.m. for six-teen drunk gays in a bar during last call with only one bump of coke left and the car running in the alley for a quick escape. She never stopped.

I loved my new apartment. Ginger had lived there for a few years and then turned it over to me when she moved. Ginger and I were Baton girls, and handing over the pad kept it in the family. Apartments were hard to find in Chicago in the late eighties. This was my first studio in Boystown by myself, with no lover, no roommates, and no one but me to count on. I was alone, and I was ready to face it and figure it out.

I hated being alone. Every moment of it. I had always been a cham-pion pretender.

"Hurry up, girl!" I yelled down the stairs.

"I'm a-comin', Chauncey!" Ginger yelled back.

I ran into the house and made sure the tea was made, the sand-wiches were on the paper plates, and the TV trays were next to each other. The apartment was beautiful. Open, airy, filled with light. It had only one room—the kitchen was separated by a turn of the corner, and I used the giant living room space with its fireplace as my bedroom. I loved that space, and I wanted to share it with my pal. This was the first time Ginger had been up to see me since I moved in, and her trip from Wisconsin had been rough.

As she rounded the corner, I heard heavy breathing.

I waited in the living room. Standing in the doorway was someone who looked like Ginger, but I thought for a moment it might be her older and much thinner sister.

"Chauncey!" she growled in that familiar gruff alto.

I carefully moved toward her outstretched arms. My eyes welled up, but I turned my head in time to bury them in the nape of her neck. My knee grazed her walker, and I threw my arms around her

tiny frame. Her bones stuck out a bit, and I released her gently so as not to break her.

"I gotta sit down, girl. I'm pooped!"

I guided her to the couch and brought her tea. Her walker stood propped against the wall. Her once golden-blue eyes sparkled less, and her luminous face was sunken and sad.

"How are you, girl?" I asked, not really wanting to know. "How are things going?"

"Great! I feel really good today," she lied. "That trip, though. Whoo, sister! That was a looong one!"

"From Milwaukee?"

"Long, girl. Long."

I walked to the TV and opened the drug drawer, where three or four packages of cocaine lay, wrapped and ready.

I picked one up and shook it above my head.

"Oh, girl. No. I'm done. No," she refused, holding up her hand.

She was done? With coke? That didn't make any sense.

I shrugged it off, assuming the later it got, the more likely she'd say yes. I went into the kitchen and got our lunch.

"You cooked!" she teased a little too loudly.

"Shut the hell up."

We ate in silence. In the gayest part of town, where a parade of sickness meandered through the streets, my best friend ate my soggy tuna sandwich and slowly died in front of me.

Maybe a year later, Ginger's daughter, Mimi Marks, called me and told me Ginger was very sick and wasn't going to last much longer. I had been to funerals and burials and wakes, and sat shivas and given testimonials, and sung hymns and show tunes and lullabies—all for my queer family who were dying, day by day. I had done all that and had never wept. I was too busy doing things, all with a smile and pounds of drugs.

I wanted to see Ginger, and I didn't want to see Ginger.

I refused to make that long trip just to help one more person die. I was barely thirty and the number of deaths I had already witnessed was enough to last four lifetimes. I didn't want to do it. I didn't want to do it with Ginger. Ginger was going to live. She was on that new AZT thing that came with the beeper everyone was wearing, and she was going to get better, goddammit.

God.

Dammit.

She was going to get fucking better.

Ginger's house was a large two-story white A-frame in the middle of a beautiful neighborhood in Milwaukee. Far from downtown and the noise and the madness and the drag, Ginger lived like I did, quietly and without sparkle. I arrived with one bag, as I wasn't planning on staying long, just long enough to see how she was, stay for a night or two, get a little high, maybe do a number at Club 219, her home drag bar.

"Hey, Chauncey!" she greeted me as I stumbled through the front door.

That trip was long when you ran out of coke.

Any trip was long when you ran out of coke.

She was even thinner than I remembered. Her face was gaunt and gray, and her hair was falling out in clumps. There were small places where I could see her bare skull. The light was gone from her.

Completely gone.

"I'm so tired. And I'm straight." I smiled that smile she knew.

"I don't have anything, girl. Maybe tomorrow night we can score from Chuck, but . . . I'm tired, Chauncey. There's the spare. I'll see you in the morning."

She vaguely pointed up the stairs, half covered herself with her flowered robe, and slouched back into her bedroom. I walked upstairs, praying that the next night we'd be able to get that packet.

The next few days are muddled. I can only tell you what I recall in snapshots. Like a play in fast-forward, where you pause for the parts you want to remember:

I woke up and did the dishes, which were stacked high. They smelled, and the glasses had brown stuff caked on the bottom of them. I washed them and thought, "If I wash these, am I going to get it? What if you can get it by washing someone's dishes? I guess I've got it. Because honestly, these dishes fucking stink." As I washed, I trembled.

I fixed breakfast. I made French toast and bacon. She ate and then promptly threw up all over the table and herself. I cleaned her up and asked her about an hour later if she wanted something to eat.

"I'd love some French toast."

"Piss off."

Her pill regimen was impossible to figure out. She took them at regular intervals, but keeping everything straight when you're high as a kite isn't easy. There were a few times I might have mixed up the green ones with the red ones. There were times she had terrible stomachaches, but I could never tell whether that was because everything she ate came back up, or that I might have given her the wrong color pill. She shat herself regularly, so changing her sheets became routine. Washing shit out of sheets takes practice, because you can't just dump shitty sheets into a washing machine every few hours. You must hand-wash and then clean them off, and then you can dump them in the machine. I also had to contend with the barf and the pee that usually followed. Wash day was something else.

Ginger had some form of dementia. It wasn't full-fledged madness, but there were fever dreams and then moments where she'd fly off into a different sphere.

"You wanna watch TV?" I would ask.

"There's a duck in your ass," she'd answer.

"Do you want to watch TV?"

"If you don't believe me, stand up and reach in your ass."

"Ging. Stop it. Focus on what I'm saying . . ."

"I'm as focused as fuck."

"Then do you wanna watch TV or not?"

"You wanna watch TV with a duck in your ass, I'm fine with that."

I got up, turned on the TV, and started flipping channels. We flipped in silence, me in my big, comfy, ripped, and a bit stained chair, and Ging on the couch, wrapped up in fourteen blankets with her barf bucket nearby.

I came across an old Vivien Leigh movie. She worshipped Vivien.

"Hey. How about this? This looks good."

"I'll bet *she* doesn't have a duck in *her* ass."

"Will you stop with the fucking *ducks!*"

After she fell asleep, I was on my way to the kitchen, and as I passed my reflection in the full-length mirror by her bed, I noticed a yellow triangle on the back of my thigh. I turned around and saw a flat, plastic Donald Duck appliqué stuck to my left ass cheek.

I know people dropped by, and I know we performed at 219, and I know her friends in Wisconsin all knew what was happening, and I know none of us were supposed to talk about it. We had no words for this. We had no experience except for what we were all going through at the moment. Together.

It was around the time I was getting ready to leave. It was late, and I remember it was evening, and there was a candle next to her bed. She hated scented candles, but the smell of death and chaos permeated the walls of the room so deeply, I needed to cover it. Ginger was in her bed, covered up and freezing and boiling. Her face was red with blotches. Her eyes fell into themselves, and her body barely made a dent in the mattress. Her voice was very, very soft, and when she spoke, I had to lean in to hear her.

"You're pretty great, Chauncey," she barely whispered.

"I don't know . . ."

Silence.

She swallowed.

"I like it when you sing. You should sing more."

"You do?"

"You sing and something happens. I didn't really know . . . will you sing more?"

"Yeah. I will."

Silence as she looked around the room. She looked at things hard. Her black and gray eyes focusing on one thing and then another.

"Do you want me to get you something?" I asked, leaning forward.

She pointed to a pile of dirty clothes in the corner.

I walked over and picked up the first T-shirt on the pile. It was her Tina Turner shirt. The live concert she went to where she screamed for so long and so hard that her cords were bloody. This shirt was a talisman. She rarely wore it.

I held it up with both hands.

"Put it on," she demanded in her half voice.

I took off the top I was wearing and put on the Tina shirt.

"Tina sings and the world fucking blows up. I want you to blow up the fucking world, Chauncey."

I couldn't move.

There was more silence. This one hurt. I could feel it in my chest.

I didn't want to blow up the world. I just wanted to go home, and I wanted everyone to be okay, and I wanted Ginger to get out of the bed and take back her shirt.

I wanted it to stop.

I wanted it all to stop.

~

I stood in the middle of the street and looked at the flickering lights. They grew larger and wider. The wind blew a little harder, and with the mic still in my hand, I flipped back my hair and sang. I was singing "Let the River Run" by Carly Simon, a song given to me by Chrisanne and one I loved and remember Ginger loving.

As I sang in the street that night at the Gentry, the table of boys who had walked in late turned in their seats to watch. Their eyes welled, and the crowd in the club grew larger. And I sang, and the wind blew, and the lights in the distance began to move. They marched in silence, and I saw them flicker. Slowly marching were men and women and others and children, and all of them bundled up and carrying these candles in front of them, lighting the way. Their faces were half shaded by the night, yet as they got closer, and I sang louder, I could see them smile in the glow of the candles, as they walked toward me down that street. And as they did, I moved aside, and they passed by.

And there we were.

All of us.

The humans in the street in a silent prayer, and the humans in the bar in a silent remembrance, and as they went by, human by human by human by human, I remembered it was December 1. It was World AIDS Day.

I finished the song, and there was no applause.

"Can we take a minute, please?" I asked everyone as the march passed in a steady and glorious silence.

I stood there.

I was angry and resentful. I was selfish and filled with irresponsible madness. And at the very end of the line, as all of us held space, the last woman in a large fur parka turned to face me, her candle barely lighting the edges of her blue eyes and red lipstick, and she smiled. She waved and thanked us all and smiled.

And I blew a kiss. As they disappeared into the night, the silence reverberated through the room and through the very center of us, and the loss and the grief and the power of resurrection and forgiveness swept across us all. I wept. My eyes filled up and my stomach heaved, and I put my head in my hands and made sounds I hadn't made in decades.

And a hand was on my shoulder, and it was the man with sad eyes. And he was weeping. And we stood in the street, holding on and watching the line of candles go farther and farther away, and all I could think was how much I missed those humans who gave their lives in battle so I might be free enough to stand in the street and celebrate the life force that is our tribe. And when I got home that night, I went to sleep wearing one of my favorite tees . . .

It's a white shirt, a bit tattered now and aged, and the sleeves are ripped in two places, but it is emblazoned with the greatest picture of Tina Turner . . .

NINETEEN

Sick and Tired of Being Tired and Sick

When I was finally hired at the Baton in the mid-1980s, I had achieved the unthinkable. It simply wasn't possible. There I stood, on the stage of the most well-known, sought-after club in our business, and occasionally, as I lip-synched to Barbra or Liza or Eartha, I'd peer to the right and see those full-length glass doors where I had once stood, watching from the outside dreaming of the inside, my hands pressed against the glass. I had stood there, in ripped hose with a half T-shirt falling off my shoulder and my hands and thighs sticky from the lack of a shower, filled with impossible longing.

But there I was—Miss Continental, the titleholder of a city-wide pageant for female impersonators. Jim Flint, the club's owner, finally hired me and was willing to take a chance on the hooker with a thousand stories. Kelly Lauren, a beautiful blond with an obsession for that Madonna girl, was hired the same day as I was, so we moved up the ranks together. Every girl had their own private dressing room, which was a necessity when you're working six days a week, doing three shows a night, arriving at the club around 6:00 p.m. and leaving around 3:00

a.m. That small private space became our home. We didn't live anywhere else, because there was no time. Being a Baton girl was about rehearsals for production numbers, and costume fittings, and constant gown upkeep, and new shoes, and designer clothes, and wigs, and makeup, and trying to find new numbers, and touring, and never sleeping, and lots and lots of drugs.

The cocaine flowed.

We partied and found boyfriends. Kelly and I became very close and eventually roommates. We fought like mad and made up like mad—and the cocaine flowed.

Every once in a while, I was awake as I selected my chosen family. Occasionally, I chose well.

When I first met Michael, he was eighteen years old, dressed in a white and pink tee and Jordache jeans, leaning up against a blinking pole in the middle of the dance floor of the Bistro, one of the hottest discos in Chicago. He was blond and blue-eyed, and Kelly fell madly in love with him.

I walked up to him as "Fields of Gold" blasted over our heads and tore through the soles of our feet.

"HI!" I shrieked over the thump thump of the floor.

Man after half-naked man passed us, shaking their asses, gesturing over their heads, and occasionally making that familiar 1970s disco sound from the middle of their throats:

"WHoo*OOOP!* WHoo*OOOP!*"

Like a gaggle of sick geese snorting too many poppers.

Michael smiled. He was absolutely beautiful. If Prince Charming were real, he was standing right in front of me, handsome, strapping, lean, and golden, and trying desperately to score coke and get laid in a local gay bar.

"GOOD! YOU?" he shrieked back.

More geese flew past us. I hated this damn song.

"I HATE THIS DAMN SONG!" Michael screamed, leaning his head toward my nose.

"WHY ARE YOU SCREAMING IN MY NOSE?" I yelled, smiling.

"YEAH! I WANT SOME BLOW, TOO!"

I knew it.

We screamed at each other for another ten minutes and then went upstairs where the beat was a little less pronounced and the geese muted.

We never stopped talking. We talked about his mother, whose temper rivaled mine. We talked about Chrisanne and my need to have her back and my deep shame in that longing. We talked about men and women and what drag meant, and how much coke we both had left, and how much we needed more. We were certain that with Michael's surfer-boy good looks and my warrior-like aggression, we were sure to succeed. And succeed we did.

We shuffled to my apartment and stayed up until the next morning, talking, snorting, laughing, watching Judy, and falling into each other's arms with great relief. It wasn't sexual. It wasn't romantic. It was familial. We were lost: he a younger me, and me an older him. I had spent what seemed like years wandering the planet searching for parental guidance, finding it in my chosen family sometimes, but this was the first time I became the protector. I understood Michael's need to be loved, to be nurtured, and to be safe. So I set out to make sure he got all those things, no matter what. It was my first dive into some sort of sense of responsibility.

"Can I stay here tonight, Shanté?" he asked, batting his lashes at me like Mary Pickford.

"Don't try that shit with me, Michael. It ain't gonna work. I'm not one of your tricks, ya know. You're not gonna *work* me," I declared defiantly.

His head lowered. He was high and getting higher, and he began to break a little. I reached over the brown card table where we sat and touched the back of his hand.

"You can stay here," I said in a voice I didn't recognize. "But just for tonight."

Michael and Kelly and I didn't leave each other's sides for the next decade. None of us really moved out.

Then there was Chili Pepper.

"Mary," she would say with her Zsa Zsa Gabor/Colleen Dewhurst lilt. "Mary . . . mira! Mira! Come here! Looooook what Mother has for youuu!" Chili, when excited, would sometimes sing the ends of her sentences.

Chili's presence stood ten feet tall. We were all female impersonators, which even back in the eighties didn't really make sense for us, as no one at the Baton ever took off their feminine self to hang in the closet next to their galoshes. This was who we were, and this was how we lived. Diana and Daphne were also called female impersonators, but none of us were really sure who we were all supposed to be impersonating. This made for some twisted and heated debates, especially when men loved us publicly.

"Are you a fag?" women would ask.

"I'm straight," the men would answer.

"You can't be straight and go out with a man pretending to be a woman."

The containers remained rigid, and we were the enemy, and it was perfectly acceptable to hunt us down. We weren't really women, and we weren't really men, we weren't really human, and we didn't really matter, so beating us and raping us and stabbing us in alleys for sport made perfect sense. We were the enemy. We were taking all the good men. We were the villains in the minds of the eighties' straight female, and punishment was what we deserved.

Chili's short, bobbed hair framed her round, expressive eyes. The mystery of where she came from, how she got to the States, and how long she'd really lived here added to her mystique. Oprah adored her, as did the *New York Times* and the *Chicago Tribune*. I'd never known another Transsexual who had not only mingled with mainstream society but had found major success in it.

"Mary. Oprah's throwing my birthday party and I want you to come. Come and sing and dance and be merry, Maryyy!"

"Okey dokey!"

Chili went to the Pump Room in the Ambassador East and was seated at booth number one, where Judy, Frank, and President Kennedy had sat. Her fingers were covered in diamonds, and her wrists shone with bracelets from Neiman Marcus. She had furs and racks and racks of shoes, and when she made tips, they came from the audience in long lines of bills taped together, one right after the other. Chili was famous, and I wanted to share her fame. I also loved her, truly and deeply. Chili wasn't without ego, and she and Leslie Rejeanne, the Baton's only Diana Ross, would battle for first place. Leslie's idea of a good fight was the soft, breezy whisper of a cut: "Oh darling, just because you're old enough to be my mother, please don't act like her."

Leslie's Diana demanded attention and was central to the Baton's legendary status. She was also the show coordinator and put together the lineup every night. The New Girls were put first to open for the seasoned entertainers.

I wanted that last spot.

I wanted to close the show.

I should be closing the damn show.

I'm the actress.

I'm the one with the talent.

That should be me!

Fucking drag queens and their bullshit politics.

I'd plot and scheme and cast incantations, and bring coke and more coke and buy booze, and snuggle up and be charming and try my best to figure out how to get that star spot.

It was at the Baton that I met the rest of my chosen family from among the many showgirls who crossed that threshold. Despite my selfish and sometimes overly vehement behavior, they loved me. And I loved them all back. I was riddled with jealousy and venom. I believed that everyone was prettier, more gifted, and more sought after by men. I froze or panicked or, more often, punched and threw things, but I could never calm the burning anxiety.

Occasionally, Chrisanne would come to my shows at the Baton.

"What did you think of my new Streisand number?" I would ask.

"Good. I liked it."

"Whaddya mean you 'liked' it? You *liked* it? I worked on that thing for months! I got every single fucking syllable . . . and you 'liked' it. You don't fucking understand entertainment at all. Why the fuck am I talking to you anyway?"

My insecurity would rumble, and I would rage and swing and stomp my feet and cause a scene. Throwing public tantrums was expected of me. I vividly recall chairs thrown out of windows in our house, clearing off tables in restaurants when the waiter called me "he" instead of "she," or grinding a woman's face into a potted plant while her husband and three children looked on in horror as we waited in line at a disco.

"Mary! Mary, come in quick, now," Chili bellowed.

Our dressing rooms were across from each other, like Lucy and Ethel (in season three).

I put on my shoes, and half naked I walked across the yellowing carpet to the frame of her door in bra and underwear and black pumps, my hair teased out to the side exits. I paused, waiting for Chili to either

shower me with praise, spill some T, or reign with supreme grace and read the hell out of my underwear.

Her head sank into her hands. She was wrapped in her multicolored robe, her famous legs crossed, shoes off and kicked under the makeup table.

"Girl. What is it?"

"Stephen has it."

I had just done a bump in my room, and I had a needle loaded and ready. I was able to handle more AIDS news. The eighties staggered to a close, and the Reagans appeared to take even more pleasure from the mounting death toll, although they pretended to care that the queers were dying. There was this AZT drug everyone was taking, that came with beepers that went off every fifteen minutes to remind us to continue poisoning ourselves. When one went to a bar, beepers would sound off intermittently, as if we were in the middle of a gay air raid.

Which, let's face it, we kind of were.

"He's purple and his face is red. He's blotchy, Mary." She teared up. I had never seen her like this before.

My body stiffened. My eyes welled up, but nothing was released. Not a tear, not a sniffle, not a moan. Just blind, red-hot anger. I turned and walked into my room and slammed the door. I opened my mouth to scream, but nothing happened. I began ripping clothes off their hangers, throwing them across the room. I smashed the giant mirror that covered half my wall. My hand began to bleed from the shards of skin I tore open from making a fist and using it like a hammer. My door began to shake.

"Girl! What the fuck, Shanté!"

Leslie's usual ease and whisper had changed to a sharp yell. And fear. There was fear.

I raised my arms. I curled my fingers. I began an incantation, a spell over the evil that was permeating us, raping our people. Spinning in

circles, I waved my hands around the room, and I chanted, I crowed. My voice became laser-like, focusing my fury on those who were murdering us.

~

I sat on the couch. My back felt twisted. My legs hurt. I lifted my jeans a bit, and there were long red scratches running up and down my calves. I didn't know how long I had been on the couch. The last thing I remembered was that the guy I was living with was about to go out and get more, and the sun might have been coming out. He was one of those guys who loved being surrounded by the girls. He loved the girls. He loved me, and he loved the girls, and he was fucking me, and he was fucking the girls. I knew it, and at this moment I couldn't have cared less. He was hitting me, and I was hitting him. We'd throw each other into walls, and then we'd make up. I remember Chrisanne came over one time to help clean up after one of our fights.

"Why don't you leave him?" she asked, sweeping up broken bottles of scotch and vodka from the kitchen floor.

"I love him. He loves me. That's why."

The apartment didn't have much furniture in it, as most of our money was going to drugs and gowns and more drugs. We had this couch, though. My brain flipped on just then. Like a light switch.

He was getting more. Ah. That's right. That's where he was.

I tried to get my legs to work so I could hobble to the window. They were too spindly and ragged, so I slid off the couch and rolled to the filthy wall that boasted the one window in our living room. The sun blasted in and tore a gash on my face.

I pulled back fast.

I was flush against the TV with the VCR hooked up underneath it. We had just bought the VCR so when we got high we could put in

any tape we wanted and waste ourselves in front of Judy or Liza, or in Jerome's case, John Fucking Wayne. I put my head back, and it bumped a little too hard. I reached back to pat my head, my eyes still half closed, and as I pulled my hand away, a small chunk of hair came with it. I looked at it, a straggly and broken tuft in the palm of my hand. That was my hair. I reached around again and yanked out another small clump. It made me giggle. I was like a doll. I was like a giant witch doll.

I blinked my eyes and felt the crust almost sealing them closed. I braced myself in an attempt to stand on my feet. I grabbed the TV, my tongue began to roll around in my mouth, and as I was lifting myself up, trickles of blood drooled from both corners. I was shrinking—becoming less and less. I walked to the bathroom, holding on to the slimy walls for support. I turned the corner and flipped on the light. The hum of the overhead stirred in my ears, and I went to the sink to wash off.

There was a mirror above the sink.

In the sink were two or three bloody, used hypodermic needles. Liquid blood ran from the needles; runny blood still came from my mouth.

I swallowed water.

It tasted like metal and barf.

I glanced up into the mirror. I didn't remember buying that painting. Why would we buy a painting of that sad human with those pinched eyes and that sunken face? When my eye twitched, so did the painting's. I raised my hand and realized that the reflection was me and not a painting at all. I froze, and I saw myself becoming less and less, growing smaller.

My skin was purple, and the weight I had lost made my collarbones stick out. My face was pinched and eroded, and my eyes were as gray as a rainy sidewalk. I couldn't feel my heart. My hands were bones. There was no flesh on my belly and legs. I was walking on two thin sticks.

I hurt. I opened my mouth to scream, but there was no sound. My tongue was bloody. Drops of blood fell into the middle of the sink and splashed the needle.

Then I cracked open. I burst like an overfull balloon headed toward the sun. Tears melted the cake that surrounded my eyelids, and a sound I'd never heard before emanated from the pit of me. I thought there must be an animal out front. It wasn't me at all. It was the sound of the murdering of a spirit and the annihilation of the past.

"Help me," I howled, shattering.

Then something remarkable took place. I was moved. I don't mean to say I walked or made a decision, or even that I was compelled to action. It was something else. I was literally moved out of that room. I left the bathroom, weeping and gasping. Still wailing as if I were being interrogated, and still moving as if I were being led, I picked up the phone and dialed a treatment center whose number I knew by heart.

"I. Need. Help." I gasped for air as more bloody tears fell onto my hand. "I'm going to die. I don't want to die."

I don't want to die.

I did not want to die. I was finally sick and tired of being sick, and tired of being the villain in my own fairy tale. I was the witch, and although I didn't mind being a witch, I didn't want to be wicked.

The next thing I knew, I woke up in a gray room, covered by a stiff sheet, lying on a brick mattress with a woman in a cheap suit sleeping in a chair across from me.

TWENTY

Underneath the Showgirl

B eing sober is like getting slapped in the face with a dead fish.
Repeatedly.
"How do you feel?"
"Huh? What the fuck do you mean by *that*?"
(*Hops in a circle for no apparent reason*)
"You okay?"
"I'm fi-i-i-ne!"
(*Runs screaming into a wall*)
"I love you."
"No you don't."
(*Hits own face with a pie*)

~

It was 1988, and I crawled into recovery like a snake with no stomach.
I was leaving entrails and blood droplets all along my way. I found a
seat, sat down, and said nothing for the first month or so of my sobriety.
These meetings with these people all smiling and patting each other

on the back and shaking hands and hugging and weeping and being honest . . .

Schmucks.

I couldn't figure out how to speak without lying. And even when I found the courage to speak, I lied. I lied about my feelings. I lied about other people's feelings. I lied about having feelings about other people. When I was called out on my lies, which happened constantly, I lied again, but I felt it. I felt a wave of shame go through me. I could still lie, but the horror was, I didn't enjoy it anymore. It was still easy, and I still did it, and most of the time people still believed me, but something was shifting. Something was moving, and it was leaving a large scar on my insides.

I hated it.

I hated being without cocaine and heroin and booze. I hated watching other people get drunk and high and laugh and giggle. I hated every single person in those fucking meetings. And yet, I went. I went to churches and basements and people's garages and living rooms. Sometimes I sat in corners of coffee shops and talked sobriety with other sober humans, and I hated every single fucking minute of it. This sharing of feelings thing was for the fucking birds.

I didn't get high because I was sad. I got high because it was Tuesday.

So I lied, especially about how I was feeling and how I was doing. I stayed sober, but I didn't stay accountable. I couldn't have cared less about them, or being of service to them, but they'd never know it. Because I knew how to fool them, how to charm them, and how to make them laugh. I knew how to do everything except tell the truth. I knew how to hide. I was a champion at it. So, I hid. And it worked. It worked for a long time.

Until one day, it didn't.

"God grant me the serenity to accept the things I cannot change . . ."

I was sitting at the bar, tucked in the corner on the very last barstool, with bathrooms next to me. When I was getting high, this was my safe place—my quick escape from humanity. I could sit and watch the crowd, and the minute I began to come down and shake and feel myself present, I was able to duck into the men's room. The women's room was always full and incredibly inconvenient if you wanted to do a line on the sink counter. Men generally peed and left. Washing their hands was sacrilegious.

So, there I sat.

I was perched above the audience as they filed out in twos and threes, linking arms and laughing, some still aghast that we "looked just like women." I sat, sipping my Coke with three cherries, and watched as some of them eyed me, pointing at me, the women tucking their heads into the crooks of their spouses' or boyfriends' shoulders. They were laughing. They pointed up at me as I sat there, covered in my black-and-gold half-open robe, my left breast partially exposed, and my hair and makeup perfect. And the men would pass. The men would pass, and I would see in their eyes a longing or a desire or sometimes a loathing. They would lower their eyes and speed up and hold their friends tighter, and their upper lips would curl. I could feel my innards churn, and it was all I could do not to throw a glass at their heads or run down and slam my fist in their faces.

And sometimes, floating just above Donna Summer's vocals, I'd hear "like a chick with a dick."

And then they'd leave.

They'd scamper out the front door and pour onto the street, beers still in hand and dressed in their office attire. And I knew, as the men went home that night at midnight, with their women hanging on to their elbows and stumbling into their cars, that when these boys made love that night, they made love to their women, but they saw our faces. I knew this because I knew them, and I slept with them. They paid

me, and loved me, and haunted me, and beat me, and slipped me their phone numbers on cocktail napkins as they left the club.

"I want your cock. Call me."

A man with a bowler hat stood at the bar and stared.

"You're beautiful," he said, tipping his hat.

He had a kind, round face and deep-set eyes. He was tall and dressed in a black overcoat and seemed to be on his way somewhere.

"Are you going somewhere?" I butted in.

"Here," he wheedled. "Can I talk to you beautiful ladies?"

My friend Kelly and I knew exactly what that meant. Since I was between men, and Kelly was blond and gorgeous, I assumed I'd fade into the background while the two of them flirted. He pulled up a barstool and sat between us.

"Who said you could sit here?" Kelly said coyly.

"Oh." He blushed, eyes lowered.

She laughed that big, wide-mouthed laugh.

"I'm kidding! I'm totally kidding!"

"What are you two up to tonight?" he invited, taking off his hat.

"We're working. And you?" I answered.

I wanted him to get to the point.

"Just watching you two. You're both really beautiful."

"And?"

All three of us laughed.

That night we lay on his bed—him half naked, his torso barely covered, as Kelly scrambled about looking for her shoes and her earrings.

"What are you doing?" I whispered, putting on my jeans.

"Those earrings are Betsey Johnson, bitch. If you think I'm leaving them here, you're crazy!" she spluttered, frantically searching between the pillows and blankets.

He lay sleeping, oblivious to our escape plan. He was silent, just a slight snore and a breath of air. As Kelly ran around the room like a

bottled-up tornado, I sat in the chair across from him. His hat lay on the floor, and the sun peeked over the bedframe. It was 5:00, maybe 6:00 a.m., and I was wide-awake. I walked over and sat on the bed next to him. I stroked his hair, half hoping he'd open his eyes and ask me to stay. He would look up at me and smile a bit, twisting his mouth and smacking his teeth. He'd stretch his great arms to his pillows, and the sheet would fall off his naked body. I would put my hand on his chest and ask if he wanted breakfast. Then I'd go down and get it for him, if that was what he wanted.

"No, babe. I don't want breakfast. I just want you. C'mere," he'd say, pulling me closer.

And he'd pause a minute and look at me and see me, and his hands would roam down my hips, and he'd smile.

"I love you," he'd say.

"I love you too," I would answer.

And we'd almost kiss, but we couldn't stop looking at each other.

"Girl. We gotta go!" Kelly announced from behind me.

I got up from the bed, found my bag, and headed out the door. I turned back and there he was, in the same position, in the same shape, breathing big and deep. Kelly started down the stairs, and I stood in the threshold, holding on to the open door, and as I stood, breathing and weeping, his eyes opened.

He looked at me.

I waited.

And he breathed a sigh and rolled his eyes and laughed at me, and slowly turned over.

He laughed.

At me.

And I knew in that moment, standing in the threshold of another half-open door, that if I didn't do something, it would always be this way. It was not going to change.

And I simply did not want to live like that.

Not one day more.

"*. . . the courage to change the things I can . . .*"

The overture was winding down, and the girls came down the stairs, giggling, exhausted, and dragging their feet, into their respective dressing rooms, sequined trails of dresses and a flurry of hair spray and bobby pins. When we finished the final of three shows on a Sunday night, the movement from fabulous showgirl to worn-out working woman was immediate and loud. We made noise, the ten of us.

"Girl!"

"Mary!"

"Oh, sister, this tape! Girl, I have to set myself free, honey!"

The magic of our gender was hidden beneath a slice of silver duct tape. We'd stand, spread our legs, grab the head of our penis, wrap a little toilet paper around it, so as not to rip off the skin at the end of the night, tape it to the base, and then tuck it between our butt cheeks. The testicles shoved up inside us, back where they came from, and the scrotum folded and taped up by the penis with one last sliver of silver. It created a smooth, Malibu Barbie groin, so that the main question from the audience, if we dared to come up between shows, became "Where do you put it?"

It.

My groin was constantly referred to as "it."

When I was in my twenties, there wasn't a day that went by when I didn't have a conversation about my groin—mostly with complete strangers, but if there was a talk show involved, with millions of viewers.

The day I was asked to appear in the audience of the *Phil Donahue Show*, along with many of my Club Victoria showgirl friends, was my first attempt at trying to field this question. Although we were not the main guests, they sat us in the front row.

"What bathroom do you use?" a woman from the back yelled angrily and with great force.

"I use the women's room," I snapped back, standing up and not waiting for Phil. "Have you ever tried to use a urinal in a Norma Kamali?"

This initial TV appearance was made before I got sober, and the day had been spent at Diana's, shoving blow up my nose in her bathroom and guzzling the scotch I swiped from her kitchen. By the time we all got to the studio, I was a quivering mess, ready to attack anyone with a vagina.

My relationship with my genitalia rarely took up much space for me. I asked the men I dated if they considered themselves gay, and all of them identified as straight. The kind of sex I had was varied. I slept with women, with men, with Trans men, and with Trans women (but only with a cis man present). I had sex with people because I wanted to have sex. There was never attachment. I never let myself go. It wasn't that I didn't have satisfying sex; I did. It wasn't that my life wasn't filled with wonderful offers; it was. It wasn't that I didn't enjoy the people I was with; I enjoyed them. I just didn't enjoy the time wasted. I grew up and was living in a time when gender was specific, and what I grew into was defined as a Man Who Became a Woman.

It was simple, and it began to make sense to some people, and some people accepted it. As I got clearer and more sober and more present, I believed it was my penis that was stopping other people from accepting who I actually was. Rules and expectations and norms were getting in my way. Rules were still ruling me. The rules gave meaning and made sense. They were what Mimi always talked about, what I always saw in Dad, and how Bobby always seemed to live so effortlessly. The rules erased me. I had no place in art or education or history or casual conversation.

I wanted to be normal. I wanted to be like the rest of them.

Even as I got sober, the rules strangled me. I needed an escape. I needed an alternative plan or I knew I would perish.

I never once considered sex reassignment.

"Mary. If you do that, that's it," Chili once said to me. "It isn't like there's a return policy."

And so, I lied.

For a very, very long time.

The voices rumbled down the hallway as doors closed, some slammed, some left ajar. At the end of the hall, I heard Leslie's voice, that half whisper as she began to de-Ross-ify herself.

"Miss Shanté!" she called out. "You know I need you, sister!"

I put my earrings in their box and headed down the hallway, passing the girls in half dress, some gabbing, some in stoic silence breathing heavily, as they shed their showgirl selves.

"Girl, what a night. You coming over?" she asked as I unzipped her.

"No, girl. You know I can't," I said slowly.

"Oh, that's right. You be all sober and shit." She saw me in the mirror. "You know I love that 'bout you, sister. You know that," she repeated.

"Yes, ma'am," I replied, smiling. "I know that."

And I did.

I finished helping Leslie and entered my room, my Eartha Kitt dress spilling over the back of my chair, and shoes and gloves and wig pieces strewn about the floor and hung carelessly in my closet.

I sat back down in front of my mirror and grabbed a glob of cold cream, and as I was about to smear it across my face, I noticed a stack of papers sitting in the center of my table. It looked like a script of some kind. I wiped off my hand, picked it up, and read out loud: "*Vampire Lesbians of Sodom*. By Charles Busch."

What the hell was this? What's happening?

Chili appeared at my doorway, leaning against the frame, her coat slung over her shoulder. She smiled and pointed her multiringed finger at the script in my hands.

"Mary. Do it," she said.

"Huh? What is this, girl? What's going on?"

"There're a couple of producer men upstairs, Mary. They're veh-eh-eh-ery fancy, and they wanted me to do this play, but you should do it. Not me. You should," she stated matter-of-factly.

"I don't understand, girl. I don't . . ."

My heart was beating so fast that it was becoming difficult to catch my breath. I wasn't an actress. And even if I was an actress, I wasn't a woman. I was "a chick with a dick" who belonged nowhere, and the Baton was my life. This was my life: Chili dressing next to me, Leslie down the hall, Kelly bellowing to customers, Chrisanne occasionally coming to my shows, and entering contest after contest after contest but never winning Miss Continental—this was my life.

I wasn't an actress.

I was a Tranny.

"They're upstairs. I'll go with you and introduce you. Get dressed," she said impatiently.

"But, girl. They don't want me. They want *you*."

"Mary," she said, stepping into my room. "Listen to me. Are you listening to me?"

I looked up at Chili, her eyes lined and lashed, her flaming red hair peeking out from a small ski hat. She bent down as if to whisper, and yet with a pointed strength and a voice steady and calm, she announced, "This is your ticket out. Take it."

I couldn't move.

"Now, hurry up. They won't wait all night. You're not Madonna, bitch."

Then she was gone. Down the hallway, the click of her heels blended with the rising chattering from the rest of the girls as they planned their night.

I held the script in both hands and looked in the mirror.

I took a breath.

And then I took a big glob of cold cream and began to wipe off the showgirl.

"*. . . and the wisdom to know the difference.*"

~

I read she was in town, but only for six weeks. I had heard the name, but I wasn't entirely certain who she was. I knew every actor in my orbit was jumping up and down at the thought of her being in Chicago, and this was before the internet, before cell phones, before instant information. If you wanted to do research on someone, you had to get on a bus and schlepp down to the public library. Since both numbers and walls of words turned my stomach, I realized that reading other people's reactions took far less time, effort, and money.

Not to mention responsibility.

She was taking only twenty-five students, and I was determined to be one of the twenty-five. I had to get downtown, and then the requirements seemed easy: show up on time, dress to move, and bring a headshot and resume. If a call time was noon, I usually showed up around noon (ish). I always thought it best to make an entrance. After all, the host of the party doesn't greet the guests at the door. The help does that. She makes her entrance coming down the stairs.

Lit.

Backlit.

With a key light and the Doris Day filter.

I wore my *Flashdance* outfit, which was guaranteed to turn heads—a red T-shirt, cleverly cut to fall provocatively off my left shoulder, a pair of blue jean short shorts, white socks, and white sneakers with a bright-pink racing stripe down the side. I carried an oversized black off-the-shoulder bag that I stuffed with newspaper and towels, as I didn't really own much of anything else, and I wanted to look actor-y. I brought along a La Toya headband just in case she asked me to do a little dance. The only eight-by-ten I had was from a Shanté shoot a few years back, with my hair pulled so tight it contorted my entire face. It was glossy black-and-white and had me in a long, beaded gown, earrings bigger than my head, and posed like a Greek fountain.

Shanté—headshot

I was ready for my very first adult acting class.

When I arrived at the studio downtown, there were over a hundred other actors, exuding both fear and excitement. I wasn't quite sure what

all the fuss was about. This was just another acting class. I realized she was an acting teacher from New York, but how famous was she, really? It was the people she taught who gave her this prestige, right?

"Name?" the girl behind the small desk asked.

I gave my name with a hint of attitude.

After all, I had performed as Shanté for the last ten years, and I was now starring in *Vampires* in the cabaret space of the Royal George Theatre, where we had been running for almost two solid years, and were now considered a bona fide hit. How could she not know who I was?

This was a formality, anyway. Who was she? Just some girl behind a desk.

I gave her my name. She gave me a time slot and told me to wait. We all gathered in the same, small room, waiting for *HER*. I stood against the wall, dying for a cigarette.

Then she came in.

Her hair was a tousled silver blond, short and full, surrounding her chiseled chin. Her eyes were a soft blue. She was dressed in brown slacks and a white top. I think she wore an ascot. Kind of butch, I thought, but you know . . . New York. They are afraid of nothing. She was followed by a taller woman, more brittle and edgy, her features sharp, with a voice to match.

"Please don't lean," the assistant commanded.

SHE unwrapped her ascot as her assistant moved to get her a chair and scoot her closer to a table, where a large pad and a pen lay neatly stacked next to a box of tissues, a coffee cup with steam emanating from it, and an ashtray. I had my eye on that ashtray. I'd sell my mother for a smoke. She sat and took out a small, white cigarette. I started to do the same when a hand grabbed mine and whispered gently, "She's the only one who smokes."

I put the pack back in the bag between the newspaper and the towels.

One by one, each actor came to the center of the crowded space and proclaimed the words of Shakespeare and Chekhov and Williams and O'Neill and Shepard and Hellman and Churchill. I didn't know what to do, because this was supposed to be a class and I had nothing memorized. In fact, I had never prepared an audition monologue. I had gotten into *Vampires* by auditioning for the director, and I had been in the play for two years. The only material I knew was from Busch's play.

As I watched the other actors struggle through what seemed to be incredibly difficult monologues about death and pain and loss and reverie and forgiveness, in which they took chances and gave themselves fully in great leaps of faith to a room full of beautiful strangers, I remembered the words I had absorbed by sheer osmosis. After all, years and years of lip-synching don't just disappear. I remembered a monologue I used to lip-synch by the great Shelley Berman. In it he is trying to talk a woman off the ledge of a building by calling from a pay phone across the street. Instead of speaking directly to her, he gets sidetracked into speaking to the central operator working in the lobby.

The monologue is hilarious.

If you are Shelley Berman . . .

Which I was not.

As I began to impersonate this iconic 1950s stand-up comedian, *HER* face turned toward her burning cigarette, and a silence fell over the room, as if the air had been sucked out by a gigantic vacuum. The angular assistant with the pointed voice raised her hand. *"Enough!"* she thundered.

I looked around the room and saw the actors trying to maintain their best hopeful smiles and nods of encouragement. As I grabbed my black bag, it rustled with the crumpled paper. I flung it over my shoulder and left the room.

I walked down the hall and passed the girl at the desk, who was busy writing furiously. I sat in the lobby, and my head fell into my hands.

"It's okay, Alex," a voice next to me murmured.

It was the owner of the acting studio. She was a jovial, kind woman whom I knew through the friends I was beginning to make in the acting world. Everyone knew Sarah. Her smile and her way with other humans, her ability to calm and to appease, even when things went as badly as they just had, were legendary.

"But I have to tell you something. There are some things you can change, and some things you can't. You must take responsibility for trying to figure out which is which. And you can't treat other people like this."

I looked up.

"Like what?" I asked incredulously.

"Look at yourself. You don't give a damn. You have no idea who was in the room. All those actors gave of their time, and a chunk out of their lives, not only to be here, but to learn from you and teach you. But you basically told them to fuck off. Didn't you?"

I put my head back in my hands.

"Get serious. Make a decision. And when you do, come back."

And she left.

When you're sober, God moments are pretty hard to define. But when they are that blatant, you'd have to be living underwater not to notice them.

I went back to the girl behind the desk.

"Excuse me. I'm sorry I was such an ass. Could you find another spot for me?"

She looked up.

"No," she replied, half smiling.

I breathed through my anger.

Amends, Alex. Remember, you were wrong.

"Please? Please? Look . . . I'm really sorry for the way I acted when I came in here. I'm . . . really scared and I didn't do my homework, and I really want another chance. I don't know if I'll get one, you know?"

She looked me up and down for a moment, sighed and said without apology, "Okay. I'll give you a spot for the callbacks. But if you come in looking like Hooker Barbie, I'll punch your face in."

I wasn't permitted to work. There was a group of us who were accepted into class as auditors only. We sat in the back and were not allowed to ask questions, read scenes, or give our opinions. But we were there. We got to take notes and speak to the actors after class. Even more significantly, even more than receiving the great gifts from these other humans as they worked and dreamed and created, we all got to watch the glorious Uta Hagen teach fucking class.

During those weeks with her and those artists, something shifted in me.

I realized that wherever it was I was headed, mine was not going to be an orthodox career. I was going to have to figure it out, step by step. Each moment was going to have to be lived. I was a terrible planner, but I was a pretty good dreamer. Through my experiences in Uta's class, I began to wake up. Who I was wasn't making sense to me, but what I was doing began mysteriously to fall into place.

And, I woke up further. My life became more specific, and more strange, and more resentful, more angry, and more beautiful.

I realized possessing Wisdom was completely different from being Smart. And, fortunately for me, the prayer was about the search, not the answer. So, it began. The awful wonderful search really began.

Being sober is like getting slapped in the face with a dead fish.

Repeatedly and often.

~

"How do you feel?"

"Huh? What the fuck do you mean by that?"

(Hops in a circle for no apparent reason but decides it's bringing other people joy so continues to hop and finds a purpose in serving someone else for half a second)

"You okay?"

"I'm fi-i-i-ne!"

(Runs screaming into a wall and realizes "fine" is a lie and the truth is filled with rage and pain, thus the damn wall becomes the damn gift)

"I love you."

"No you don't."

(Still hits own face with pie)

Well . . . you can't have everything.

TWENTY-ONE

Like Everyone Else

They all had a look, had a walk, and a way of speaking to each other. They all congregated and giggled, and knew how to recite, and they spoke well and about many, many things. I said "girlfriend" and "Miss Thing," and I had to concentrate. I had to get my vocabulary correct when I was in the room with them. I couldn't just say things. They didn't just say things. They smoked, and gestured, and talked about agents and managers, and said things like "my next project," and "casting calls," and "I'm so tired of the typecasting," and "Me too. I'm so tired of it too."

I wasn't like them. I wasn't like them at all, but I wanted desperately to be. I desperately wanted to be "tired of it all."

"I can't believe you have a dick. I mean . . . whoa. It's amazing to me . . . I mean . . . do you? Have one?" a man asked outside the theater one night.

I was smoking and had most of my makeup off, with a few remnants of blush dusting the tops of my cheekbones.

I blew smoke in his face.

"I've had the change," I lied.

His face fell. He turned around and walked away.

That was the extent of his response to the performance I had just given. He had been a member of an audience who laughed and guffawed and loved it when I fell or tripped or made faces I stole from Lucy and Carol Burnett. He had loved it when I sounded like Tallulah, or skipped across the stage half naked, dressed as a vestal virgin and with my breasts up and my ass hanging out, as I fought to avoid becoming lunch for the dreaded succubus.

The audience laughed, because I acted like Jerry Lewis.

They laughed, because I was a clown.

They laughed, because I was silly, and ridiculous. They laughed, because I was sexy. But I was safe, because I wasn't real. I wasn't like those other girls. I was a fetish and an afterthought, like a mint after the main meal. And they believed they had every right to examine and prod, because in the 1990s in Chicago, as I was trying to squeeze my way into mainstream theatrical storytelling, who did I think I was anyway? I was a drag queen named Shanté from the Baton, who was also a hooker and a junkie.

"I want to change my name," I said as Ginger and I walked up the stairs to my apartment.

"You do? Aw, Chaunce. I just got used to Chauncey," she half mocked.

I was about a month into rehearsal for Charles Busch's *Vampire Lesbians of Sodom*, and the publicity had "Shanté" splashed across all the ads. I hated it. I didn't want to be Shanté. Shanté said "Miss Thing," and gave hand jobs in the coatroom, and got beaten up by boyfriends, and wore too much blush.

I did not want to be Shanté.

"I don't wanna be Shanté, girl," I repeated.

We got to the top of the stairs and stopped as I put the key in the front door.

"Who you wanna be?" she asked directly.

"My great-great-grandmother's name was Alexandra. Alexandra Rebecca. What if I was Alexandra? Then Mimi could call me Alex, and maybe she would stop calling me Scott."

I don't know how or why it came to me at the top of the stairs, or how or why I decided that picking my name was about my parents' comfort, but Alex felt good. It held me to the ground, and it sounded like the rest of them. It made me feel a part of something other than sequins and satin shoes. The history of who I used to be rumbled around me for a minute. As I opened the door, I noticed a picture of my great-grandmother, Mony, and her husband, nicknamed Doc, on the nightstand next to my bed. I walked toward it and started to ramble off the names in my family:

Mony, Doc, Dody, Spike, Nana, JG . . . Mimi.

"It sounds like the seven dwarfs."

I knew none of them by their given names. These names were chosen. By them. For them.

And so, I did the same thing. I christened myself, and blessed myself, and gave myself the name that I cherish and hold close to me still.

"Alexandra Scott Billings."

That was me. It felt like me when I said it out loud.

I kept Scott and put him in the middle. Like Jan Brady—surrounded by family, but always a little left out. Just as a reminder.

The director and the producers of *Vampires* flatly refused to accept my name change. The owners of the Royal George Cabaret space weren't too happy either. That's a lot of names to put outside on the billboard: Alexandra Scott Jeff Franklin Billingsley, or whatever it was. My friends didn't like it. My family hated it, and Mimi said point-blank in a drunken fury one night, "I don't care if you change your name to Winnie the Pooh! You're still going to be my little Scott-a-roo!"

Which, I reminded her, rhymed.

I was the star of this show, and because I was hired at a time before the word "Transgender" existed, I was still labeled a pre-op Transsexual (who was in fact lying about being pre-op). All the publicity revolved around me and what I represented to the community. And, to the community, I was Shanté. I was a trophy the PR people had won and from whom they were not about to part. Shanté they could sell. Alexandra appeared to be just like everyone else.

So, we fought. We argued, and I walked out, and they threatened, and tried to recast. I stayed home, went back to hooking, and finally, they relented. So, in 1991 at the Royal George Theatre, my name was placed above the title for the Chicago premiere of *Vampire Lesbians of Sodom*. The reviews were mostly awful, and focused their analyses on wondering which "sex I was," speculating about whether I was a "female impersonator," or gleefully dissecting my bad comic acting. We tanked in the eyes of the Chicago critics. A few papers refused to print the entire word "Lesbian," so we were saddled with a few carefully placed asterisks. The critics wanted the show to disappear, and me along with it. They really hated us.

But we ran for nearly five years.

Despite the rotten reviews, my ego was running rampant, and even though I wasn't like them, I began to collect a new family—actors. I remembered actors well from those blissful summer musicals with my dad. I was in awe of what they did and how they did it. And as I went from show to show, from cast to cast, through the madness of how critics saw me and the bizarre way audiences reacted to me, I discovered that these wayward lost souls were just like me. All of us Chicago actors were in our twenties and thirties. All of us were aimlessly wandering, trying to figure out what it meant to tell a story, and struggling to become famous at the same time.

There was Jonathon, with his impish smile and his too large heart, who became one of my first straight, white, cis male protectors. I eventually moved in with him. Another good friend, Jackie Hoffman, was kind, witty, vulnerable, and the funniest woman I ever met. Her house became a refuge for me, Rose Abdoo, and Jimmy Doyle. As the cable TV thing began to take off, the three of us would climb into a cab and arrive at Jackie's tiny house on the North Side, and sit transfixed, watching *Nick at Nite* showing old *Bewitched* reruns, or *Rowan & Martin's Laugh-In*, or *The Dick Van Dyke Show*. We'd eat, and laugh, and talk about Second City, or wonder what was going to happen next. Sometimes I'd bring along Chrisanne, who'd giggle for a few minutes and then escape into Jackie's bedroom, where she'd promptly fall asleep.

Jimmy was a brilliantly funny, charismatic, and compassionate human with wide eyes and a wider smile, and Rose was a glowing, radiant actress whose passion and biting humor fell out of her like sugar from an open bag. They both helped save me. They befriended me. They understood me. And most of all, they treated me like an actor—just like any other actor who was trying to figure it all out. I was still lying and trying to stay sober, still hanging on to friends who were dying of AIDS, but I was also someone who wanted and needed the very same things they did.

I felt just like them. I had found my group, my community.

"I don't think Second City's ever gonna put me on the mainstage," Jimmy would complain, leaning back on Jackie's blue-and-gold couch.

The Second City mainstage, back in 1990s Chicago, was filled with hilarious humans: Stephen Colbert, Ian Gomez, Steve Carrell . . . and my pals. But Jimmy's climb into the center ring was fraught. It was different. It took more than was expected of most.

"Why? I think they will. They will, Jimmy! They will and they should and I know they will!" Rose would retort.

"They need to if they know what's good for them," I echoed.

"Second City's a fucking man's world, you guys," Jackie chimed in from the kitchen.

"Jimmy's a man," Rose said.

Jimmy smiled. "Fuck yeah, I am," he said, sounding like Elaine Stritch.

"You know what I mean . . . Jeezus fucking Christ!" Jackie said. She entered the room, a snack tray in both hands. "They're a bunch of *guys*, who want *guys* to do *guy* shit," she said, emphasizing the word "guy" like a truck driver on a long haul.

"And I'm a fag," he murmured softly.

"What the fuck did you just say?" I asked.

"You know what I mean. That's what they think!" he answered loudly. "I'm a fucking fag."

"They don't think that, Jimmy . . . do they really think that?" Rose asked.

I don't know whether they thought that. None of us really knew whether they thought that, but that's what it felt like. And if they did think that, it made perfect sense to all of us that they would think that, because that's what most people thought. Jackie was a Jew. I was a Tranny. And Jimmy was a fag.

Nobody could quite pin Rose down. She was famous for saying, "The biggest question I ever get in any audition room is . . . Rose Ab*DOO* . . . so . . . what exactly *are* you, anyway?"

Because I guess, none of us was in fact like any of them.

I sat in the hallway, my knees to my chest, and tried to position myself into a place of nonexistence. I was gaining a reputation in Chicago theater, but only really in the off-Loop area. Mainstream success eluded me. So, I auditioned. For anything. I loved working. I wanted to work. I wanted to act. I wanted to keep doing the thing I wanted to do in the body I was designing to live in.

As Alex.

As me.

Sitting in the hallway of a local rec center with a dozen or so other Chicago actresses, where the producers of a new musical had rented out two of the rooms, I backed up against the wall. We waited our turns, and one by one, a boy with yellow hair and ripped jeans called out our names.

"Please have your pic and resume ready."

I had those. Finally. I had those.

My picture had been taken by a local photographer, and as I had barely any money, the black-and-white photo was not exactly professional. My head was tilted. I wore a black turtleneck sweater, and my hair was frizzy and matted. I didn't quite understand the idea of self. I couldn't really show *Me* because I was still trying to find *Me*. I looked like an ad for a glamour shot from Sears.

We all sat, and one by one we went in. Further down the hallway I saw a group of *them*. I looked at *them* with great envy. I wanted to be in that group over there. I wanted to be in the group that was chatting, and giggling, and talking about where they were going after the audition. They dressed like actresses. They looked like actresses, and they were surrounded by other actresses.

And, as if someone had flipped a switch, three of them saw me way down the hallway. They pointed, whispered to a fourth actress, and they all laughed. They threw their heads back, and they laughed. As they stared, their laughter sliced through the middle of me, ringing down the tiles of the hall.

The previous year I had spent time in jail. I had been walking down the street, on my way to get a pack of cigarettes. I was dressed in a white sundress with bright yellow wedgies and a small brown bag. I was walking. I wanted cigarettes, and it was a hot, hot day. As I made my way across the street, a police car pulled up beside me. A large man got out, took me by the hands, and pinned me up against the car. I knew

I didn't have a whole lot of money, so I assumed this was some sort of gay fashion police.

"You know," he spat very close in my ear as his hot, awful breath blew onto my neck, "you can't walk around this way unless you have two articles of male clothing on."

He began to handcuff me, closing these round steel things to my wrists. Tightly.

"Two articles of male clothing?" I repeated. "What . . . you mean like, tube socks?"

I spent the night sleeping on a cot that smelled like fish and dried semen. They handed me a doughnut that crackled when I held it in my hand, and a cup of coffee so thick I could have used it to plant a rosebush. I slept next to a man of about sixty who threw up on himself every so often.

So, when the girls pointed at me, I twitched. I wasn't wearing my two articles of male clothing. Maybe they were from some undercover Transgender-arresting office and were masquerading as actors in order to trap me. I had spent five or six nights in jail over the past few years, and I really wanted this part, so I didn't have time for bail or overnight stays. Real actresses didn't get thrown in jail or need to worry about their underwear.

A girl with flaming-red hair grabbed me by the hand.

"What?" I screamed, thinking it was a soft-handed cop.

"Let's go over here."

Her voice was easy. Her eyes were a deep green, and she reminded me of Barbra Streisand in *What's Up, Doc?*

"I'm Jamie."

"Alex."

"Those girls are assholes."

Jamie kept me close to her that day. She really didn't understand how she had saved me. I had been about to leave, but because of her, I

didn't, and I was cast. The show was a send-up of 1950s horror movies and musicals, and was written by Jeff Richmond in the style of *Grease*. Jeff went on to *Saturday Night Live* fame, and into Tina Fey's loving embrace as her husband and father to their children. The show was called *Lobo A Go-Go*, and once again, most of the reviews focused on my ability to portray a female rather than addressing my acting.

I should have said something. I should have done something. I should have stood up and said no, or stop, or wait a minute, or what do my genitals have to do with the story? But I didn't.

Another time, I auditioned at a fancy theater, and I was in the middle of singing "Losing My Mind" when the artistic director got up and walked out. She took her coffee, grabbed two or three loose papers off the oblong table, and left the room. The accompanists, one man reading a newspaper and the other looking at me helplessly over the brim of his glasses, and I, stayed. I finished my audition, thanked the men in the room, and, heartsick, walked back to the lobby, where Chrisanne stood, eyes flashing and feet tapping.

"Are you ready?" she seethed between gritted teeth.

I assumed she was angry because the audition took longer than expected, and she might have been waiting for a while.

"I am. I'm ready," I said as quickly as possible.

We got into the elevator and rode to street level in complete silence, which was odd. When we got to the car, she exploded.

"What the fuck! Did you hear that woman?"

"What? Huh? What woman?" I yelled back.

"The woman with the gray hair who walked out of your audition! She came into the lobby and called somebody and said, 'You've got to be kidding? You sent me *that*? *That's* what you sent? That Alexandra Billings? This has got to be some kind of joke.'"

I stood there in the middle of the parking lot, my head spinning.

"What?"

"Well, we're gonna fucking *sue* her! We're gonna sue her, for sure! That's what we're gonna do!" Chrisanne was fuming. Her neck stretched out, and the veins in her face popped purple and blue.

We got into the car, and she screeched all the way home. We never did sue, because who were we going to sue? Who would take our side? A review I got once called me a "drag queen," and I asked a lawyer if I could sue for defamation. She answered back very simply, "Well, are you?"

They didn't have to deal with that. *They* walked tall and traveled in groups and had nice shoes. And their monologues were from classical plays, and they complained about the size of dressing rooms, or having to bring their own wigs or costumes or stockings or lashes. I loved what I did. I was thrilled that I was working. But I wanted what *they* had.

Every year, hundreds of actors from across Chicago congregated for the general auditions at *the* major Chicago theater. This was the chance for any nonunion actor to be seen by the artistic director. This theater, with its regional Tony Award and its many award-winning productions, was the pinnacle of achievement for local artists. I just wanted to be there—to be there in a play or a musical. I wanted to be with all of them, there, in this mainstream theater with all the other mainstream artists.

I was more nervous than I think I had ever been before. Every audition is awful. Standing in front of strangers, hoping against hope to get the job, and most of the time being told, "No, thanks." I had worked a lot, but mostly on friends' recommendations. I rarely landed a role from an audition. So here I was once again, sitting on one of the hard, wooden benches that lined the massive, circular walls, with dozens and dozens of other non-Equity hopefuls, all nervously pacing, reciting texts, reading books, or sipping their Perrier. I sat alone, going over my lines from one of Titania's monologues from *A Midsummer Night's Dream*, when a lanky man with a long, thin tie and a brown suit came

directly up to me. As I looked up, I could feel every head in the lobby turn toward us. There was an audible intake of air from the entire room.

I looked up into his brown eyes, expressive and a little sad. I knew he was someone tied to the theater, but I just couldn't remember who he was.

"Alexandra?" he inquired politely, as he pretended to smile.

"Yes."

This was it. This was it! He came out because he didn't need me to audition anymore. He had a role for me, and he was going to give it to me, and it was about freaking time that I was recognized in this goddamn city.

"That's me," I said.

The skinny man in the brown suit sat down next to me. He smiled again and took a breath before he spoke. He was definitely preparing the way for something.

"I . . . I just want you to know there's really no point in your coming back here."

"What?" I asked.

"It just doesn't make any sense. I feel it's not fair to you. We can't cast you here."

"You can't?"

"Of course not. If I put you in a show. . . the entire audience would spend the whole first act talking about you and your history. It doesn't make . . . it simply won't work. I'm sorry. I really am. I hear great things about you. Good luck."

He got up.

Straightened his tie.

And left.

I sat there, looking around the room at the women. I looked at who they were and how they saw me. I looked at their faces. Their eyes

shone with hope and promise and newness. And I picked up my bag and pretended to go to the restroom.

When I got home, Chrisanne was furious. She told me we should call HR.

"That's illegal. He can't say that to you, honey. He can't say that legally. You can't tell somebody they're not going to get a job because of who they are."

"You can if you're the only one," I said plainly.

I was "it."

That was that.

They sat against walls and pointed and laughed, and when the time came for them to stand up, to extend a hand, they were strangely absent. But still, I wanted to be one of them. I wanted to be just another actress—to fit in and be one of the girls, one of the girls in a show. That's all that mattered. And there were times when it did happen. I worked. I got cast, and I kept getting cast. I worked and worked and got to tell stories. Occasionally, I'd make friends, like Jackie and Jimmy and Rose, and occasionally, I'd meet a human with magical powers, like Jamie. But that happened infrequently. That wasn't the norm. Usually, I was left on the outside looking in.

I wanted very much to be seen just like the rest of them. I wanted to blend in. I wanted to erase my Transness and become something else entirely. I wanted everyone to forget the Baton, and Club Victoria, and hooking and heroin and booze and recovery, and I wanted everyone to see me the way I wanted to be seen. But that was not what happened. People see what you show them, and many times, what I showed them had very little to do with who I was.

I wanted to be *them*.

I wanted to be an actress.

I wanted to be anyone who wasn't me.

TWENTY-TWO

Honey's Joyful Sound

I had always heard of a joyful noise, but I was never really sure how it sounded.

I was jealous of her. I was jealous of her blond hair and the way she walked. Like Rita Hayworth. She slid and floated. Her feet barely touched the ground. It wasn't a performance. When I first began my transition, I assumed that it was all about how to Act like a Lady, how to Be a Girl. So, even though Scott swayed when he walked, and Shanté strutted when I put on heels, and my ass seemed to gyrate like a glockenspiel clock, I moved deliberately and with specific intention. I thought about it. But for Honey, it came naturally. It wasn't practiced like most of the Trans girls I knew, including me. We prepared. Up and down the hallways, and up and down the stairs, and mostly it was bullshit. And I have to say, I was jealous. Jealous of her being blond, being beautiful, round and catlike, and jealous of her walking without rehearsal.

"I can't go to the grocery store," she confessed to me one afternoon.

"Why not? What have you got against the grocery store all of a sudden?"

She looked at me. I stopped. She was accustomed to my using humor to disguise my fear, but when her eyes narrowed, I shut up and I listened. She and Chrisanne were the only two people who could see through the clownish facade that had served me my entire life. I guess by this time it was getting a little old, because I was hearing impatience from them a lot more often.

From people I loved. Annoying.

"I was standing in line and this woman passed behind me," Honey began, "and called me 'he,' and turned to somebody and said they shouldn't let 'that' happen in a place where there are children."

I lowered my eyes. My heart broke.

Let *that* happen.

We had been turned from an "it" to "that." I wasn't sure if this was a promotion. Honey began her transition later than I did. By the time we became friends, I was already in my thirties, and her journey had just begun, so the road from one pejorative term to the next didn't really make much sense to her. From "it" to "that" was a sort of movement, at any rate.

Honey and I knew how to hide, how to duck and cover. We knew, as Trans women, what it meant to be hunted and spotted from across a room, ridiculed and stereotyped on TV, and what it felt like to be publicly shamed. The public shaming ran deep and buried itself in our souls, eating away, bit by bit, moment by moment, human by human.

"You got clocked?" I asked.

Honey had a strange attitude to assimilation. She seldom made overt choices to be "feminine." Although sometimes, in order to save her own life, she was forced to make an attempt. Just like all of us, really. Depending on the place, I was able to blend in, but I was always keenly aware. I assumed from the moment I walked into a restaurant that everyone knew I was a man and I was dressing as a woman. And as much as I felt that was untrue, I still didn't have words for what I

was. "Transsexual" started to feel clinical. It felt uncomfortable, as if I belonged in a textbook. My assimilation test would begin from the moment I entered the room, and last until the first insult was hurled. If the staring, or the whispering, or the pointing never occurred, I was free and clear. The minute it began, my disguise was revealed. And although I never lied about it, or lived in stealth, my shame was so deep, it felt as though I did. So although I appeared to assimilate, I didn't.

When people initially looked at Honey, all they saw were her expressive face and her big baby blues, flashing from across the room. She was striking, but when they turned to look at her in awe, she mistakenly took their glances for disdain and hatred.

We understood each other. From the inside out.

"I did. I get clocked a lot, Alex. Grocery stores. Banks. Drive-thrus."

"You do not. Do you? I'm sort of shocked."

"You're not around when it happens."

"I'm around you all the time."

"Yeah. But you see what you want to see. So even when you're around, you're not around."

Honey lived as Don, and Don lived as Honey. She was Honey when I met her, performing in a show called *Dirty Dreams of a Clean-cut Kid* in Chicago, and although she was billed as Don Auxier, I knew Honey West.

Don had come from a small town in Indiana, where his closest relationship to his Transness was his mother's clothes and a small tutu that belonged to one of his sisters and used to hang on the line outside, drying in the breeze. At five or six years old, Don would squeeze his round little body into the tutu and be his sister. He'd dance around the living room, smiling and laughing. Truly laughing. And everybody loved it, until they didn't. Everybody clapped and smiled and took pictures, until they didn't.

"Did you ever stop to think that maybe you were one of us?" I asked her.

I still couldn't make heads or tails out of my own Transsexuality, but I knew a sister when I saw one. No matter what name we were given at birth, we all knew the truth.

"I saw you from the very beginning," I confided to Honey as we stood in my kitchen.

"I saw you too," she confessed, staring blankly at the small prescription bottle in front of us. "And when I saw you, I knew right then . . . you needed that unibrow plucked."

I smiled.

"And I remember thinking . . . is that her hairline or does her wig really need to be yanked into place?"

I held her hand. There it was. No matter what was happening, there was that joyful noise. She was trying her best to guide me toward it.

Well . . . perhaps both of us.

"That was you, sitting in the back of the Cairo, wasn't it?" I asked, still staring at the bottle.

Honey's hands fidgeted.

"I thought you were singing directly to me," she said honestly.

"I was."

"You're a lying sack of dog dung."

When we sat at Fathers and Sons, a year prior to this, she was talking about how sad she was.

I asked, "Are you sick and tired?"

"Yes."

I asked, "Are you sick and tired of being sick and tired?"

"Yes."

I asked, "Have you ever considered that you might be Trans?"

And she answered, "No . . . no . . . I'm just . . . yes."

And I saw a hundred pounds of brick and mortar lift off her shoulders. Just as they had off mine decades ago. Because we saw each other. Because we knew each other. Because we were family.

She asked, "Do I have to wear a dress now?"

"Come to my house and I'm gonna give you your first hormone pill out of my own stash."

"You will?"

"I will. It's made from pregnant horse urine."

"It's made from what?"

"Shut up. They work."

Chrisanne had made an enormous meal. She was downstairs watching TV because she knew Honey and I would watch *America's Funniest Home Videos* and talk incessantly. Chrisanne would much rather watch her Holocaust documentaries or shows like *A History of Christianity*, neither of which were known for their comedic content.

"What's the holdup, Honey?"

"I . . . I don't know what's going to happen after I take one."

"Well, what do you think is going to happen? It's Premarin, not meth."

"You don't know that."

"You're right. I'm making an uneducated guess that the doctor who prescribed these pills is an actual certified doctor and not a prison inmate."

"Something else you don't know."

"Take the fucking pill, girl."

She opened the bottle, took out a small, purple pill, and popped it into her mouth. She downed it with a gallon and a half of water. The threshold that was crossed as we stood there was lost on the two of us and didn't really resonate until many years later. But we were there for each other as one human began a transition into their truth and their power, and the other, holding their hand, bore witness. To hold the

hand of a spirit as it finds its natural birth is profoundly moving, but at the time, as my emotional life was still suppressed and crowded with voices of rage and loss, I simply said, "Now . . . let's sit here for a minute and watch your tits grow."

She laughed, choking a bit.

"Now that would be America's funniest home video."

~

All the Transsexual girls I knew began as I had. We all lip-synched. We all hooked. We all dated men, and we all got lost in a world where no one saw us. There was very little mingling with the outside for us. We belonged in a very small space, and that's where most of us stayed. There was Chili, who ventured out and conquered the straight world with her wit and her charm, and occasionally a few others dabbled in the outside, but most of us stayed where we were told. There was no space to be made. And then I heard of Honey West, playing down the street in a show she had designed, written, and produced, and directed by an actual theater director. She was singing. She was using her own voice, this Honey West person.

Honey West. Honey West. The only Honey West I knew was Anne Francis.

I didn't understand.

And then I heard her sing. Her voice was soft and powerful. She belted and she purred, and her sheer musicianship was incredible. She possessed the extraordinary ability to sing harmony and to improvise lyrics in front of a live crowd as she flirted with the front row or collected requests from the back. She held the audience tightly, like the hostess you always wanted to have at dinner. Every club she headlined became her living room, and we were her guests. Honey welcomed everyone to the table. I tended to attack a song from the outside, while

Honey navigated through the center of the piece. She was trained. I was not. She read music. I did not. She could sing on pitch. I could not. And yet when we finally joined forces, when we finally teamed up after two or three years of friendship, we found our differences to be our greatest strengths.

There were many nights when I fell off the barstool as we sang next to each other.

"We have a guest with us tonight who traveled very far to see us," she cooed one night, over the smoky haze of the Gentry on State Street.

"We do? How exciting! I hope it's Liza. Is it Liza?"

"It's not Liza."

"Then I'm not interested," I shot back smugly.

"It's my gynecologist."

The crowd roared.

"Your what?" I choked.

"My gynecologist," she repeated.

I climbed off the barstool howling like a monkey.

"You don't have a gynecologist, girl."

"He's a specialist."

And so, it went on, and I found something I had lost, something that I had never even realized had gone. This buoyancy and this familial love from a Trans voice.

I was finding my voice, and she was finding hers.

Mimi's closet was filled with treasure. When I opened the two sliding doors with the mirrors attached, my face would get red, red, red. At five years old, the sparkle was blinding. I would take things down and put them on, and walk around her bedroom, and parade and smile and laugh, and turn around in the mirror many times, and every time I had on a new outfit, something somewhere would light up in me.

The sparkle in the closet made me happy, and the sound I made shook the planet.

For Honey, it was the tutu.

"I loved that tutu. I remember dancing in the living room, and people around me loved it."

"You danced in drag in front of your family?" I asked, eyes wide.

"Yeah. But . . . it wasn't until later that I stopped, and I couldn't ever do it again . . ."

Honey and I lay on her bed. I was sideways, eating a bowl of Pringles. She was propped up with the remote in her left hand.

"Why? If you were able to do that in front of your family, why did you stop?"

"Because someone told me to. I remember they told me to stop it. They told me to stop doing it. And I just felt this . . . this enormous shame, girl. I was stained. I was permanently stained. And really . . . I never knew I was doing anything wrong, until someone told me."

I never knew I was doing anything wrong, until someone told me.

Until someone told me.

Here was this terrible thing I was doing, and I was doing it to other people. And although the sparkle and the tutus made home an unsafe space for both of us, they felt just fine until we were told they weren't.

I simply never knew.

Not until someone told me.

Us.

Her voice was melodic and powerful, and Honey and I continued to hold on to each other through the musicals and plays we did together, plays I directed her in, and cabarets we costarred in. We made up our own rules, and through it all, we tried to remind each other that no matter what anyone said, we were going to be heard and seen, and we weren't doing anything wrong, despite the many who whispered, made laws, and voted for humans who made sure we got the message.

We really weren't welcome, not really.

"They come in to see the freaks, girl, but they leave knowing the artist," she would say.

Her voice flew into me. It gave me hope, and it gave me breath. I was tired of being Judy and Liza and Bette, and Honey was tired of pretending to be Don. I began to cast off my disguises. The human I had begun to understand and speak to, the one standing in front of the sparkle in the closet, was the one I was trying to free. Although Ginger and I had shared huge moments in my life, Honey took up more space in me. Not only was she my teacher, but she also became my student. We gave and took from each other. I began to see clearly, and I began to shed who I wasn't.

People were leaving us, and there were funerals, and illnesses, and lesions on people's foreheads. Honey and I were doing benefits and concerts, trying to pick up pieces of people we knew.

After another night of seeing me walk like Bette Midler, hold the mic like Judy, and gesture like Liza, Honey erupted: "Look, girl. I like when you do that . . . you do it really well . . . but I miss . . . you."

"Huh?"

"Why do you do that? You're so good. You don't need to do that. I like it when you're *you*."

As I saw her, she in turn saw me. Honey was the first human in my life to do so. It shifted something profound in me to hear someone I loved this much see me so clearly. Her voice crashed like a cymbal, and I hated it. I got angry at her self-righteous psychoanalytic crap, shoving it down my throat just because she was in analysis and I wasn't. I had given up heroin, cocaine, and booze—what more did she fucking want? The shedding hurt. The more that came off, the more pain I felt. I stumbled and fell, but as pissed off as I was at her, she'd always be there for me.

"Did you know we're Transgender now?" I announced as we were on our way to a show one night.

"We're what?"

"We're no longer called Transsexuals. We're called Transgender."

"Sounds like a detergent."

"Well, that's what we are," I proclaimed flatly.

"Where did you hear this?"

"The library."

She paused as she turned the corner.

"What the hell were you looking up?"

And so it continued, as my Transgender sister and I grew up together. She reminded me constantly of the truth of who I was, and I reminded her that who she was becoming would always matter. I began to let go. I began to unravel. I saw a new path, and because I was led by this human, I began to forge it with her. I began to rediscover a voice I thought I'd lost. And hearing myself, I began to shatter and fall apart. I was held by Chrisanne, and I was seen by Honey, and I slowly realized, like Dorothy had in her own fairy tale, that this magical sound I thought I'd lost had actually been with me all the time.

It's profoundly funny when you rediscover the sound of your own laughter. Honey made me laugh so hard I would fall off furniture—couches, beds, chairs, stages, tables, desktops—and once, I rolled around in the back seat laughing so hard, Chrisanne had to pull over and stop the car. The sound I was making was moose-like.

That laughter was necessary when our Transgender tribe appeared to be nonexistent and inconsequential. I couldn't find us anywhere, so leaning into the sound of joy was everything to me.

We laughed, Honey and I. And we continued to laugh. We held on, and slowly, I began to hear myself. And although I could feel the rumbling in our world, and the black dresses in my closet piled up while

our friends fell away, I kept searching for that joyful sound, that noise I had heard so much about. Honey and I decided that no matter what anyone said, no matter how many times they told us we were wrong, this time . . . we would refuse to believe them. This time, we'd tell them to eat our collective asses.

And we thought that was hilarious.

TWENTY-THREE

That Time I Almost Died

My eyes squinted and my head started to throb. I squirmed while reading *People* magazine and tried to focus on the pictures. Words hurt. I shifted. My legs jumped of their own volition. I held the magazine in one hand and clamped down on one of my knees with the other.

Chrisanne sat in the chair next to me, motionless. She had brought along a book and rarely looked up. Occasionally, I would put my hand near hers, and she'd automatically grab it. She'd hold on. Tight. She'd squeeze it two, sometimes three times, never looking up from her book.

"Alexandra?" the nurse called from the half-open door.

"Yes," Chrisanne answered.

I put *People* on the magazine table. Chrisanne closed her book and led me toward the threshold.

"Right in here. I'll be back to take a few vitals."

Chrisanne and I entered the rectangular room, which was bathed in white light with one small chair propped up in the corner. Chrisanne sat.

"You should have a seat on the table. You're the patient," she quipped.

"I know what I am."

"You're a cranky patient," she teased affectionately.

"My legs still hurt."

She leaned forward.

"I know they do, sweetie. I'm sorry."

There was a blue stripe that ran around the edge of the ceiling. I lay down on the crinkly white paper that covered the long patient's table, and I traced the stripe with my index finger.

The nurse came back, took my temperature and blood pressure, smiled a bit, spoke in a half whisper to Chrisanne about what had been happening to me the last few months, and then told us the doctor would be in as soon as he could.

I lay back down while my legs jumped occasionally.

"How do you feel?" Chrisanne asked.

I stared at the blue stripe lining the universe and trailing off to nowhere.

"Weird."

The doctor walked in, blank faced. His eyes were small, and his hands were unsteady. He had brown hair and no face. He was present, but it seemed like he'd rather be somewhere else.

"Well, Alexandra. You have it."

I sat in the room beneath the blue stripe and noticed how much white there was. The instruments, the paper that crinkled as my legs bounced, the chair where Chrisanne was sitting, the door, the frame, the floor, and his coat. I stared at his name tag.

I couldn't read his name; it was blurry.

Chrisanne moved over and took my hand.

"Say it again," I instructed the faceless man in the white coat.

"You have AIDS," he intoned blankly.

Chrisanne took in a deep breath, and the room got wider. It expanded, and my eyes hurt, and I tried to remind myself to breathe. I saw Leslie and Daphne and Jeffrey and that boy with whom I did that show, whose name I couldn't remember, and I remembered funeral after funeral and bullshit eulogies by bullshit people who performed their grief, when what we needed was the truth. And I decided I didn't want that. I didn't want to put Chrisanne through that. I saw the wrapped bodies in white sheets spattered with blood, and the piles and piles of clothes, and the dishes in sinks, and I didn't want our house to look like that. We'd better hire someone to come and do the dishes. I saw Ginger's face. I saw the brown-purple lesions on her, and I saw the open sores on her chin and on her forehead. I remembered the bones in her knees protruding from her jeans and the way she had to hobble upstairs and how she smelled because she was swimming in yesterday's shit that she couldn't deal with because her arms were too heavy. She couldn't eat or smile or speak or live in delight or beauty or fancy, because dying requires focus. The ones who remain behind are left to sweep up the remnants of their once beautiful lives. It is unlike anything else, and it takes up everyone's time, and no one is safe from it.

"Am I going to die?" I asked.

The faceless man took out a pen and started writing on a small pad.

"My suggestion is that . . . well, maybe you ought to give yourself a treat. Maybe you ought to treat yourself. Just max out your credit cards. Buy a house. Go on vacation. Maybe a new car or a closet full of clothes."

Chrisanne breathed again and I heard it again. The room was getting larger and longer, and my eyes began to close.

"I mean, you probably won't be around to pay the bill . . ." said the man with no face.

More words happened, and I heard a piece of paper rip out of something, and more words, and I was helped off the table, and Chrisanne

215

still had my hand. She squeezed it, and as we left, she turned to the faceless doctor and said, "Oh, she's going to be around. Don't you worry about that."

We drove, because Chrisanne had to do something. I could see her insides crumbling. The summers in Chicago were always filled with so much color: crowds of humans going here and there and shopping and picnicking and holding hands, the sun beating down and the heat rising, the city coming alive. The virus had gotten smarter in the nineties. It seemed to flourish. Rock Hudson was on the cover of *Us* and *People* and *Time* and *Cosmo*. His gaunt, skeletal features, ravaged by the virus, warned the straight community that they were next. The white, cis, het population began to worry. There was no safe place. Everyone was dying. Everyone was angry. But no matter, it was always our fault. That never changed. It was always because of the queer people, and what we did, and how we did it, and the very fact of our existence, that gave this thing breath. No matter how many famous people died, we were always to blame.

~

Chrisanne and I would take off in the four-wheel drive flatbed truck she had bought for the theater company she recently started.

As we drove through the streets of Chicago, we'd pass by people, and more people, and *more people*, and I hated them. I spat on them, and I wanted them to get the thing I had. I thought up different ways to infect them all. I could inject them with my tainted blood, fuck them to death, open my vein and squeeze drops of AIDS-ridden blood into their open sores. The lid was blown off my decades-old rage. It was intense and immediate, and it began to pour out and into the souls of everyone on the street.

I hated everyone.

Including Chrisanne.

We went home. We stayed at home. We ate. We cleaned up. We drifted around the house and we barely spoke. A week went by. Then another. I began to climb into myself and refused to come out. One afternoon, Chrisanne stood at the doorway of the bedroom as I lay in bed.

"If you're going to curl up into a little ball and do nothing, you have to do it somewhere else."

"What?" I asked, stunned.

"I can't sit here and watch you die. I can't do that," she repeated. "We have to do something . . . figure this out."

Her eyes were dull, their light dim, and her body was tired. She was spitting out words from a place of exhaustion and desperation.

"There's nothing to figure out."

"We're going to get information. We can't just sit around and do nothing. We have to find something . . ."

"You do that. You go fucking find something. I'll be over here."

Pamphlets and leaflets and posters for rallies and conferences were brought into the house. The very first home computer arrived in our tiny apartment, and she would search for hours about CD4 counts, viral loads, transmissions, and trials of new drugs besides this AZT thing that everyone was taking but that made them sicker than they were before. She'd talk to me about this support group and that doctor, and this meeting at someone's home, and inquire about what was I doing today to find more information, and did I know this, and was I up to speed on that . . .

"There's a support group at a place called TPAN, and it's not far from here. I think you should go."

"I don't want to go. You go."

"I'm not the one who's sick, sweetie."

"No," I retorted firmly. "You're not."

But I would end up going. And I would attend a rally, and see my doctor, and ask questions, and go to my recovery meetings. I would go, but I wouldn't listen. I was dying. What the hell was the point?

Nobody got it. You didn't get it unless you had it. I was on my way out of this world, and I wasn't even forty years old. Don't speak to me about what you think is good for me, or what you think might help. The only thing that would help is a cure, and that was not going to happen. It was 1996, and people were starting to become aware of us, but that was only because of Rock and Elizabeth. It was their lives they wanted to save, not mine. I'd been burying my friends for almost ten years. Maxing out my credit cards was a waste of time, and your support groups and your recovery programs are all fine for people who have a future, but some of us are merely waiting for the store to close.

I took the truck and headed to Mimi's.

~

Very few people knew. We were careful about who we told. I was an actress, and telling people I had AIDS could very well end my career. We gathered a small group of our friends—Jamie, Michael, and Joey— sat around one night after a party, and told them. Some people froze, some got up and left the room. Michael put his head in his hands and wept.

"We'll figure it out, Alex. You're made of strong stuff," Jamie said in her best Alice B. Toklas voice.

Michael and Joey held on to me, tightly and lovingly. None of it really mattered. I knew they loved me, and I knew they were trying, and I knew they wanted to manifest healing and hope, but none of it mattered. I couldn't feel a thing. I simply didn't care.

~

It was a long drive to Schaumburg, and it had been a while since Mimi and I had seen each other. I rehearsed my speech all the way up. Tried to make it sound casual and ordinary. Like any other news.

"You know I'm in this new musical, and Chrisanne and I are in love, and also, I have AIDS."

Something like that, maybe.

We sat in the kitchen. Mimi had made us tuna sandwiches and we sat, chatting about work, the new musical I was in, and her life at school.

"My students are so stupid this year," she announced solemnly.

"Mother, don't say that about your students," I chastised, munching on my sandwich.

"You asked me how things were going. I'm telling you how things are going. I'm teaching stupid people."

"They're only six."

"They're six and they're stupid."

I ate.

She stared at my breasts.

"What?" I asked.

"Did that hurt you? I mean . . . whatever they put in there. Did it hurt?"

"Yes. It hurt like hell. But I'll tell you what hurt even more—not having them."

She got up from the table and poured a drink. Half scotch and half water. It was 2:00 p.m.

"I have something to tell you," I stated calmly.

She was silent. She sipped her drink and turned toward me.

"I have AIDS. I was diagnosed last month."

She turned away. She put the glass on the counter by the sink and looked out the window. I had grown up in this house, and all my life, outside the window where Mimi did the dishes and cooked the meals

and planned the parties, was this huge, beautiful weeping willow. She loved that tree. Sitting beneath it was one of her favorite places in the backyard. She'd set up chairs and she and her girlfriends would chat and drink and giggle for hours under that tree. Bill would barbecue and grill, Mimi would set up a small table, and we'd all picnic under that tree. It was full and leafy and spread out like a blanket along the floor of the lawn. She stood there looking out of the window. No tears. No sound. No breath.

"Oh, Scott," she whispered, staring at the backyard. "My God."

The heaviness of her sound was almost too much for me. I had never heard that tone before.

"You know the tree died. I had to have it cut down. And now there's just this big empty space where it used to be," she said slowly.

I couldn't move.

"It did? When did it die?"

"And now I just go outside and stand on the porch and look at this big hole where that tree was. I don't even really like to go outside anymore. It just . . . died."

She picked up her drink and took a sip.

She faced me.

"Do you want some more tea?"

~

I was making my long walk up those damn stairs, which haunted me at each entrance and every exit. I was starring in *Son of Fire*, an original musical by Christopher Moore. I was playing Chieko Shima (a middle-aged Japanese artist) in love with a much younger Ken, a budding artist with a penchant for fame and money, played by Will Chase. The story, based on real-life events, was my first—and to date, my only— romantic lead. Once again, most of the reviews focused on my being

Transgender and not being very convincing at being Japanese, a woman in love, or an artist. Will was kind and compassionate, and his gifts were apparent to us all. We had a few love scenes together, and although I was nervous and shaky, having him as a partner gave me great strength. He constantly reassured me how happy he was to be doing this play with these people, this ensemble, and renowned director David Zak.

The virus would give me a break every once in a while, almost as if it would visit and then go on vacation. Randomly, I would be fine. I wouldn't have AIDS. I wouldn't suffer, and my hatred for humankind would subside. This musical gave me hope and reminded me that true love was possible. As Chrisanne and I blossomed, my art, too, seemed to bloom.

This was Honey's and my first show together. My dressing room was on the top floor, and since the set had two stories, every five or ten minutes, Honey, who played many roles, would race up a rickety ladder and run past me, sometimes as Don, sometimes as Honey, sometimes as a judge, and sometimes as a performance artist in a *Flashdance* outfit singing about "the bomb-a-go-go." I'd be sitting at my table, twirling up my hair and smoking. My character died in act 1, and I didn't come back as a ghost until the middle of act 2, so I could sit and smoke. And make fun of Honey.

She'd race past me, puffing and scooping up parts of her costume that she had abandoned on the second rung of the ladder.

"Girl! Don't just sit there. Help me," she'd squeal.

"My God," I'd say, blowing smoke onto the makeup mirror. "You sure are working hard."

I helped her.

A little.

The stairs that led from the bottom of the stage to the top were getting more and more difficult for me to climb. My legs were weak. My ankles would fold. And then, piece by piece, my body began to fall

apart. I grew mold underneath my thumbnail. Then two of my nails fell off. I had to wear press-on nails and glue them to an open nail bed. I developed thrush in my mouth and under my tongue. The insides of my cheeks were bloated with white, puffy cotton balls of yeast and infection. There was medication. It worked, and then it didn't. Singing became a war. I had to navigate the searing pain in my legs and the balls of gunk in my mouth. I made sure that although Will and I had intimate scenes together, I never kissed him. I knew he couldn't contract AIDS this way, but I wasn't about to take a chance on my other opportunistic infections. He never complained, and he never asked why. He would take my face in his hands as we sang about love and art and the beauty of the world around us, his gaze never once leaving my eyes as his voice soared. I will never forget his compassion and genuine kindness as I got progressively sicker and sicker. Will was really the very first white, cis, het male who was a leading man to my leading lady and treated me like an actress instead of a Transgender Actress.

As a Friday-night performance went on, and the glorious thirty-person cast sang and sang, I was supposed to make my way up the stairs but couldn't. My legs simply would not work. Mary Beidler, who played my best friend and confidante in the show, was unfailingly there to support me. Mary was an accomplished actress and singer and one whose work ethic I admired and wanted desperately to follow. Unfortunately, I wasn't willing to work for it. I wanted the adoration, not the training. I was frightened of almost everything then: of the stage, of art reflecting life, and of all my teachers, who seemed to have to scream at me in order for me to hear them. I was still battling with my own idea of femininity and what that looked like. I was bullied on the streets, harassed by people outside the theaters, and still called a Transsexual by the majority of the Chicago press, most of whom remained fixated on my genitals and what I had done to them. Only weeks before we opened, as I was on

my way to rehearsal, a car drove by and someone threw a dozen rotten eggs at me, screaming, "Faggot!"

And now, on top of all that, I was dying.

That night, as I stood there looking at those stairs, Mary came up behind me and held me. My legs toppled, my body slowed down. She scooped me up and led me up the stairs, and after the show, I asked her to take me home. I felt the vessel I was traveling in begin to grind to a halt. This was it. I could feel it in my bones.

I wanted Chrisanne. I needed to be with Chrisanne.

We piled into the truck, most of my makeup still on, and drove home. On our way up to our apartment, I fainted. Mary caught me, and as I lay in the wet grass on the summer night, partially conscious, she screamed at the top of her lungs, "Chrisanne! Help! Help!"

That was the last thing I remember.

~

My eyes were still half closed, almost cemented shut. I was so hot. My head felt as if I had been burned and my hair had been singed off. As I turned my head, blinking the sleep out of my eyes, there was Chrisanne. She was tucked in a corner, curled up on a makeshift cot, snoring, as she does.

My hands were hot. My fingers and toes and my ass and my genitals were hot. I couldn't get comfortable. The white sheets stuck to me. The blanket was too hot. I threw it off. There was water falling from my eyebrows into my eyes, and it stung. As I roused myself, the pain became more intense, and I started to cry. I was so hot and sticky. I couldn't get comfortable. And then I released my bowels in my bed, and I lay in my own feces. The heat from my belly rose up, and the smell was rancid.

"Oh . . . okay. It's okay, sweetie."

Chrisanne's voice came through a thick fog.

I could feel her hands holding mine. But I had to pull away because being touched was painful. I wanted to scream, hold her, and ask her what was happening. But words hurt.

A tall man with a beautiful smile came in. He was encased in blue. He whispered to me, and I turned away, and something cool was wiping my bottom, and then I turned, and I saw Chrisanne's shirt. I kept turning and turning and being turned, and I would hear an occasional "Oh my God, thank you" from Chrisanne through the dense, hot fog, and I would see his blue gown light up against the white walls.

Then I'd go back to sleep.

My eyes opened to more white, and there was a plate of food in front of me. I picked up a spoon, put it to my mouth, and threw up. And as I threw up, I pissed, and then the man in the blue gown appeared.

"Here. Let's try it this way tonight," he'd say.

"Oh . . . yes. Okay. Let's do that." Chrisanne was so tired.

"You grab that end and I'll grab this end," the man in the blue gown would say. "You're doing great, Alex," he'd murmur.

And I would turn and turn and turn and then be turned and . . . it was so hot.

"You should probably call her parents," he said.

"Now?" Chrisanne asked, panicked.

"Well, soon. I don't think she has much time left, really."

I heard her pick up the phone. I think I spoke to Mimi. There was a scene between us, but the words hurt and so I don't remember it. I wanted to be cooler, and I was so hungry.

And the sound kept coming.

"Help! Stop it! I'm not going! You can't make me go! I'm not going to go! Help! Help!"

The voice calling for help got clearer and clearer. It echoed down the white hallways and found its way into my room and wove into the red-hot blanket.

I opened my eyes, wiped the sweat from my forehead, and kicked off the white sheet and the white blanket. I was wearing a checkered gown with the back open, and it was too hot. I tore it off, and there was Chrisanne, still on that cot. Still snoring. She looked so uncomfortable. I wanted her to have a bed. She needed a bed. I wished she could crawl in here with me, but dying takes up an enormous amount of space.

"Help!" cried the voice from down the hall. "Help!"

I plugged my ears. I didn't want to hear this. I tried to dream of love songs, and long stairs with hidden trapdoors, but the voice kept on. It kept begging for help. Begging for help. Once it got so loud that my breath stopped. My breath stopped. I stopped breathing. I lay back down. For a moment, only for the tiniest moment, I was at peace. The heat was gone. The terror was gone. The voice stopped and I lay there. And it felt fine. My heart was beating, but barely. And as I lay there, a white-hot stream of voices flew through the air and landed in the middle of the room, and suddenly I knew if I kept going, I would never come back. I knew if I remained there, I'd never return. This wasn't peace. This wasn't peace at all.

Moments later, my eyes opened. My mouth was clear and my head stopped throbbing. I was cool. Sitting up, I could see the room, and the food in front of me smelled good, even for hospital food.

"Sweetie?" Chrisanne's voice came through the fog again.

I turned to her. Her eyes sparkled and her hands were shaky.

"Hi," I yawned.

She put her arms around me and tried to climb into bed, but the silver bars were too high, and the man in the blue gown probably wouldn't like it.

"Thank you for turning the heat down," I said, scooping up some Jell-O.

"I love you," she whispered softly.

"I love you too," I answered.

Dr. Ross Slotten walked in. His smile was always bright and vivacious. His thick hair was swept back, like Jack Lord's from *Hawaii Five-O*, and his long face was punctuated by his black, deep-set eyes. He took over as my doctor after the faceless man was fired. Apparently, telling people with AIDS to max out their credit cards and enjoy their remaining time on earth had been a monologue the faceless one repeated to many patients. Ross had enough and gently suggested he move on.

To Alaska.

Dr. Ross Slotten was another one of those tangible angels in my life. I didn't have to listen very hard to know what he was trying to say to me.

And I listened. This time, I finally wanted to truly listen . . .

"What the fuck happened to me?" I asked.

Ross sat on the edge of the bed. He put his hand on my knee, stared straight at me, and said, with a calm demeanor and no irony whatsoever, "I have absolutely no idea."

"What? Are you kidding? You honestly don't know what happened?" Chrisanne sputtered, pulling up her chair.

"Nope. We don't know why you got this sick, what brought it on, what it was, or more importantly, why or how you got better.

"Alex, your temperature was, at times, almost a hundred and four. None of us really know what happened. But . . . we're going to find out, and you're gonna be fine. Really. You're going to be okay."

"Well . . . what about that guy down the hall? Maybe he and I had the same thing. Maybe you should check on him."

Ross looked up at me.

"What guy?"

"The guy down the hall. He was screaming 'help me, help me' all night long. You heard him, didn't you, honey?"

"There was no one down the hall, sweetie," Chrisanne answered slowly.

There was no one. There was no one down the hall.

Except, there was.

There was a song in *Son of Fire* called "Gifts of Love." It was written for me to be sung to my lover as he lay dying. It's about the cost of love and the high price of living, explaining that life without love is no life at all. The lyrics revealed that in order to be found, you have to listen for the guides, that sometimes there is darkness in the search for the light.

Be led. Be taken. Surrender, Alex.

I went back into the show after I almost died, and every night I was gifted with the honor of singing this piece. I remember looking up and shouting to the top rows of the theater, trying my best to rattle the nails and shake the boards loose. I wanted to reach something farther away and give thanks. I wanted to listen. I had ignored so many guides in my life already, and I didn't want to waste one more minute trying to figure it all out and make sense of everything.

"I have absolutely no idea what happened. None of us do."

Exactly.

TWENTY-FOUR

Love Letter 1

December 5, 1996

Sweetie,

I'm writing. Look, I'm writing. It feels so great to be actually writing a letter. The last letter I wrote you was during first rehearsal of *The Tender Trap* in high school, when you lost your voice and I had to be you, and I made you one of my famous cootie catchers that told you of the magical red-horned platypus that would be your favorite pet and that your lucky number was twelve and that I was, in fact, your true love. Chrisanne and Scott. You and me. God bless the magical cootie catcher.

   Everyone's asleep. The entire apartment is quiet, the dog has finally shut the hell up, and Kelly's blond head has hit the pillow. And I do mean hit the pillow. I think there's an indentation of her face in the middle of this pillow. Michael gave us his room, so we're both cuddled in the same bed, and he took the

couch. It was so great. I mean, I know that Michael and Kelly have been much closer than Kelly and I, but you know . . . I mean, we were the Three Musketeers during the Baton years.

I'm rhyming, dammit.

Kelly and I have been up all night talking about what it was like when we were hyped up on coke and when I was shooting heroin in the men's room at Club V, and all those years of being roommates . . . and all those men. I know this sounds weird, especially to write to you now and talk about this . . . all those men. But you know my past. I know you're okay with it, and you even saved me from it . . . at times.

Remember that time when Donny had beaten me so badly my lip was turned up and there were like . . . brains coming out of my ears, and I called you and you drove down that night from the suburbs? You packed a bag for me, and we got in the car, and he came running up to the window, and I was so frightened I couldn't speak. And he said something like "Where you going with my girl?" And you said something like "Shut up and fuck off."

Remember?

And then you drove me into the sunset toward the town of Something I Don't Remember . . . with my brains still coming out of my left ear.

You saved me, and I'll never forget that.

Kelly and I were talking about that. She was always the kind of Trans woman I wanted to be. Feminine and cute and sexy with blond hair you could tie up and toss around. Instead, I feel a little like ET—square and squatty with webbed feet and a mellifluous baritone.

She asked me how it was going to work, after all the men I'd been with.

I've been thinking about that.

Remember when we first made love? Now, you know I've had a lot of sex with a lot of people. A. Lot. Of. Sex. With. A. Lot. Of. People.

But that night, when you first put your hands on me, I won't lie and say it was like being touched for the first time. It wasn't. It was like being touched for the last time. There was a kindness and a sexual ignition that happened, and I knew that this was it. If we don't do it now, it's never going to happen. I'm not talking about desperation. I'm talking about urgency. And yet, it was peaceful and slow and seemed to go on and on, and more than anything else, I felt safe. It was as if I had been searching for the longest time for this particular place, and I had finally landed. You saw all of me. And there wasn't a moment of shame.

That really was the first time.

And then you lay on top of me. We were on the couch, and we were completely naked and still sweating, and you proposed to me.

It took you twenty minutes, but you proposed to me.

I told Kelly that story, and she smiled so big and said, "Damn, that's hot."

Michael was with us all night tonight, but eventually he left Kelly and me alone and went into the other room. I thought that was so sweet. He's always been that little brother of mine, and even though his love for Kelly runs deep, he stepped aside. We got a chance to talk. I would marry you no matter what, sweetie, I think you know that. But without these two people by

my side and without their blessings, I don't know that I'd marry you totally. I mean, I don't know that it would be complete. They are part of me. Part of who I am, and Michael, with his mischievous face and his tuft of blond hair and little munchkin smile, has always occupied a huge space in who I am. I don't know how I would have survived what I have survived without Michael.

Remember that time I was going out and he was standing in my doorway with his arms crossed and his feet tapping and looking me up and down . . . I had put on the greatest outfit in my closet, and his fashion siren was spinning like a top. I said, "What's the matter now?"

And he said, with great authority I remember, "You could introduce that belt to those shoes, and they'd have nothing to say to each other."

He's been that voice in my head through cabaret shows when he's done my hair, and through benefits when he's talked me out of wearing an outfit that, he would remind me, Charo wouldn't be caught dead in.

And he loves you. And he's so excited. And he can't wait.

It was hard for them, sweetie. I guess I wanted to say all this because they knew me in a specific way, and falling in love with you was never part of that experience. So, having them here, being a part of this . . . it matters.

Also, I cannot wait for all our parents to be together. That's going to be great. I think you told me they might have met, for about half a second at a performance we were doing at Schaumburg High. They might have said three or four words to each other. But this will be different. This is going to be so amazing

and so beautiful. I can't wait to hear what our mothers have to say to each other.

I love that we decided to separate tonight. I didn't exactly want to adhere to a lot of wedding traditions, but I like this one. The house is dark, and the dog is finally asleep. The last thing I need to do, before tomorrow comes, is lie in the dark and dream.

I can see my wedding dress from here. I hung it in the corner so when I went to sleep it would be the last thing I'd look at and the first thing I'd dream of.

Even in the dark, I can see what's next for me. Right there in front of me.

I cannot wait to see you tomorrow. Happy Almost Wedding.

I love you.

Me.

My Wedding(s)

I had two.

Wedding 1
Friday, December 6, 1996
Chicago
(The day of the wedding)
4:00 p.m.

I was backstage at the Bailiwick Theater in Chicago. It was just beginning to snow. I was sitting in front of a huge mirror ringed by theatrical

lights that spread a powerful and almost supersonic glow on every woman behind me. Michael was furiously tying ribbons and bows to the halo of dried flowers and leaves he'd hand sewn to fit on the crown of my head. I had found a dress at Marshall Field's that I absolutely loved. I didn't do the big "bride shopping" thing because we didn't have the money, and when I told Mimi that Chrisanne and I were getting married, she flew into an alcoholic rage and got up from the kitchen table screaming, "This is ridiculous! You can't get married! People get married to have children!"

I wasn't sure what being childless had to do with how much Chrisanne and I loved each other, or the fact that we had decided to devote ourselves to each other, or that we wanted to share this union with our friends and our family and have it divinely blessed, but in Mimi's mind, marriage and children seemed to make perfect sense. I had asked Mimi if I could wear her wedding dress. I knew it would be too small, but I thought somehow I might make it work. I'd seen photos of it, and it was truly gorgeous.

Mimi in her wedding dress

"You can't wear it."

"I knew you were going to say that."

"I burned it."

"You what?"

"I burned it."

"You burned your wedding dress?"

"When we lived in Marble Estates. Outside in the backyard. On a Sunday afternoon."

"Where exactly did you burn it?"

"In the garbage can."

I could barely speak.

"Why did you burn it on a Sunday?"

"So it would be holy."

My dress was a long, white slip that had a box neck and a small dip in the back. It touched the tops of my feet, and when I walked, it moved like a sheath on a cloud. I wore ballet slippers, as I knew from my drag days that being in heels was not conducive to long, happy evenings on your feet. I carried a bouquet of the dried wildflowers that Mary Beidler had strewn all over the mainstage of the theater, where we set up the ceremony. There was something wonderfully ironic that Mary was onstage with me again, as this was the same space in which we had performed *Son of Fire*.

There was a performance scheduled for that weekend, and we were to be married on its set. We tried our best to cover it with sheets, cloths, and carefully placed dried rose petals; however, you couldn't help but notice the large, red doorframe, the green-and-black checkered throw rug rolled up and leaning precariously against the naked brick wall, and the huge unfinished painting of George Washington hanging directly in the middle of the stage. Above a red chaise longue David loaned us to distract from the door, the carpet, and George loomed an oversized, overstuffed maniacal boar's head complete with fangs and saliva.

Wedding 2
Monday, November 10, 2008
Los Angeles
(The week before the wedding)
3:00 a.m.

Matt always reminded me of a lithe, buoyant Elton John. He leaped from place to place—he sprang like a cheetah. He was fast and bright and fall-down funny. His wide eyes and his chiseled features could be either Gable or Lombard. We shared an obsession with the queer icons, and his Judy Garland impersonation rivaled Jim Bailey's. He was a late-night ghost like me and my pals from Chicago whom I missed so profoundly, and our friendship reminded me of those times sitting bleary-eyed watching video after video after video. Times had changed, though, and now there was the internet, so there was YouTube. The world at large was at our fingertips. I could dial up Judy's TV show, and we'd sit in our apartment in San Dimas, home of Bill and Ted (that everyone there really loves to talk about, by the way), and go through episode after episode. He was almost a generation younger than I was, but as my teaching began to shift and move into a direction of truth instead of ego, I loved being around younger people. I realized they were a powerful source of energy and kindness in my life. I wasn't sure why, but his was one of the first relationships where this synthesis of teacher/student/friend became apparent and necessary to me.

"I have to ask you something," I said to him one night at 4:00 a.m., after one of our late-night sessions.

"Please ask. And yes. That's the answer. Unless I have to be nude. Do I have to be nude? Oh, what the hell. Yes anyway!" He laughed, puffing on his cigarette and leaning back in his chair.

We sat on the cramped little porch of the apartment Chrisanne and I were renting in The Valley. I had tried to make it in Los Angeles

without her, but after six months alone, I was desperate. Chrisanne left Chicago as quickly as she could after I called her. She spoke to her job about working remotely, packed up more of our furniture, arranged the moving truck, and made the car trip from Illinois to California in early 2006. We settled into a small two-bedroom on the outskirts of Bill and Ted–Ville.

"Do you know what's happening here in California with the gay marriage law? Prop Eight?"

"Yeah. Why?"

"We want to be included in this fight. Chrisanne and I want to make our marriage legal and not be under this civil-union bullshit."

"But you're already married, I thought. Are you all living in sin? Sinners. You're dirty, dirty sinners."

"That's absolutely true, but that's beside the point. We're going down to the courthouse next Thursday just to sign the papers so we can be part of the movement and make things legal. I've had a wedding. I've been married for over ten years. No law will ever change that. This is just procedure. A statement from Chrisanne and me. And . . . a way to protect ourselves legally, our property, our rights as a married couple if one of us gets ill. Rights . . . like every American."

I puffed on my cigarette.

"Should I sing that Whitney Houston song now?"

"We need a witness. Want to come with us? We really want you there, Matt."

His eyes lit up. His knees began to bob up and down, and his voice tripped a bit.

"I . . . what, really? Yes! Wow. Alex. *YES!*"

I lowered my eyelids.

"Matt, I love that you're excited, but remember, this is just a formality. It's just a statement. We're not getting married. I'm already married. Okay?"

His eyes got even larger.

"Okay. Okay."

Wedding 1
6:00 p.m.

Michael began laying pieces into my brown hair. I had lost chunks of my own hair as a result of AIDS, so filling me out was quite a job. Piece by piece, eyes glued to his work, he would occasionally touch the back of my neck and smile at me in the mirror. I had five bridesmaids and one groomsman (Michael) in my party, and Chrisanne had the opposite. I chose the colors—forest green and red—and I'd picked out the cake, which read "Alexandra and Chrisanne" and was surrounded by a large red heart like the *I Love Lucy* logo. The two female cake toppers I found at Walgreens.

We had almost 150 guests. They arrived slowly, ready for this union no one expected. Among them were both of Chrisanne's parents as well as her brother, Jay, who also served as one of her groomsmen.

Chrisanne and her mother were sitting in the living room as the day approached. "Are you sure, honey?" her mother asked pointedly.

"Yes, Mom. I'm sure," Chrisanne answered slowly.

"I want you to be sure. You know . . . I love Alex. But I want . . . this isn't a game, you know. This is marriage. This is for the rest of your life. No matter what."

I was sick. I was very, very sick at a time when people like me died when they got sick. We didn't get better, we didn't get married, and we didn't have lives. We shriveled up and were tossed into the back seats of Chevrolets and left beside dumpsters. Chrisanne was so frightened of her parents' reaction that almost a month before, she wrote everything down in a long letter, sealed it in an envelope, and left it on her parents' staircase. She was marrying a woman they had known as Scott, who was

probably dying. Scott was one of their favorite people, but she didn't seem to be the most stable person their daughter could have chosen.

Things were complicated.

"Your daddy and I wanted to be here. You know that, don't you? We wanted to be here for you. Because we love you and we support you."

"I know that."

"One more thing"—she stood up and took Chrisanne's hand—"I just want you to know that if something goes wrong tonight . . . just one thing . . . take that as a siiiiiignnn."

Chrisanne rolled her eyes. We were marrying the person we'd been chasing our entire lives—through gender after gender and decade after decade. We were here, finally, with the love and blessing of both our birth and our chosen families.

What could possibly go wrong?

Wedding 2
November 17, 2008
(The day of the wedding)
Noon

On the last possible day, at the last possible hour, as the last possible moments ticked by, Chrisanne, Matt, and I piled into our car and made our way to the Los Angeles City Courthouse to add our names to a growing list of same-sex humans who wanted to be counted in the same way every other married American had the right to be counted. Time was running out. Prop Eight was being voted on by the masses, and this was the final day any paperwork could be filed. None of us could have predicted that same-sex marriage would be legalized and then revoked. It was utter insanity—the voice loud and clear from both our government and our populace: "We gave those gays more than enough time!"

Matt had brought us something old, something new, something borrowed, and something blue. I kept them in the car with us, and as we drove up, a small line was forming outside the doors of the courthouse.

Wedding 1
7:30 p.m.

The sounds were louder, filling up the dressing area as my bridesmaids began to surround me, hold me, and keep me in their hearts.

"Alex. There's . . . there's someone at the door for you," Mary announced.

I looked up. Michael was standing by the door, holding it halfway open. I was getting a little shaky the closer I came to being married. I walked to the door and opened it all the way, and there stood a man with brown shaggy hair, dressed as if he were going out to dinner. He smiled at me, and I knew I recognized him but couldn't for the life of me figure out how.

"How are you, love? It's so good to see you! Wow! You look gorgeous!" he shouted joyfully.

I could see he was happy for me, so I did what I usually do when I meet someone who knows me that I know I know but can't remember why I know.

"Hey, sweetie!" I said as kindly as I could.

We embraced, and as he pulled away, he looked me up and down.

"I can't believe it. This is brilliant! I mean, I've heard of these before, but I've never been to one. I'm so excited! And I'm sorry. I know you're about ready to go on, so I don't want to disturb you, but I just wanted to say that a couple of my lesbian friends did a show like this about a week ago, and it was fucking hilarious! I know this is gonna be great . . . especially with you in it! Well . . . anyway . . . just wanted to let you know I was here. I'll see you after the show. Break a leg. Love you."

He held me one more time and then disappeared into the onslaught of people filing into the theater.

Show?

Show!

He thinks this is a performance. He thinks we're putting on a show. He thinks this is a costume, that I'm in character, and that this is some sort of political comedy we're doing. He thinks it's a drag show or a parody or a farce. Do other people think that? Are the people in the audience waiting for me to slip on a banana peel as I walk down the aisle? Did Chrisanne's parents come all the way here to participate in some huge queer reality show? What's going to happen when there are no laughs? When the music plays? When Honey starts singing? When we take our vows?

I was suddenly filled with abject terror. I stood at the doorway quivering and wanting to vomit. I wanted to run out the door and grab Chrisanne by the hand and race to the truck and drive until the sun came up.

I was marrying the love of my life. I was not in a show. I was getting married. But I couldn't move from the doorway.

Wedding 2
1:00 p.m.

The couple in front of us, two younger African American men, were beaming. They filled in their papers, took some pictures, and moved on. The line was still fairly long behind us, but after an hour or so we made it to the window. The woman behind it moved her glasses to the bridge of her nose.

"You have your paperwork?" she inquired in a monotone.

Her face was red as if she'd been out in the sun too long, and she had the blackest eyebrows I'd ever seen. She seemed to have smeared

her lipstick on with a red crayon, but her hands, though crinkled, were immaculately manicured. She took the papers from Chrisanne.

"Where's your justice of the peace?"

"Our what?" Chrisanne asked.

"You have to be married by a reverend or a minister or someone," she answered.

"We do?" Matt chimed in.

"There's a justice of the peace right over there," she muttered, pointing across the hall.

"Oh. Great," I sighed. "Well then, let's just go over there and have a ceremony, and we'll be right back."

"He's gone. He leaves at noon."

I stood there looking at this woman, who seemed utterly callous. I wasn't sure why she brought up the justice of the peace in the first place, knowing full well he had gone for the day. I also didn't understand why we weren't informed about this beforehand. I also hated her damn eyebrows.

"What do we do?" Chrisanne asked, moving toward her just a bit.

"Well, I guess you try to find a reverend or someone who will marry you."

And I could swear now she was smiling just a little.

"But this is the last day. We're not going to find someone on the last day in what . . . when do you close?" Chrisanne blurted out.

"Six."

"You're giving us five fucking hours!" Matt pushed his way through.

"We close at six. Next?" the woman barked, her eyebrows twitching.

The three of us trudged out of the line. People looked at us with a combination of fear and sadness.

"We have to find someone to marry us. I'll be damned if a woman with eyebrows like that is going to get the best of us," I declared loudly enough for her to hear.

We headed downstairs to the café. Chrisanne and I always think better when we're around food. And we only had a few hours to think this one through.

Chrisanne strode away. "I need a doughnut."

Wedding 1
8:00 p.m.

It was one foot after the other as Enya blasted over the theater speakers. I walked down the aisle, moving flowers out of the way with my feet. The music surrounded me and filled me up. This song had always reminded me of Chrisanne, about places not yet seen, about paths not yet searched, about drifting into each other's arms and holding on, readying ourselves for our next adventure together. I had chased her for centuries, always in the wrong vessel, but this time somehow, we got it right. I was the way I was supposed to be.

I was Scott and I wasn't. I also knew that had I stayed that way, this would have been legal. If Chrisanne had married Scott, no one would be thinking that they were attending a show or stopping backstage to wish me luck. Scott and Chrisanne would be man and wife, and perhaps my parents would have shown up, and Chrisanne's mom never would have felt the need to make a bargain with her. But I had changed my name. I was legally Alexandra Scott Billings, although my birth certificate still stated male. Back then, it was the law that the sex assigned at birth could not be changed. It took months to sign all the papers, get things notarized, and collect notes from doctors and psychiatrists to legally become Alexandra.

As I walked and walked down the aisle, moving roses and tulips with my toe, I was both Scott and Alex. Chrisanne knew and loved Scott, and she was marrying him and me, and that was all that mattered. Legalities were irrelevant. There was a divine power that seemed

to push me together like a puzzle. I don't know that I ever thought about it until I was walking toward her, standing there, radiant in a long, green ball gown, with her hair swept up and her face glowing. Her spirit had come toward me from the back of the classroom all those years ago. And just as I had popped up from under the desk, looking around like a newly hatched chick, I was now coming toward her with my arms outstretched. Whether the law, or these people, or God saw this ceremony as a joke, we both knew how it had all begun, who we were then, and who we had both become. This was how I chose to marry. Just like this. In this dress that I had bought, in these shoes, in this holy space where I found solace and beauty, and to this human, who defied law and gender, just like me.

As I walked up to her, I could barely contain myself.

"You look absolutely beautiful."

She came close to me and breathed, "*You* look absolutely beautiful."

Then for the very first time in my entire life, I felt . . . beautiful.

Wedding 2
3:30 p.m.

The cafeteria crackled. We were all on our phones, searching for a church or a reverend. We were new to the area, unfamiliar with where to go or even where to look, and time was running out.

Finally, I got Jeff Perry on the phone. Kind. Calm. Easygoing. Never panicky Jeff Perry. Jeff, who came to my first class when I was thrown in by Tina at Steppenwolf Theatre and who saw something in me as a teacher from the very beginning. It was Jeff who had asked me to teach with the Steppenwolf and who invited me into their giant boys' club with absolutely no hesitation. His childlike wonder and amazement at the world around him bewitched me, and his ability to stand firm in his convictions and stand next to the marginalized astonished me.

Jeff was my anchor at various times in my life, especially when the harbor was filled with rising waves.

"I need help. We need help," I said to him over the phone.

I explained what had happened, about the woman with the eyebrows and the time constraint we were under. Jeff looked in the yellow pages, fired up his computer, and . . . found us a church in North Hollywood that was going to take us a while to reach. We left the cafeteria just as the chairs were being piled on top of the tables. The clock was ticking. We barely had enough time to marry each other, sign something, and then get back to the eyebrow lady.

We arrived at the church and parked out front. It was white with cracks lining the doorway and a tiny steeple at the top. It looked about as big as our apartment, and had one small, red door. We entered a tiny, well-lit, comfy waiting room that looked as though every hippie in the 1960s had slept there. As we signed in, we were greeted by a woman who was half Janis Joplin and half Joni Mitchell. Her long gray hair puffed out over her shoulders, and her voice wafted around the hallway. She seemed to sing when she spoke, and when we explained our odd dilemma, she shifted into high gear.

She also smelled as if she had just taken a marijuana bath.

"I'm Starbuck. Reverend Starbuck," she intoned.

"No, you're not," I spluttered, smiling as images of *The Rainmaker* swirled before my eyes.

Matt poked me.

"Come over here . . ." She waved us over to an altar with pungent incense burning, a few throw pillows, and a beautiful gold bowl with a giant ladle. I wondered if we were having soup, but I said nothing.

"You stand here," she said with a gesture, gently nudging me to one side.

"And you, Chrisanne . . . you stand here."

As we readied ourselves, Matt stood beside us, and she began to read. She spoke of love, of entering into a union, what that meant, and how much work it would entail, and what a spiritual gift it could be. She talked about giving, and about how being of service to your partner sometimes meant giving up yourself. She spoke of consequence and kindness. She lifted me up, and as the service went on, the clock stopped. I stood there in the jeans I'd chosen without really thinking about it, and I wore the ring Chrisanne had given me, which was new, and the bracelet I borrowed from Matt, as well as a blue scarf and the something old, the music on the mix tape we listened to as we drove to the church. Something old, something new, something borrowed, something blue, and all because of Matt. And it didn't feel like a betrayal of the first time. This time I wasn't worried about the gender container anyone had placed me in. The fact that the eyebrow lady pushed us here was really a gift. It reminded me why we did this in the first place. It reminded me that Scott was never very far away, and that Alex had always been here, because this is who I always was, and even though I was still on my way to finding out more and more about myself and my life, I was sure of one thing:

This human in front of me was my wife, and marrying her was the smartest goddamn thing I ever did.

5:50 p.m.

The eyebrow lady glared over the top of her papers. She pushed her glasses farther up the bridge of her nose and, with one final stamp, handed us back our official paperwork.

We were the last people out of the courthouse.

On the way home, I took Chrisanne's hand as she drove. She and Matt were chatting, the sun was setting, and Los Angeles seemed new. I had been born there, but it seemed new tonight. I was in the front

seat with my wife. Starbuck had asked us whether we were committed to each other, and we had both said yes, and she had pronounced us married.

That was all. Married.

This time, I didn't think about whether I was born with an *M* or an *F* assigned to me by some random doctor based solely on my genitalia. This time, I sat in the car and held my wife's hand, and I felt married. I didn't feel like a bride, and I didn't feel like a groom. I felt as if I was married to this human next to me, and that this was a sacred and holy venture. It was much simpler than I remembered it.

The next day, Proposition Eight passed and suddenly, because I was a Transgender Female and I had fallen in love with a Cisgender Female, what we were last night was no longer what we were this morning. But just as it had been the first time . . . there was nothing anyone could do about it. There was no law that could take Starbuck and the magical spell she had cast the previous day away from us.

That evening we went out and had burgers, fries, hot dogs, ice cream, and chocolate shakes. And that's how we celebrated—surrounding ourselves with food . . .

And an ancient love that had survived the ages.

Wedding 1
10:15 p.m.

It was freezing outside, and as we passed by the flatbed truck filled with wildflowers, Chrisanne's brother Jay filmed us on our way to our new life. Whatever was going to happen to us, we'd discover it together. The ceremony left us exhausted, and I directed Chrisanne into the black limo I had rented for the night.

And that's how we drove off. In style.

Our first dance was at a famous gay bar in Boystown called Sidetrack. We danced to Ethel Merman's "Everything's Coming Up Roses" from *Gypsy*. Neither of us knew what was next, but that was really the point, I guess. And that's how we celebrated: in wonder, in curiosity, and utterly and completely in love.

Love Letter 2

December 6, 1996

My Love,

You're sleeping next to me. Your body is so beautiful. I can't stop looking at you or believe it happened. Your cream-colored skin and your back turned toward me. I keep touching your back and making sure you're here. I cannot believe it. My God, the snoring. I cannot believe the amount of sound that comes out of a human this tiny. Honestly. Did you swallow Aerosmith? It's uncanny. I've actually never heard a human being snore quite the way you do. The United States Air Force could use you as a secret weapon.

I thought it went really well, didn't you? We make a good team, you and I. You directed it, and I made it into a fabulous musical!

Go, Us! It didn't feel like opening-night jitters to me. I don't know about you, but I wasn't nervous for one second. Isn't that funny? With all the self-doubt I carry around like luggage, not for one moment was I scared. I was completely sure I was doing the right thing.

For the very first time in my life. I was doing the right thing.

And then I saw you, and I saw those eyes, and I remembered what it was like when I popped my head up from underneath the desk. It always feels like the first time. I am always looking for you every time I pop my head up.

Do you know I miss you when you go to the store?

I do.

I think that means we're codependent. That's okay. I have so many other diseases, one more's not really going to make much of a difference.

I missed my parents. I have to say, I really missed them.

Mimi's refusal to come and Dad's "terrible cold" were cowardly and wrong. Both your parents and your brother showed up—not only showed up, but participated. Your dad walked you down the aisle, your brother was in your wedding party, and your mom made you wear a girdle.

It was beautiful, though, wasn't it? The *I Love Lucy* cake, the disposable cameras left for the guests so everyone could take their own pictures, and all our friends. Seeing Chili and having Honey sing, and Jen and Michael, and Bill playing the piano, and that beautiful poem by Cin. Seeing her, and bringing her back into our lives, meant everything to me. I felt a blessing when she came out and spoke those words, sweetie.

She was my first kiss. You are my first love.

She gave me away, I guess.

I have loved you for centuries. Do I tell you that enough? I have been with you since the beginning. We have lived our story of Sebastian and Viola, and we have ended happily ever after as Olivia and Cesario. And we are one, and we are each other. And the fact that you said yes when I proposed to you, after you proposed to me, and the fact that you have always been here even when you weren't, and the fact that we are together in a place where no one can touch us and where we are finally safe and finally home is, for me, proof of a divine source that is constant and powerful.

I mean, remember that time I almost died?

You quoted our journey in your vows, and we promised to behave and do well by each other, but I fully expect to fuck this whole thing up. And so, I pray that when I do, you'll forgive me. And we'll forgive each other. We live in a world that hates us, doesn't recognize this marriage, and tells us it is illegal. The world may declare that you are not my wife, that we do not have equal rights, and if we die, or if we are fired, or if we buy a home, you are not my spouse. We will live here anyway, and by the lives we lead, we will hopefully proclaim a message of clarity and kindness.

Let us love, and fuck right off.

I am yours, my love. I always have been. In whatever vessel I have traveled, I always have been.

The water is overflowing; I think I have to go. My legs are twitching again. I have to get back in the tub. This pain. Ugh. These shingles. I know you're tired. You have spent most of tonight putting me in and out of warm baths filled with oatmeal to try to soothe this

pain. But today, nothing hurts: not my legs, not the AIDS, not Mimi's disappearance, not the people who mistook our wedding for a performance, not Dad's fake cold, and not your too-tight girdle, which went careening across the room like a slingshot when you took it off tonight.

You hated it. I thought it was hilarious.

We ate. We opened gifts. We shook the flowers from our hair. And so, my wife, I cherish you in celebration. Here's to many more years of being married to you.

I'm super excited about the whole thing!

I love you.

Mrs. Alexandra Billings-Blankenship

Our first wedding

TWENTY-FIVE

Love and Marriage

*(and a whole bunch of other stuff no one tells you about
cuz you grew up with Bob and Eloise Billings instead
of Mike and Carol Brady, and you expected everything
to be resolved in thirty minutes with no commercial
interruptions, and besides that, who was supposed to be
Mike and who was supposed to be Carol, anyhow?)*

Part One

H i, honey! I'm home."
Mike puts his briefcase gently on the side table next to the
potted fern by the TV that was never on. Carol rushes out,
apron blowing, hair shag intact.

"Oh, Mike . . ."

Her wistful tone is cut short by a kiss and an embrace so loving a
small gasp of air leaves my lips as I sit transfixed by my television.

The Bradys defined family for me. As a child, I was a Brady, and
as a married adult, I was a child who was still a Brady and was shocked
when I discovered I wasn't a Brady at all.

And neither was anyone else.

I don't know what I expected to happen. Maybe that was the problem. I had zero expectations about what was supposed to happen, how I was supposed to behave, or how she was supposed to behave.

On the day of my wedding, shingles erupted on my legs, popping pus regularly, leaving white, oozing open sores on both thighs and hips (which can really ruin a white satin wedding gown). Consequently, I ended up walking down the aisle trying to keep my thighs apart like John Wayne. Our biggest worry centered on what was going to happen if my opportunistic infections kept getting worse and I had to go back into the hospital. They don't let roommates into the AIDS wing. Only family. And to the outside world, Chrisanne was simply my good pal However, her angels on the AIDS ward, where I was eventually admitted, had shone brightly the time I almost died, and they had let her in, no questions asked.

But that wasn't the norm. Our world was not always that kind.

She was working in the health insurance industry while also starting a theater company. Theater was her love, and directing became her voice, although she would regularly tell me, "I have no real passion. You have passions. I just like to do things." I didn't buy that for a second. Chrisanne's fear of failing was overwhelming and tended to oppress her.

I was on disability from the state because, although Chrisanne made a good salary, we needed both our salaries to survive. We spent our honeymoon at Disneyworld, which really is the happiest place on earth. And although it was hilarious and sexy, and we ate our way through most every land they had, we could not ignore the undeniable feeling that my life on this planet wasn't going to last much longer. We dove headfirst into our joyful union, but neither of us could really surrender to it.

There was the gender thing.

Carol was a baseball coach for the boys one time, and Mike helped Marcia in the kitchen. But Carol threw out her back, and Mike made such a mess, and Alice all but quit. The roles were defined. You didn't cross the lines. You knew what you were supposed to do, and you knew not to ask for help.

I liked that. Most of me did, anyway.

I was very married to my Trans Femme identity. I wanted my cigarette lit, my doors opened, and my chair pulled out. Chrisanne was very married to her notion of self as well. Hers manifested in the need for her intelligence to be respected, her well-being to be addressed, and yes, even in moments of learned female behavior.

"The trash needs to be taken out," she announced one night after dinner.

"I don't take out the trash," I stated firmly.

"Neither do I," she snapped back.

The trash piled up for almost a month.

Mainly, we were tormented by our gigantic egos. Hers manifested in her dependence on logic and her analytical ability, which she believed afforded her the right to think through every possible situation and then instruct me—whether I asked for advice or not. She was always right. About everything. If there was a conversation I was having on the phone with someone, after I hung up, she proceeded to tell me exactly what I should do and when and how.

"Who asked you?" I would say.

"Oh, that's right. You don't need any help. I forgot."

My focus was on all the ways to change the world, and why people weren't doing what I was doing and behaving the way I was behaving. Why weren't they letting go and having fun? Laughing more? Fighting for change more? Good times were good for the soul, and if you weren't having one the way I thought you should, I'd let you know.

And I certainly let my wife know.

"You're not following your dream," I would say every other week or so.

"I'm doing exactly what I want to be doing."

"No, you're not. I can tell. Here's what you need to do . . ."

"Who asked you?"

A union needs to be nurtured. It needs attention, and I don't think that I was doing either of these things very well. I was ill, and when I wasn't ill, I was working on becoming famous, and when I wasn't working on becoming famous, I was still behaving as if I were single. All my closest friends remained unchanged, and I assumed I could too. Just because I had a wife at home, I saw no reason for me to come in before my usual 3:00 a.m. If Chrisanne didn't understand that, it was because she didn't really know how to let go.

"You don't stay out until three a.m. and then just come home whenever you feel like it, Alex."

"You're trying to control my life."

"I'm trying to get you to act responsibly! I want a marriage like my parents had!"

I did not.

I didn't want a marriage like anyone had, and yet I was tormented by the Bradys. Their perfection was idyllic. I wanted my own marriage, but on my own terms. I wanted to be loved fully and completely, but I didn't want to be wrangled, pulled too close, told what to do, silenced, or manipulated. I wanted to have fun . . . with Chrisanne. With this particular human. We'd been chasing each other for a lifetime, so I wanted to make this time count. No matter what, I believed that love and devotion would pull us out of any mine shaft.

Marriage for me was about learning to love the chaos, and I simply didn't have the patience or the know-how to make the necessary adjustments. Neither of us did.

There was also the "real world." Chrisanne's courage to tackle everyone at once always amazed me. During the nineties, when the virus was still steeped in stigma, she placed a picture of me from our Disneyworld honeymoon on her desk at work. Chrisanne displayed her wife, prominently and without apology.

"What if someone asks you who that is?" I inquired.

"I tell them. That's my wife."

I followed her lead. When I introduced myself over the phone to the electric company or the credit card people, I'd introduce myself as Mrs. Blankenship. And when they asked what my husband did, which they inevitably did, always assuming I was heteronormative, I would correct them. Firmly.

"Oh. You mean my wife?"

The pause at the other end of the phone was usually long. This kind of information wasn't given freely back then, and it certainly wasn't given in a business setting. Chrisanne taught me. Logic. Analysis. No big signs, screaming, or pounding on doors; it was the simple everyday gestures that enabled us to interject our marriage into mainstream society.

Conversely, Chrisanne met this openness with constant paranoid and bizarre questions about my love for her. At least once a week, while we were in the car, at a restaurant, getting gas, cleaning the house, or watching TV, without warning she'd turn to me and ask, "Are you sure you love me?"

It never made any sense. I was never sure why she asked it, and I got tired of reassuring her. It was not my problem. I should not be blamed for her self-doubt, but tension began to build.

The gender wars escalated as well. She had learned that being a woman was supposed to mean something, and I had been taught very early on that being a man implied certain privilege. We allowed these ghosts to creep into the center of our marriage. There they waited.

When we argued about the garbage, or the dishes, or the bills, or my health, these ugly gender wars would explode. Chrisanne's volatile temper got worse. She nagged me and treated me as if I were truly stupid. Her conviction that I couldn't do much of anything made me begin to believe it. Her need to dominate and hold power became a source of emotional violence in our house. She was the woman. I was not. That was that.

"Didn't your mother ever teach you anything?" she would scream at me.

Well, no.

I had been foisted into male childhood. What I had learned was that I was supposed to take charge, take care of things, be responsible for everyone's well-being and happiness. I wasn't entitled to seek my own bliss, and the hidden shame of who I actually was manifested into public shaming and bullying. I forced every feeling I had, except rage, deep into the pit of me. I was good at rage. We both were. I couldn't figure out how to balance the male privilege I had taken for granted for the first nineteen years of my life with my blossoming Trans Femme identity.

As the years passed, I grew increasingly aware of Chrisanne's profound sadness. She called it "The Well," and it had been with her for as long as she could remember.

"It's like I've fallen down a well and I can't find my way out. It's weirdly comfortable, but the grief is overwhelming."

When these moods struck her, there was nothing left to do but leave her alone, which was extraordinarily painful, or come toward her and try to change her completely . . . which made far more sense. Instead of allowing her to be and live in the sadness, I needed to attempt to change it. I cast myself in the role of court jester and tried to do what I did best—make her laugh. I knew I was good at it. I certainly knew I could do it for her. And so began the pattern of her deep well of grief,

loss, and childhood trauma being jollied out of her by me. I tried to get her out of bed or into the car so we could romp in the garden or go to Denny's for a big plate of Moons Over My Hammy.

When "The Well" began to engulf her, it would pop her like a balloon. Ordinary things that should have been dismissed as mundane squabbles grew into mammoth scenes, with her throwing herself on the hood of the car as I was trying to get out of the house, or getting so aggravated that the dishwasher wasn't loaded "correctly" that she'd throw jabs at me like a nail gun. It became increasingly difficult to stay in a marriage where my role as wife was no longer working, and where my wife's unpredictability had become lethal.

Then one morning, in September of 2001, the world exploded. And in the wake of that, Chrisanne began to come apart.

She began to unravel. To the man crossing the intersection, the woman in the car with no turn signal, the couple parked in a handicap parking space: "Hey, fucker! What the fuck? Get the hell out of my goddamn way! I fucking mean it!"

The veins in the front of her neck would bulge, and her face would turn red, and her hands would grip the steering wheel, and finally it got so bad that I screamed at her to stop. I had to tell her I couldn't be in the car with her anymore, and that she wasn't allowed to drive. The white-hot rage followed her into the bedroom, the kitchen, her work, no matter how we tried to run from it. I was caught under the falling debris of her moods, and clouds of thick, gray smoke filled our lives.

Finally, the dam burst open, and I found myself throwing her clothes out our front door, piece by piece. I had lost the ability to reason, and my unexpressed anger erupted. Chrisanne came toward me, eyes dead, with an anger equal to mine, and as she did so, I wrapped my arms around her and shook her. I then picked her up off the floor and began to try to throw her out of the house, like the clothes, like the bodies, like the billows of smoke.

I stopped.

Dead.

On my feet and completely still.

We were breathing hard. Her face had a look of madness and fear. She backed away from me slowly.

"I can't do this anymore. I'm not good for you. This isn't working. We have to stop." I took a breath and stepped away from her. "I'm leaving. I can't be around you. I'm no good for you. And you're no good for me."

She stood. Neither of us made a sound except for long, gasping breaths as we tried to keep standing.

"So . . . you're leaving," she said matter-of-factly.

I stood and thought for a moment . . .

"I'll stay if you go on medication. But that's the only way. That's the deal," I said, staring at my hands.

"So, this is an ultimatum?"

"Yes, sweetie. I guess it is."

So . . . she went on medication.

The world had changed, yet it hadn't really. We were stuck in this limbo of not being married in the eyes of the outside world but still being married. My fantasy life was starting to beat its head against the wall. No one was the Bradys. No one real, anyway. And yet I couldn't help my need for them. I ached for that perfection and longed to run screaming into the very heart of my television family.

As the nineties came to a close, and more AIDS medications became available, things shifted again. Chrisanne and I began to rediscover each other through therapy and through kindness to ourselves and to each other. It was hard work. This marriage thing was work. I discovered that some things couldn't be resolved, and we'd fall apart. I slowly learned that sometimes I wasn't right, and she wasn't either. But there was this

incredible, indescribable thing between us that caused me to still look at her the way I had when I popped out from underneath that desk.

Yet I was still running from this thing I could not define. I felt closer and closer to my Transgender identity, which at one point in my life had been clear and clinical but now seemed to be getting blurry and unidentifiable. My *Brady Bunch* squares seemed to be breaking apart.

If I wasn't Mike and I wasn't Carol, who was I?

TWENTY-SIX

It Always Comes in Threes

I spent most of the play soaking wet. And not only wet, but cold and wet. Cold and wet and late at night and half dressed. I was supposed to have run out into the night in the middle of a rainstorm and then get struck by lightning.

I was cold and wet and tired and half dressed . . . and charred.

The acting passion of Jamie Pachino, my brilliant Alice B. Toklas, had given way to a budding career as a playwright, and her first play, *Children of Cain*, had a wonderful role in it for me. I was to play a character called Devlin, a wisecracking, mostly misunderstood sister in a three-sibling family, living under an age-old curse. Chrisanne and I had formed our first production company—Night and Day Productions— and this piece was to be our first venture.

Devlin was a soft, gentle, and sexy character. I had an entrance where I stand in the doorway in an oversized man's shirt and nothing else. I emerge from the bedroom, having just made love to my boyfriend, and proceed to have a conversation about family, standing shadowed in the doorway. It was a helluva entrance. And mostly, it was

a beautiful scene and powerfully written. Jamie had become a hugely influential part of my existence.

We had shared the stage in both *Gertrude Stein and a Companion* and *Lobo A Go-Go*. She had attended our wedding despite a debilitating case of bronchitis, and now we plunged into developing her plays together. She was an actor first, so working with her always felt collaborative. Jamie understood the ego, the artistry, and the deep commitment necessary to build a role from words on paper into relationships of the heart. Years ago, when we began *Gertrude Stein and a Companion*, I remember that the houses got bigger and the work got scarier as the reviews praising our work and Chrisanne's direction were published. And I kept trying to sidestep my own Transgender identity. Not only was the press obsessed with it, but I was too.

~

We hadn't opened yet. We were still rehearsing, and I was still figuring things out. I was still trying to work my way through this text of curses and sex and lies and separate my true feelings from those of my character, Devlin. I was split right down the middle.

"Alex. You have a phone call," the stage manager called to me.

"I do?"

I had never gotten a phone call at rehearsal before. Not ever . . . so this felt very strange. I walked up the short flight of stairs, into the managing director's office, and picked up the black phone lying on its side.

"Alex? This is Frieda," my mother's closest friend said calmly. "Bill died this afternoon. We're at the hospital, and your mother needs you. I think your mother needs you," she added protectively.

"I'll be there in about half an hour," I spluttered and hung up.

"What is it?" Jamie asked, arms beginning to rise toward me.

"He's dead."

"Who's dead? What?" she asked, horrified.

"My stepdad, Bill. He died. I have to go."

"Yeah. Ya do. I'll tell Ed. Go. Get outta here."

After letting Chrisanne know where I was, I drove down to Schaumburg. I remember them dancing. Beautifully. With grace and an air of fantastic sophistication. He would hold the small of her back, and she would swirl around the room, her smile broad and indelible in my nine-year-old brain. Their feet would intermingle as if they were walking across the planet as a single entity. They never faltered. Never toppled. Never lost their balance. Not once. Not ever. They danced on weekends by themselves when they didn't think anyone could see them, and they danced at the parties they gave, when they knew everyone was watching. Mimi was a performer. She always loved that part. Waving, smiling, hearing something no one else heard. The attention filled her up like a vase with colored water.

Bill was mostly stoic and quiet. Like a tree. Rooted and firm, with long branches you could hold and sit on. His hands were enormous. When, for a very brief moment, I was in the Cub Scouts, I had to make a small race car from scratch. As I had neither skill nor desire, Bill and my brother, Bobby, took over for me. They glued it, cut out pieces of this and that, and attached things onto other things, while I sat in my room and played Judy records. When it was time to race, Bill took the car out of the tiny package he'd wrapped it in, and held it in his hands. Huge. Big. Palms like baseball mitts. He smiled and looked at me with those slits of blue eyes. "You ready? I think you're gonna win," he said with a smile, his face happy and hopeful.

We did win. He was right. We won.

~

When I finally arrived at the house, I could hear mumbling and dis-connected voices. I opened the door, and there were Frieda and Mimi in the kitchen. Mimi was holding a drink, and Frieda sat at the table. I walked over to Frieda. She looked up and half smiled. I then walked over to Mimi, who was standing, looking at nothing.

I went to hug her.

She stepped back and pretended to see something on her shoe.

"We're going to donate all his clothes. Don't you think?" she said, looking at Frieda.

"I like it, Eloise. Good idea."

"I'm glad you're here, Scott," she said, taking a sip.

"I'm really sorry, Mimi. I thought he . . ."

She put her drink down and walked to the hall closet. She rustled through some things and emerged with an American flag. Turning to Frieda and me, she instructed, "Let's go."

We followed Mimi outside into the sunshine. She went into the garage, grabbed the small ladder, stepped up on it, and put the flag in its holder. She stepped back down and gazed at the flag. The afternoon sun bounced off the red, white, and blue. Mimi wiped a small some-thing off her face. I wanted to weep. I wanted to throw my arms around someone and let go, but the stopper that kept all that emotion repressed pushed farther and farther into my belly. I stood there, watching the flag and wishing.

"He would have liked that," Mimi said calmly. "Don't you think so, Frieda?"

"He would have, Eloise. I really think he would have liked that."

They disappeared into the house and left me in the driveway with the flag and the faint sound of a siren. Bill's voice had been soft and gen-tle. He had smiled often and had never yelled at me. Except maybe that one time. And I really deserved it then. I watched the flag. I watched it wave a bit, and watched the breeze rock it back and forth. And I wanted

to fall apart. I wanted to sink into the ground, because I was going to miss him, and I did love him, and I had never told him.

Not ever.

I wanted to split open, but I didn't.

Besides . . . I didn't have time. I had things to do. I had to get back to rehearsal, to Jamie, to Devlin. I had a show to put on.

~

"Alex? This is Bobby. Mimi's had a massive stroke and is in the hospital in California, so . . . um . . . I think we need to . . ."

~

Pinch. Pinch. Pinch. The strings tightened, and all my breathing stopped. I tried to prop my breasts up with both hands, but the corset was so tight that my poor bosom ended up looking like raw dough stuffed into a mattress.

I hated period pieces.

Kate pulled tighter and then yanked one last time.

"You're going to look fabulous, Alex!" she said, half out of breath.

Kate Collins was playing Nora in Ingmar Bergman's version of *A Doll's House* at the Court Theatre, and I was to be Mrs. Linde, complete with pulled-back hair, a basket of knitting (which I had requested), and a corset (which I had not). Kate, a fierce, delightful, and charismatic performer whose movie-star looks might lull you into taking her for just a pretty face, was a glorious scene partner and a truly divine dressing-room mate. The culmination of her long career in television and onstage was her maniacal, almost demonic turn as twin sisters on *All My Children*. I was never a true soap-opera fan, but everyone in the world

knew *All My Children*, and everyone in the world came to see Kate and talk about *All My Children*.

When I told Mimi what I was doing, where, and with whom, she immediately said, "Please remind Natalie that her sister is never to be trusted. She keeps making the same mistake over and over and over. It's aggravating."

Kate's final moment as Nora, with all of us sitting in the front row of the audience watching, was a master class in grief and spiritual freedom. I had never been that close to acting like this before. I had never been able to witness, from birth to performance, an actor taking a moment of ultimate truth and turning it so far inward that it became less about acting and much more about something else. I couldn't seem to define it. I wanted to know what it was, how it worked, how she did what she did, and her ability to do it every single night, at every single performance. Her process was fascinating, but being so near to it frightened me. It was too honest. It made me very uncomfortable. As Nora said goodbye to her children, to her life, and to the only husband and security she had ever known, she seethed and wept and pleaded and went to her knees. She groveled and finally stood up tall. The door slam that was heard around the world echoed through the rafters of the theater.

And it was absolutely Nora. And it was absolutely Kate.

Charlie Newell, one of my favorite theater directors and, coincidentally, Kate's joyful and truly hilarious husband, placed us all onstage, where we had to walk precariously across a steel grate beneath our feet. The world was gray and sharp and dangerous. This was really my first attempt at a classic role, and I finally felt I had been cast because I was becoming an actor, rather than a Transgender Actor.

Rehearsal felt like class, like studying with masters, scary and incredibly exciting. I was working with champions: humans who knew the art of the possible, who studied it constantly and applied and reapplied it. Kate was experiencing moments, tiny, fragile, huge impossible

moments, and I had no idea how she did it, and that made me angry. I was saddled with ego yet overwhelmed by joy and elation. I was sharing this space with an artist, and simultaneously I was drowning in jealousy.

Kate showed what was possible both as an actor and as a human being.

~

I found myself on the floor . . . I had never fainted before in my life.

"What the hell happened?" Chrisanne shrieked from the couch. "Are you okay? What is it? What the hell is it? Alex!"

I was teetering, trying to get up.

Chrisanne grabbed the phone out of my hand as my eyelids began to flutter, and she listened to the rest of Bobby's message.

"She's had a stroke," she said quietly, repeating every word. "California hospital . . . you have to get on a plane . . . maybe . . .

"We have to call the hospital," she said directly.

She found the number and began speaking to nurses, finding out exactly what was happening. I sat on the couch. My head felt heavy, and my arms tingled. After two years of married life, and just as Mimi was beginning to send apology presents for having dodged our wedding, she was lying in a hospital in a coma.

I never knew my mother to be sick a day in her life.

She was sixty-two years old.

~

I held the book close to my lap and put my head back on the headrest. Bobby, now in his late thirties with a mop of brown hair and a thick belly, leaned over to me. "What is that? What are you reading?"

"Oh." I was startled. I was always startled when my brother asked me a question. Years of conditioning made me incredibly fearful of him, and reticent. I was always a stupid little boy when I was around him. No matter what. I chose my words carefully. After all, Bobby had paid for this flight to see Mimi. Chrisanne and I owed him.

"It's a bio of Nancy Reagan," I managed to answer.

Nora had recently closed, and my angel in waiting, David Zak, had just cast me as a character based on Nancy Reagan in a play by Larry Kramer. I was very excited to meet Larry. I was hoping he'd like me. He was a huge influence during the difficult stages of my early diagnosis, had introduced me to protest, and impressed upon me the necessity of finding my voice in the theatrical community based on social justice and change. I was thrilled that he was going to be at rehearsals, so I was doing as much research as I could. By living through, and continuing to survive the plague, I felt that I knew Nancy's heart and her soul. Both, I felt, had been blackened by ignorance and stupidity and lacked any kind of compassion for the gay community and our mounting death toll.

"Who is that, Kitty Kelley?" Bobby asked, his brown eyes lowering.

"Yeah. Um . . . why?"

"She's a liar. She's an idiot. You should read something truthful if you're going to research someone."

"How do you know she's a liar?" I asked, sotto voce.

I could barely get my breath. The fear was like an apple stuck in my throat. He literally scared the hell out of me.

"Jeezus . . . you know the good thing about her? You know? Do you know the really great thing about Nancy Reagan? She stood by her man," he said in a sanctimonious tone. "You know that? Do you know that?" he reiterated, the fierce rumble in his voice beginning to swell.

He turned away and looked out the window as we passed cloud after cloud after cloud.

"You know I have AIDS, Bobby. I have AIDS, and her husband did absolutely nothing."

He turned to me, and with a calmness as if he were ordering extra ketchup for his fries, he patronized, "He couldn't take care of everything, could he?" Then he turned back toward the floating clouds.

I tapped his shoulder. "I want you to look at me, Bobby. Turn your fucking head and look at me. Do you see this? This is the face of AIDS. Do you know that? I am your sister, and I am not an idiot, or a child, or your punching bag, or your gofer, or your steward, or your pacifier when your emotional life turns into that red-hot rage we both inherited. I am not afraid of you, or your temper, or your idiotic tantrums. I am your family, and we're on our way to see our mother, who may or may not wake up again, and you want to sit here on a plane and argue about a bunch of people who, I happen to know, were solely responsible for murdering every single one of my fucking friends. I am your family. I want to love you. I want to hang out with you, and all I've ever wanted was to be with you, and sometimes be just like you, and you've hated me ever since I can remember, and now is no different. Have you ever seen anyone die of AIDS, Bobby? Have you ever walked into a house so stinking of feces and cat piss that you could throw up before you get to the hallway? Do you know that's probably going to happen to me, and do you know that it will happen to me because of people like the Reagans who won't say a word? They want us all dead, and the reason she 'stood by her man' was because she had no voice and no other way to wield her bigotry and hatred of queers, except by manipulating her husband, whose meticulous plans turned out to be my community's worst nightmare. Stand by her man. She stood by while this fascist American traitor wreaked havoc upon a tribe of humans by ignoring the virus that's eventually going to kill not only everyone I know, but everyone you know as well. I'm sitting right next to you, Bobby, and I

have AIDS. Look at me. Fucking turn your head and see me. For once. Stop being such a coward!"

But . . . I said nothing.

He turned his head and took a nap, and I clutched my book and wept.

Quietly, so I wouldn't wake him.

～

Mimi looked tired. Not worn out or exhausted, but tired. Her breath was shallow, and her hair was matted along her face. Her usually bright eyes were closed, and her pale skin seemed even paler. It seemed elastic and fake, as if someone had dripped a thin layer of plaster over her and allowed it to harden.

She was there. But she wasn't.

I leaned down to her. My dad and Bobby were instructed to wait in the hall.

"Mimi," I whispered in her ear, putting my hand on the top of her head. "I know you can hear me, and I know you're trapped inside this thing you've been walking around in. But here's the thing: No one knows what you're going to be like if you survive this. You might not be able to drive, or go to lunch, or teach, or make phone calls. This might be it. I really don't think you want to be like this, do you? Bobby and I are here, and I know you've been waiting for us to fly down. So. We're here. So, go. I love you. With all my heart." I kissed her forehead. "Go."

She died that night.

Three days later, Chrisanne, Bobby, and I were rummaging through Mimi's things in her condo in Laguna Hills, sorting papers and clothing and desks and drawers and cabinets, and having performed this ritual for friend after friend during the plague, I assumed this would be no different. But when it's your parent, and when it's your parent whose

relationship with you was fractured to begin with, and that relationship was gradually mending, trying to decide what to do with her sparkly top or her cabinet full of candles became almost unendurable. Had my wife not been there, I don't know that I could have done it. Bobby was making his way through the paperwork, which was a big help, actually, and keeping track of most everything else.

As I walked with Mimi's open jewelry box, he stopped me dead in the hallway.

"Hey!" he shouted. "Put that back. We have to have that stuff appraised."

"I just want her amethyst ring, Bobby. I'm not going to sell it. I'm going to wear it."

"Nope. You're not. Put it back," he ordered, his fingers waving toward her bedroom.

I walked mechanically back into the bedroom and put the box where I had found it.

I went to her closet, knelt down, saw shoe box after shoe box, and remembered how I had felt being in here while she was at school. Her shoes. Her dresses. Her wigs and her belts and her fancy pantsuits. I took her clothes and began folding them. When we went out to lunch in public for the first time and she had called me her daughter, she wore this. When we drove to go shopping on the pier during that gorgeous day by the beach, I bought a sundress, and she had said I looked beautiful . . . she wore these shoes.

I had survived so many burials, but this one was different. I hoped Chrisanne would hold me, and I would lie in her arms so a well of grief could wash over us both. I would weep and fall apart.

"She loved you so much, sweetie," Chrisanne would say.

And we would sit up and tell stories and remember her. We would try to keep it balanced.

But I wasn't in that place.

She was gone, but I couldn't really feel it. In her immaculate house with everything in its place, Bobby kept count and rifled through more papers. And every so often Chrisanne would remind me, "Let's make sure we all get a say in everything."

Because I could not.

Through the eulogy, the wake, and the funeral, I had my wife by my side, and I held on to what little spiritual belief I had acquired through my recovery. As much as Mimi and I had battled, and as often as we had left each other and come back together, there was a finality to this moment. We had spoken almost every Sunday for the last few years, and we were reaching a place of evenness and truce. But whatever it was right now, that's what it was going to be. There was to be no more healing, and there was no more fixing or solving to be done.

This was it.

My mother was dead.

I wanted to crash through a wall and break something fragile. If I listened very closely, I could have heard a snap. It was a heartstring snapping, and that sound has rung in my ears ever since.

I went on antidepressants for a little over a year because cutting myself and relapsing to heroin began to seem like increasingly appealing, tempting options.

I wanted to be free of it. I wanted to shake myself loose from it. I wanted to feel my way through the grief. I really wanted to.

Because . . . I had a part to rehearse and a show to put up. I was readying myself to play a Reagan. I was on my way to meet Larry Kramer.

That would certainly solve everything.

$\sim$

It was a language. It wove my dad and me together. It bound us. It flowed through the deepest part of who we were, and who we wished we were. He wanted two sons. He wanted a house and a wife. He wanted to fly planes, and fill stadiums, and create magical worlds filled with mythology and stories about the best parts of our humanity, the parts of us most of us wished we had known. Except he never really took the time. He didn't know me, and he didn't know himself. He probably should never have had children. But there I was, his Transgender child, and here he was, a decorated war veteran communicating through the language of music.

And we needed nothing else.

~

Standing in a recording studio is the scariest thing in the world for someone who hates standing in a recording studio. Ralph Lampkin Jr., producer, friend, confidant, and cop, pushed me kicking and screaming into the booth. "You can do this and it's gonna be a big, big hit, Alex. C'mon! We'll sell a million copies. We'll just do what you've been doing in your cabaret act. It'll be great! Great!"

He would twitch manically, flipping his jet-black curly hair from one side to the other. His hands would point and sway and jab the air, and he'd underline almost every word he uttered. Ralph was like a wind-up toy that never wound down. He spoke fast. He produced concerts for me all over Chicago, in New York at Feinstein's, and in the famed Emerald Room along with Amanda McBroom. We had found each other in my Shanté days and sort of grew up together, seeing each other occasionally and finally coming together personally and professionally once I began singing at the Gentry with Honey. Ralph was complicated. He had an ego, and he was bombastic.

"I'm going to speak to Michael Feinstein about those lights! I hate them! They're unflattering, darling. Really. You look orange, and I hate it when you look orange," he would yell.

"Ralphie . . . calm down. It's okay. We'll fix them."

Ralph's need to make things happen, while simultaneously making sure I was taken care of, sometimes resulted in strained and fractured relationships with other people in the business. Although strangely, his obsessive, controlling temperament worked well for the two of us. People didn't bother me much with insignificant details, because they knew I had Ralph. I was singing in nightclubs where, in the mid-1980s and 1990s, there weren't a lot of other Trans people around. I was playing mainstream rooms with mainstream audiences and some of Chicago's top musicians. I was simply a singer, making a living and working the nightclub circuit, and that was mainly a result of Ralph and his boundless belief in me.

~

I stood behind the glass, huddled in the booth of Southport Records in Chicago, gigantic earphones over my ears and the mic staring me in the face. I peered through the glass partition to where Ralph stood with Joanie, our fearless engineer. With exaggerated grimaces, Ralph tried to communicate what was wrong and how to fix it, how to dig into this song that I'd been singing live for almost five years, but couldn't seem to get this time—not here in this glass booth without an audience and lights and a stage and musicians and all the things that made sense to me.

I put my head in my hands. I tried to shake something loose. I knew this song. Why couldn't I do it?

And then my dad's voice came over the speaker in the booth.

"Alex," he said.

I jumped a little.

"Yeah, Dad?"

"It's the vowel."

"It's what?"

"It's the vowel on the end of the word 'alive.' You're flat because you're not opening your mouth, and you're not singing the vowel. Think *ah* instead of *i*."

Dad was visiting Chrisanne and me, and his visit happened to coincide with the recording of my first CD. He'd been in the studio all night, standing next to Ralph, and as badly as it was going, he hadn't said a word. Until now. I was getting direction from my father. I couldn't believe it.

I nervously began to sing the *ah*. It was better, but I had lost everything else. There was nothing behind it. I was singing, but my gut was empty, and my legs felt heavy. I could see Ralph, his black hair waving like a Muppet's as he and Dad conversed, whispering back and forth about what to do.

I stopped the playback.

Joanie smiled her big, wide smile at me. Warm and kind, and a great singer herself, she chimed in with a few helpful suggestions, but nothing seem to resonate. I was lost, and my father's presence wasn't helping.

"Alex?" he said calmly over the mic.

I was wearing the big earphones, and his voice was small and gentle. I rarely heard my dad speak this way. He was all but whispering in my ear. He was so close to me I could feel the same heartbeat.

"I want you to close your eyes." I did. "I want you to remember what it was like before Chrisanne. Imagine it." I did. "I want you to breathe very deep into your chest, and then into your stomach, and I want you to imagine her leaving."

I saw Chrisanne turning her back on me. She took a step, and then another step, and as she began to walk away, I rose up slowly on my toes, and my eyes opened. I saw my father's face through the glass, leaning forward as if his hand were on my shoulder.

I couldn't breathe except to implore her to stay.

"Sing," he said lightly.

I did.

That was the take we used.

~

I had begged David Zak to do *Gypsy* for almost two years. Rights were an issue, then money, then both, and then time, and finally, without warning, he walked into the Gentry one night, halfway through my set, and announced over the microphone, "Ms. Billings? How would you like to be our Madame Rose in Bailiwick's production of *Gypsy*?"

The crowd squealed, and I sat, flabbergasted.

I was trying to figure my character out. I was trying to find the reason for the constant push and the ever-present need for attention and love. Although her ego made sense to me, the rest did not. I was only in my thirties at the time, which strangely is how old Rose Hovick actually was when the musical begins. I instinctively understood that playing Rose needed an actress who was fearless in her search for self and relentless in her ability to rip off her skin and let herself bleed.

I wasn't ready for any of those things.

I worked on her walk, on her gestures, on her ability to love those children and get what was best for them. I wanted to be liked and I wanted to be worshipped. I was acting. I was performing. I was not revealing, either onstage or off.

"I want to work on 'Rose's Turn' tomorrow," David announced.

Zak, as we affectionately called him, had had a messy life path, but for me he was a comfort and constant producer of opportunity. To others, he was a miser. He was followed by threats and accusations for permitting terrible working conditions in his theater. I have to acknowledge that some of these accusations must have been true, as I know some of these things had happened to Honey and others I knew. But none of these things had ever happened to me. David had given us his space when Chrisanne and I got married, and he gave me a theatrical home when Mary and I decided to present my first one-person autobiographical piece, *Before I Disappear*, which had an original score, with lyrics by Chrisanne and music by me. The show would not have happened had David, with his oval-shaped cherubic face and his jovial demeanor, not bounced by me in the hallways of his theater and said offhandedly, "You know, your life would make a really good musical. Think about it." And he sped on his way.

David created space for me as a Trans performer at a time when all we were really known for was lip-synching or hooking. There was me and there was Honey and that was it. Whatever problems David may have created himself or been involved in accidentally, he was never anything but kind, compassionate, and overly protective of both my practical and theatrical life.

Ralph, David, Mary, Chrisanne, and I became a family. A chosen family. During the late nineties in Chicago theater, when the plague was still raging, and when our Transgender family was still slithering out of the shadows, I was blessed enough to be surrounded by these artists, who not only believed in me, but pushed me to do more than I thought was possible. This fractured family of actors, producers, writers, and dreamers created a safety net I had never dreamed possible. We fought, and we left each other, and we came back, and we created.

Creating together—that I understood. It lived in me and allowed me to make sense of our life even when the words failed and the meaning

got lost. As many problems as Chrisanne and I might have had in the beginning of our marriage, creating together was never one of them. It was making love for us. We surrendered to the thing in front of us. And that was true of all of us. And the rare sanctity of that contract was not lost on me. Not for a moment.

Rose's need for love made sense to me. But her passion did not. Because you see, there was that empty space. It continued to echo. Imagined emotion made sense to me—real emotion did not.

The reviews for *Gypsy* came out and the show was mostly well received, but the reviewers were once again stuck on the fact that I was Transgender, and that I was playing this person who was not. Although they praised some of the musical moments, they reminded me once again that I was not to be taken seriously.

"My God," my dad said on the way home.

"What?" I was exhausted. We were still in previews for *Gypsy*, and doing this show was a herculean challenge. I wasn't even forty years old, but I can tell you, it almost put me in the hospital.

"I . . . I just . . ." he stammered. I wasn't quite sure what was happening.

"What, Dad?"

"Tonight. I just . . . you know I've never seen you before."

"You've seen me sing a hundred times, Dad. What are you talking about?"

He looked at me while I was driving, his blue eyes like steel across my temples.

"You're really good. I mean it. You are really, really good."

I kept driving. Through the red light and past our turn, he kept silent, and finally, pulling up to the driveway of our condo, he made a sound. "Okay," he muttered, as if something had finally dropped. "Okay."

I got the courage to look into my father's eyes, and the shift that happened between us was remarkable. His face softened, his hands moved toward mine, and he smiled.

Opening night came and went, and the night before we opened, David let my dad come back and greet the cast during our note session. When my dad was introduced, he stood up, and in a great proud voice, began to recite the story of my life—through his lens, of course—from the time I was seven up to getting cast in *Gypsy*. After delivering his fable, he proceeded to give the rest of the cast his personal notes. Actor by actor.

As unheard of and bizarre as this was, I was strangely flattered. This was my dad boasting about his daughter. That was life changing.

Chicago in the winter is an assault. The cold is unforgiving, and the wind is merciless. That night, Dad and I sat inside and watched TV. Chrisanne had gone to bed, leaving us alone on our last night together.

"Let's go smoke," he suggested.

We walked out onto the porch, bundled like two snow people.

"Can you tell me what happened?" I asked, blowing smoke and watching it mix with the intense cold.

"When?"

"You and Mimi?"

"When we first met?"

"No. The second time. Just this last time."

"We'd been away from each other for a long time, you know that. Well . . . Bill died and then I married Karen, and then I lost Karen, and Eloise and I were alone. Eloise moved to California. I really didn't think we were going to see each other very much. I was teaching and she was retired and then, we just . . . we just started seeing each other."

"Mimi called me and told me. I asked her if she loved you. She said yes."

He smiled and took a drag.

"Did you love her?"

"Ever since I can remember." He blew smoke out into the air. "You know what I mean."

"Chrisanne was the one who said you two were going to get remarried," I interjected with pride.

Then I smiled. My dad loved Chrisanne. Deeply and profoundly.

"I don't doubt it. She has some kind of radar thing, doesn't she?"

"Like a German sub."

I took a seat across from my dad and bundled up, pulling the cap over my hair and wiping remnants of Rose off my forehead.

"So, what happened?"

"So . . . we saw each other, and we went places, and you know your mother and I never stopped loving each other. So, I asked her to marry me again and she said yes."

"And then she asked me to sing at your wedding. Did you know that?"

He nodded and smiled.

"And then what happened?"

"Then we went on sort of this pre-honeymoon and found this great little townhouse in Santa Fe. And we were sitting in the living room and she was acting . . . well, funny. She'd been trying to quit drinking for a long time, you know that, don't you, Alex? Well . . . she had. But she had a cold that night, and I thought she had taken too many Sudafeds and mixed them with whatever she was drinking, because she wasn't making any sense. I couldn't understand her. And she said, 'I think you need to call the lawyer.' And I thought . . . aw, jeez . . . she wants out already and we haven't even done anything yet. Well . . . I told her to go back in the bedroom and lie down, and a couple of minutes later I heard a great big thud, and your mom had rolled off the bed and was lying on the floor heaving and . . . her eyes were . . . and she wasn't really moving. She'd had her stroke."

"What was with the lawyer?"

"I think she was trying to say 'doctor.' She was trying to say, 'I think I need a doctor.' I didn't listen. I wasn't paying attention."

He shifted in his chair. His head lowered. His eyes wandered. He sipped his drink and he smoked. We sat in silence as the wind howled through the slats beneath us. I shivered, and then Dad looked up at me and asked very plainly and without irony, "Why?"

I knew exactly what he meant. How do you answer someone who wants an answer to something that has no answer? I was what I was. I was this. This was the gift of my birth, and even back then, at that moment, I knew what I was. I was not a mistake, and it was not a choice. But I certainly didn't know why. Does anyone know why? So, I did my best . . .

"Dad, I don't know. I really don't know . . ."

He smiled a half smile and sipped his drink. We never talked about it again.

~

Three weeks later the police found my father's body in a pool of his own blood in the living room of his condominium in Lake Point, California. He'd been there for a few days. Harbor College had fired him because of his temper and his drinking, and he had made few friends and knew even fewer people. There was a woman who lived next door whom I met only once when Chrisanne and Bobby and I went back to do to Dad's house what we had done to Mimi's, but I cannot remember her name. She was seeing Dad after Mimi died, and she was very kind and brought over a large casserole for the three of us.

That was it.

My father was buried a lieutenant colonel in the United States Air Force, and my uncle Chuck let me know that when they folded the flag,

they usually give it to the oldest living female of the family. He asked if I wanted to receive it. I refused it. I didn't want a flag, and I didn't want a ceremony, and I didn't want guns going off, and I didn't want a reception. I wanted my parents back. You see, no matter what happened now, no matter how many amazing things happened, they would be missing. They wouldn't know. They wouldn't be there. As much history as I might make, there was no parent there to be proud of me. No parent would be there to wrap their arms around me and tell me how well I was doing, or what I needed to do next, or how it was going and how it might be improved. I was on my own now. Out into the universe and traveling down the yellow brick road alone, linked to no one.

Something seemed to break apart then.

A piece here and a chunk there, and through it all, I began to feel freer. As much loss and as much grief as I felt, there was a sense of letting go. It wasn't about these two individuals and their behavior any longer. It was about me and mine. What was I doing? Why was I doing it? Who was I doing it for? For me. For me. I was reminded of the lyrics from Gypsy: *This time for me!*

It took the loss of my parents for me to understand exactly who they were, because I did not see them, and I did not pay attention.

I was the Transgender child in the house, and my life revolved around secrecy and fear.

Mimi had sent her spies to our wedding. Friends. Teachers. People she trusted. And after our wedding, as I stood in the reception line next to my mother-in-law and we were both shaking hands and beaming, these women came up to Chrisanne and me, teary-eyed. "It was . . . it was beautiful. I'm . . . I'm so sorry your mother wasn't here. It was just beautiful," one of them said, her hand still shaking mine.

After all, it was illegal. What would the neighbors say?

I was in Mimi's spare bedroom and going through the very last closet. As I put something beside her TV, underneath the stand I

noticed a small square object, an old white handkerchief draped over it. Unwashed and stained, this thing didn't seem to belong there. I picked it up and uncovered an old, brown box about the size of a toaster.

I opened it, and inside were small pictures, newspaper clippings, trinkets, a bracelet or two. I began taking things out, one by one . . .

There was a clipping of a review of a show I did years ago. And another one. And another one. And then ten more. All my work at the Steppenwolf and the Bailiwick was carefully preserved. I could see the faint markings of a yellow highlighter. There was a videotape of me on *Phil Donahue*, and another of me singing at the Gentry. "Scott on *Phil Donahue*," the tape was clearly marked. "Scott at the Gentry," the other one read.

And underneath it all was my CD, *Being Alive*, with a picture of me on the cover, standing in front of a statue in Chicago, and on the inside flap, Ralphie and me walking down Lake Shore Drive, wind whipping through us, laughing hysterically. There was a picture of Mimi and Dad at the front desk of some hotel. She looked rested and happy and content, and her eyes weren't red from booze or her face pink and puffed from the lack of it. She was bright and smiling. As I continued to rummage, there was the picture of Bill. His finger rested on the front end of the toy car he and Bobby built. He beamed as he pretended to have a conversation with me about that car, the building of it, and the inevitable trophy. All I could see of myself was my left elbow protruding behind the tiny rear tire. Next to that, there was a picture of her and me. Just the two of us, sitting in this very condo in front of the fireplace that she never lit. My hand is resting on her knee, and her head is tilted toward me. I turned the card over.

"Alex and me," it read.

Alex and Mimi—our final photo

Bracelets and a pair of earrings I thought I remembered telling her I liked once, and then more pictures. Pictures of her in giant bunny ears, of her and her friends jumping off the back end of a boat in clear, blue water, and of the two of us at lunch at a restaurant . . . eating tuna sandwiches and smiling.

And a picture of Chrisanne on Mimi's balcony. Chrisanne's face is bright and beautiful, seeing Mimi and trying to forgive her—to love her for who she was, and not for who we wanted her to be. A picture of us in our wedding dresses. Chrisanne in her long green ball gown, with her parents and her brother and Honey and Michael and Kelly and Mary and all of us holding the space Mimi should have filled but hadn't.

Way at the bottom and wedged in the corner was a small pin. It was about the size of my thumbnail. I picked it up. It was a red-and-gold AIDS ribbon. It shimmered, and I turned it over in my hand. I closed my fist and held it to my heart. I closed my eyes and imagined her going to the store and picking it out and telling the man behind the desk that her child was infected, and she needed a pin. She would have insisted that it had to have sparkle, and she would've demanded

a selection because just one wouldn't be good enough. She'd want to choose the right one. Because someone very close to her had AIDS, and if she was going to wear something for this person, it had to sparkle.

I took that pin with me, and now it sits in a drawer in my house, and whenever I cannot feel any of these humans near me, I take the box out and I see them all and what they gave me. Bill brought me compassion, my dad gave me tenacity, and my mother gave me hope.

After losing Bill, Mimi, and Dad, I set out on a journey to discover how to fill the vacant space inside me without constantly striving to satisfy my need for attention. I wanted to find out what performing meant—how to be truthful without shame.

I had to discover that there was something more than me pretending to be someone I wasn't.

That simply wasn't working anymore.

I was on my own. And yet, not alone at all.

TWENTY-SEVEN

Me and Pootie

T here's a period at the end of that sentence, dammit!"
There seemed to be a separation. His body and his spirit appeared to be glued together at the seams, as if at any moment they could come apart, ripped from the foundation of the volcano that bore them both. He wasn't easy. He wasn't soft, and he wasn't in one piece. Larry Kramer was fractured.

He paid attention to absolutely everything. Nothing got past him.

"You've got to have balls. Skin in the game. This isn't everyone's fight. It's ours."

Larry never fluttered. His gestures were measured and careful. His gait was tempered. He didn't shuffle. He didn't glide and he didn't float. He walked purposefully. His feet on the earth were the patterns of his past. There was no mistaking Larry—from the soles of his feet to the creases in his smile. And he smiled a lot. There were articles and articles and articles written about his anger, about his rage, and his vehement attitude toward the world at large, and they were all right.

And, they weren't right at all.

"You've got syrup on your chin," I observed, handing him a napkin.

"What does that have to do with what I'm saying, Alex? I'm making a point."

"With syrup on your chin."

"Well, listen to my words and stop staring at my chin."

"It's like a small city of syrup."

He grabbed the napkin, and jumping into our familiar shtick from *The Mirror Crack'd*, he said in his best Liz Taylor, "You know, there are only two things I really dislike about you, dear."

"Oh? And what are they?" I Kim Novak–ed back.

"Your face."

I was a teacher now. After my third show with Tina Landau at Steppenwolf, one summer during the intensive session, she tossed me into her room like a free throw from center court.

"I can't teach Viewpoints, Tina. I've never taught anything before in my life. I can't do this."

"You're gonna be great, Al. You've been working with this methodology for three years now."

"Well, yeah, but that's been you and me and the shows we've put together, that's not teaching . . ."

"You understand how to apply the Viewpoints to your acting and you understand how to apply them to story. Teach that. Teach what you know."

"I don't know shit," I said defiantly.

"Neither does anyone else. You're gonna be great," she trilled, already halfway out the door.

I was a teacher!

I was a young teacher.

I was a young, terrible, egomaniacal, self-centered, whimsical, ignorant, sometimes mildly entertaining teacher. But I was not, in fact, teaching. Not really.

There I was, standing in the rehearsal room at the Steppenwolf School, trembling in front of fifty actors, all waiting with bated breath for me to do something that would change their lives. The child of two teachers, with years of practice putting the Viewpoints to use in Chicago theater, and having had a handful of acting classes, I was no teacher. So, because I wasn't a teacher . . . I simply acted like one. Using all the training I had had as an actor, I walked into the room as a teacher. For a while I spoke a little like Miss Jean Brodie, but after a few weeks, I began to surface and create a voice in the room.

"You're a teacher, Alex, and you stand in a room and teach straight theater to a bunch of gay artists," Larry complained, sitting in his big black chair in David's office.

"How do you know they're a bunch of gays, Larry? There actually are straight people who are artists, you know."

"Name three."

"You're ridiculous."

"I'm talking about the chance you're pissing away, and the fact that art is ours. There's Shakespeare, who is brilliant and necessary, and then there's us, who are silenced and murdered. And we created it. We own it. It belongs to us. And you're not doing shit. You're not talking about anything. You're just trying to make people love you. You're a teacher. I guess. Are you?"

We didn't speak for almost a year after that.

~

There was death, still. You would think that by the late nineties, the deaths would have diminished some. That we'd had enough. But the deaths kept gnawing at me as if someone were scraping out my insides with an ice-cream scoop. And the plague was eating Larry. He would sit at the table between rehearsals and take pill after pill after pill. The

blue one, then the green one, and two of the little brown ones. We'd talk about having AIDS. I told him there was this thing called a clinical trial that I was involved in. After I almost died, Dr. Slotten told me about it. You got AZT and then two other pills that worked in tandem with it to try to corner the virus and stop it from replicating. This was far from a cure, but it might at least slow the disease so I could have a few more years, instead of a few more months. Larry's finger would wag, and his voice would rise, and he'd inform me that the idiot doctors knew nothing, and that they were guessing, and the only reason these trials were around was so that more of us could die, and make room for the sick straight people.

We were the canaries, and they were the coal miners.

"You have no idea what the hell is going to happen to you when you're my age because of this shit you're taking, Alex."

The AZT made me throw up most mornings, caused chunks of my hair to fall out, made me so light sensitive that any kind of sunlight burned my retina so badly that two pairs of sunglasses weren't enough, and my general appetite was iffy at best.

Then someone would die, someone else would get sick, another human would get their first lesion. A friend would have to drop out of the play because his neuropathy was so bad that he couldn't feel his feet and he would lose his balance onstage. We'd find bodies in alleys, on street corners, and stuffed in garbage cans. The war was still on, and it was getting worse. The spread was uncontrolled and commonplace. We were on TV, and straight people hated us for killing Rock, and Brad, and Michelle, and their mother-in-law. Then Ryan got it, the entire world fell apart, and the shrapnel landed on us.

And so, Larry was needed. His hands, his voice, and the way he could stand in front of people and demand they listen. I'd go to rehearsal, then to the doctor, then to a funeral, then to my students,

then to my wife, and then to a funeral, and then to a meeting, and then to a funeral. I wasn't really doing a good goddamn thing.

"You're a teacher. I guess. Aren't you?" he would bellow at me in the early days of the plague. He'd reach across his podium, and he'd let us all know that death was no longer an option. We were not expendable. Just because we were a bunch of fairies, the rest of the world could no longer ignore us or use us for experimentation. Like the Pied Piper, he started gathering gay human beings together. I didn't know him in the beginning of the plague because I was mostly asleep. I lived as Shanté in the drag world, where my primary worries were dresses and eyeliner. I wasn't paying attention. But I knew *of* him and I knew of the humans who lay down on their backs in the streets, daring the police to run them over. I saw them bunched up like sardines, with flickers of light bouncing off the moonlit streets of New York, as they walked in vigil for the hundreds who were dying. I heard the curses and saw the raised fingers at the cowardly Reagans hiding behind a makeshift bible filled with pious nothings barfed up by all the president's men. Groups of activists lay down in churches, and on beaches, and in city cafés, and they painted signs, and made speeches, but it was Larry who begat the movement, because he saw it first. He paid attention to the details of the war.

I did not.

I was not awake.

I was not aware.

ACT UP began in his living room. The Gay Men's Health Crisis was born out of his inner life force, and these two groups of people gave their lives and took us all in, even if we didn't know it and didn't care that they had. When we couldn't walk, they did. The divine hand of something I wasn't quite sure of yet drew him and me together for the Chicago premiere of his play *Just Say No*. I met Larry Kramer for the first time in 1996, and it split me apart forever.

I lay in his arms and wept.

I remember my chest heaving, and my arms giving way, and my spitting out words about Chrisanne's love for me, and the conviction that I was dying, and everyone was leaving the planet, and I really hadn't signed up to bury so many people before I was thirty. I spat out the joy of being an actor, and what happened when I was truly seen, and how famous I wanted to be, and complained about why I wasn't famous and asked when I would be famous.

Larry sat in a big fluffy chair in the lobby of a theater. It was daytime, during a break from rehearsal, and people occasionally passed by. I lay in his lap, and although he didn't hold me, his breath and his chest and the sound of his heartbeat were clear. Larry whispered to me. He leaned down and gave me something profound and moving. It didn't stop my grief, but it seemed to open a portal.

He whispered.

And I said, "Yes."

I was portraying Mrs. Potentate, a thinly disguised Nancy Reagan, in *Just Say No*. Mrs. Potentate nicknamed her hubby Pootie, a moniker I immediately bestowed upon Larry. Once again, I was at the Bailiwick Theater being directed by my *Son of Fire* director, David Zak, who was slowly becoming part of my chosen family. He gathered us all together in this rollicking, door-slamming comedy about the plague and the couple in the White House with their closeted son, beautifully played by champion swimmer and gay icon Greg Louganis. We fixed and redid and reworked and added and subtracted from the play, and through it all, my husband, played by the hilariously insane Marc Silvia, kept the show going, never leaving the stage.

Larry was all the things the world thought he was. He was indeed angry. He made me angry. He was filled with ego and bravado and had a fabulous sense of the theatrical. He blew things up, and he sewed them back together again. After our run in Chicago, he and I went to

New York and tried to remount his play Off Broadway. Sadly, our plans never materialized, but the time we spent in the city together more than made up for it all. We would go years without speaking to each other and then one day out of the blue I'd get an email congratulating me on an opening, or a benefit, or a concert I was doing.

"You're still doing it. So great. Remember what I told you," he'd write.

I never forgot it.

I returned to Chicago, and in between singing gigs and plays, I would run across town and teach. I would go into room after room and do whatever I could to pay attention and remember that I was a Trans woman standing in the middle of the room teaching straight people's work. My encounter with Larry had not changed that, because I was still figuring out my authentic voice. But there was a shift, a small sound nagging at me. I had moved a bit, and instead of trying to make everyone love me, I realized I had a different job and other responsibilities. As part of the queer fabric that wove together our fragmented artists' lives, I needed to do something else in the room besides beg for attention.

I began to listen. I practiced paying attention to the slightest things. "There's a period on the end of that sentence," I would say, as one young student would begin to talk themselves out of doing what they feared the most.

I saw things that I didn't understand, but I stopped trying to figure everything out. I tried making signs and holding them up. I lay down in places of prayer, and I tried to hold others in moments of loss and overwhelming grief. Together, my students and I began to work with each other and lift up the smallest voices in the room. And I started to see what he had told me was true, and that my "Yes" mattered much more than I had ever imagined.

Larry passed away in May of 2020. I don't think the noise that he shot through me has quieted down just yet. I don't know that it ever

will. The last time I saw him was in a hallway of a show I was doing in New York. I ran around my dressing room that night, so excited to see Pootie. We took a picture. I got him tickets in the sixth row, because when I walked out onstage, I wanted to see his face. His shining, smiling, beaming, long, lined face. I wanted to see my teacher pal. Because that's who he was to me. He was mine. He was total, and rich, and real. Sometimes I feel as if I made him up, because his voice was so powerful and profound that it couldn't possibly be true. But I always felt him. In the room. In the street. At the gravesites. On the lip of the stage. In the moment.

I want very much to share what he whispered to me that day in the lobby as we sat in the fluffy chair. But to be honest, I feel as if it was just for me. Just between me and Pootie.

TWENTY-EIGHT

The Lying, the Witch, and the Wardrobe

I was annoyed that I had to get a costume together to drive downtown to yet another audition for a TV show in which I was not going to be cast.

"You're going to get this one," Claire reassured me.

"No, I'm not, but at least I get to see you," I answered gently.

Claire was, and still is, the most beloved casting director in Chicago. Every Chicago actor knows Claire Simon and the hilarious, compassionate, and attentive humans who work in her office. Claire's careful and highly intuitive demeanor was reinforced by her outrageous and delicious sense of humor. Walking into Simon Casting was like breathing air for the first time. Claire gave me precisely the same kind of sides she gave any other working actress in her late thirties. My being Transgender was honored by her, never exploited. She coached me with a deft hand and a firm tone in every audition. She never forgot to ask about Chrisanne, and she greeted me with an open heart and a glorious smile. She loved actors. Claire was one of the first humans in show business with a direct link to Hollywood who believed I had a story

to tell. She recognized that my being Trans was powerful, but it wasn't everything.

"I think you're great. I think you're funny and great, Alex, and no matter what, I want you to be happy. I want other people to hear you. More than anything. I really want other people to hear you and know who you are," she would say, spitting out each phrase in rapid succession.

I gathered everything I needed, or everything I could find, anyway, and began piecing myself together. The long black skirt, the weird sparkly slippers, a black towel I found in the back of our bathroom stuff, and a stupid black cone hat. I was auditioning for the part of Witch Number Two and a Half, in a commercial for the Chicago lottery. Dressing up for parts had become the norm for me.

I stood looking in the mirror with the sides of text in my hands.

"And now (cackle, cackle, cackle) I'd like to draaawwww your attention to the ball with the red dots! And the spell I have cast as we . . ."

I stopped. I looked down at my pointy red shoes and then up to my reflection. I looked like someone had emptied a laundry basket on my head.

I called Claire.

"I'm not doing this, Claire. I'm done."

"No, Alex. You must! I have everything ready, and everyone wants to see you!" I felt her smile over the phone.

"I've been auditioning for TV stuff for five years and I never get anything. I'm done. They don't want Transgender people in Hollywood, Claire. Let's give them what they want."

"Well . . . you'll change your mind. I'm not just going to give in to these stupid-ass prejudices, Alex. And you're not either," she argued, gaining speed and momentum.

I was exhausted. My body hurt. I was working all the time: singing, getting cast in wonderful plays with wonderful people, telling

wonderful stories, doing readings, working on new plays with new authors and new actors. I did two more shows at the Steppenwolf. I was teaching class constantly, and I was very grateful, and very happy, and utterly and completely bored.

And I was sick and tired of doing the same thing with the same results in the same way over and over again. I saw my life stretched out before me, and all I wanted to do was go to sleep. I'd teach, and then I'd audition, and then I'd sing, and then I'd audition, and then I'd do a play, and then I'd go to another funeral, and then I'd audition, and then I'd march down the streets with my gay family with giant signs that demanded more HIV clinical trials, and then I'd do another play about AIDS, and some more of our friends would die, and then I'd sing, and then I'd bury someone, and then I'd picket something. Then I'd wake up and do it all over again. Every day I'd get up and wonder who was dead, and which march I was supposed to be at, and had I remembered to take my meds, and how much blood needed to be drawn today.

I resigned myself to being semi well known in Chicago theater: singing occasionally, making CDs, doing concerts, and intermittently traveling to Eighty Eights, a New York nightclub that welcomed Transgender performers. I had performed my one-woman show, *Before I Disappear*, Off Broadway. This wasn't a terrible life. I was living the dream I honestly had never thought possible. I wasn't a sex worker. I was sober. I was in an amazing marriage, which, although it certainly had its share of problems, was a marriage of souls. I was blessed. I knew I was blessed.

"Alex. It's Claire. I have something for you."

I called her back . . . reluctantly, and she told me about an audition for a small independent film written by a writer who didn't have much experience or money. She explained that the lead character was Transgender, and that she was funny, intelligent, caustic, terrified . . . and on her way to meet her son, whom she'd never known. It was a

movie about a journey to the heart of forgiveness. I loved it. And I didn't want any part of it.

"What's the catch?" I asked skeptically.

"No catch. There's no catch, Alex. It's yours, I'm telling you. Who else are they going to get?" she said excitedly.

"Glenn Close."

"This is a great script, Alex. Seriously, a great, great script."

I sighed.

"Okay . . . one question."

"What?"

"Do I have to dress up like an egg salad?"

I went down, and Claire was absolutely right: the script was fantastic. The rides were funny and smart, and even though the writer wasn't Transgender himself, the sensitivity from which he wrote was universal and resonant. This was a story not only about this Trans woman, this was a story about family and truth telling, about love and its pitfalls, about acceptance and its many gifts. I loved it. I wanted it. It was a tiny film for no money, and I wanted it. I had never played a Trans character before, with the exception of *Time to Burn* at the Steppenwolf. This was the first major Transgender movie role I had been offered, and I desperately wanted in.

The audition went well. Claire sat across from me, with her assistant working the camera. We read, and we read again.

"Try it this way and without so much anger. You're a little too angry," Claire instructed. "Now this . . . try this, Alex. Lighter. Lighter. Lift up and let's do it again. Laugh a little. Even if it's not right, just try laughing while you're talking to your son."

Acting for the camera was completely foreign to me. With all the outfits I had put on, and all the words I'd had to say, that tiny piece of architecture sitting on a tripod with its one black eye staring at me, seeing everything . . . I never got used to its presence. It was intrusive.

It didn't breathe or cough, or applaud, or groan or leave its seat when it had to pee just as you reached the climax of your death monologue. It sat there. It winked at me and never smiled. It never let up, and no matter what I thought about, or how I manipulated my emotions, it caught me in all of my lies.

I hated that thing.

"Pretend it's Chrisanne," Claire suggested. "Pretend it's part of you and isn't sitting in judgment," she said matter-of-factly.

Yes. It was on my side. It wanted me to win. I was not ready to be seen.

"I think they want you," Claire announced over my answering machine about a week later.

They wanted me. They what? They did?

I got it. They wanted me.

They wanted me for this role, and I loved this role, and at almost forty years old, I was finally going to star in my first movie. A movie about a Trans person starring a Trans person. We could really say something important. Even if they had no money, and it was a tiny film, and it played to only a few people, we had a chance to really do something important. I was a part of something.

A day later the writer called me personally to apologize and let me know that the role was being given to another actress, someone more famous than I was. The only way the movie was going to be made was if they cast her instead of me. No one would back the film if I was in it. He was very kind and very apologetic. I was a Trans actress and I should have been the one to tell this story. It should have been me. I was fine with it all. At least the story was getting told. At least our stories were beginning to be noticed as part of the human experience. That was a victory. At least . . . that's what I tried to convince myself of.

The actress who replaced me was Felicity Huffman.

The movie was *Transamerica*.

Ms. Huffman received rave reviews from every major critic. Her performance was hailed as "revolutionary" and "brilliant." Among the numerous awards that she and the film received was the Golden Globe Award for Best Actress. She was on the covers of magazines, on the sides of buses, and on massive billboards that towered over the streets of Chicago, and finally she was nominated for an Academy Award.

I saw those billboards on my way to shows and doctor's visits. I ate dinners with Chrisanne as TV commercials hailed Huffman's miracle of a performance as this Transgender woman. And I saw row after row of magazine covers with Felicity in drag, her wrist limp and her head cocked to one side, as if she were listening at a door. I saw the film. I sat in the tenth row, and I watched Ms. Huffman lisp and shuffle her way into the Trans experience. Her voice was pitched low, and her hands flopped from side to side as she flailed about, seemingly swatting at flies. I had been around Transgender women since 1980, and I never once saw anyone behave in this way. I didn't know what she was doing, and I didn't care. I don't know, had I in fact played the role, whether I would have received the kind of adulation and acclaim that was heaped upon Ms. Huffman, but it hurt. Felicity is a wonderful, powerful, and enigmatic actor. This isn't about a comparison. This is about visibility. And at that time, I didn't understand the ramifications of being rejected and asked to make way for a cisgender female to play the lead in one of the few successful Hollywood films about the Transgender experience. Larry Kramer's voice did not ring sufficiently loud in my head.

I think the most horrifying moment was that at one point in the film, the character and her son are on the road, and they pull over. Felicity stands in the dirt by the car and takes out a strap-on plastic phallus and begins to pee standing up. It was mortifying and insensitive.

I watched this actor put on the clothes of our community and try to represent what she couldn't possibly understand. I watched her play dress-up. And that March, as I sat at home and watched her in the

second row at the Academy Awards, I tried to count how many actual Transgender people might be in that audience. Not the ones you could see. Not the ones outside the theater carrying signs or waging wars or changing dialogue, but the ones hiding in stealth, the ones still living a damn lie because to the Hollywood community, we didn't exist. We were still being represented by cisgender people who felt it necessary to show our dicks in our hands while we peed standing up.

I didn't see anyone in that audience. We weren't there because we were all too frightened to be authentically seen. We pretended we weren't there or we stayed home, as I had done for so many years, and watched from the couch. We'd been there since the beginning of Hollywood. We weren't new. We weren't an ideology. I knew that. My chosen family knew that. My wife knew that. But Hollywood did not know that. This is not a costume. I am not dressing up. None of us are.

Felicity lost that year. And that year, I took a deep breath and forgot all about Hollywood.

~

"Do you have a blond wig?" Claire asked.

I hung up.

She called back a few days later.

"If you have a blond wig, I can put you on tape for this, and I think . . ."

I hung up.

A few minutes later she called back, and I let it go to voice mail.

I just couldn't do it. I couldn't go through it again. It was pointless anyway. Being a Transgender person in Hollywood made no sense. Theater was the only place for me. It was the only place I was going to get any work. After all the lines I'd waited in, and all the sides I'd read, and all the scripts I'd gone through, I knew in my gut that I wasn't like

every other Chicago actress. As much as people pretended that I was no different, it wasn't true. My Transgender experience was not being honored. I wasn't Blanche DuBois, I wasn't Mama Rose, I wasn't a Japanese sculptor, I wasn't Hamlet's mother, I wasn't a magical bird in Dr. Seuss' land of make-believe, and I wasn't the queen who slipped the pea under the mattress. But those roles had been offered to me because the roles of Norma Desmond, and Carlotta, and Mrs. Lovett all went to cisgender actresses in the mainstream theaters who didn't provoke comments and whispers at intermission. They could tell the story, which according to many producers, I could not.

But I was still working. I hadn't gone anywhere, and neither had any of my Transgender artistic family. We just continued to live the lie when we were forced to, dress up when we were told to, and find the gnome costume in the back of the closet so we could get the job and be on our way.

"Do you have a wig, girl?" I asked calmly.

"What kind?" Honey asked, shuffling through her closet. "I have a million wigs. What do you need? Zsa Zsa? Eva?"

"What's the difference between Zsa Zsa and Eva?"

"Bangs."

"I think I want this gig, but I don't know. I don't know that I fucking care anymore."

"Then why are you doing it?" she asked.

"I honestly don't know. It's Claire. I love Claire. And she's never given up on me. I feel bad saying no."

Honey put the dress she was holding on her bed and stood next to me. She put her hand on my knee and turned my head toward hers. "You're such an asshole."

I stood up. I wasn't in the mood.

"I mean it. You're a little ungrateful. Here's another Transgender role and this is for Walt freaking Disney, and who else do you think

they're going to get? Felicity was last year. That's a done deal, girl. That ship has sailed. Look . . . if you don't do it, another Felicity Huffman will."

And then she handed me a blond wig in a bag. I wasn't sure if it was a Zsa Zsa or an Eva, but I took it.

I got the role.

~

I had never had a dressing room before. Well, not in a trailer anyway. I had never in my entire life been inside a trailer, nor set foot on a film or television set. I had no idea what a "mark" was, or what "picture up," "back to one," or "stepping in" meant. People spoke in their own vernacular, and they did it incessantly. "Back to one now so we don't lose money!" and "Don't be the idiot who's lagging behind." I had no idea where "one" was, and certainly had no idea how to get back to it. I knew what "Miss Thing," "Mary," and "Miss Two" meant, but this language was foreign. I had been flown first class and was ensconced in a five-star hotel not far from Warner Brothers studios, where our Disney "backdoor pilot" was being shot. I assumed, at some point, someone on set was going to show me where this back door actually was, but that never happened. I was in Hollywood for a two-week shoot, and early on, a young man knocked on the door of my three-room suite and handed me an envelope with three hundred dollars inside it.

I immediately called Chrisanne.

"Someone dropped off an envelope with money in it."

"What do you mean? Who? And why are you answering the door?" she asked incredulously.

"Because when I do, people hand me envelopes with cash in it."

We found out it was my per diem, but that phrase, too, had to be explained to me. I was in my forties, and this felt like walking into my

dad's rehearsal while the cast gathered around a central microphone and sang "On a Wonderful Day Like Today" from *Roar of the Greasepaint* as I sat in the audience, scrunched like a ball in amazement and terror. But this, I reminded myself, was what I wanted to do. This was where I wanted to be. Here I was, almost halfway through my life, flown first class across the country from Illinois back to LA where everything had started, and standing in my trailer getting dressed for my first scene in my first TV movie for Disney. I realized that I was putting on gowns and wigs and dressing the way I used to dress when it was illegal and immoral. Those voices of condemnation still lived loudly in my head. Even as I stood there in my trailer, gazing into the full-length mirror, with the costumer fixing, hemming, and asking me how it felt, whether the garment was acceptable and was I comfortable, I heard those voices.

The movie was called *Romy and Michele: In the Beginning*. It was directed by Robin Schiff and starred Alexandra Breckenridge and Katherine Heigl. It was a prequel to the enormously successful *Romy and Michele's High School Reunion*, with Lisa Kudrow and Mira Sorvino, and featured the same two characters as they graduated from high school and began their lives. The plot involves them finding a pair of red ruby shoes, bumping into a wicked LA agent played by Rhea Seehorn, and being guided by a blond, bewigged Trans woman, a cabaret singer with a Southern accent, which I borrowed from my mother-in-law. The magic three—Romy, Michele, and Donna (me)—all end up in jail.

Naturally.

The movie featured a cameo by Paula Abdul, which is a whole other book.

"Right over here, Alex. You're going to enter here, and your mark is on the other end of the walkway. Do you see it?" the girl with the fourteen pencils in her mouth instructed.

"Yes. I see it," I replied quietly.

I stood in my pantsuit in the midday sun on a path lined by rose-bushes and apartments. Behind me were the two girls I'd met at the audition weeks ago. One, brown haired and mischievous with a constant grin and a throaty laugh, named Alex, and the other, a glorious blond with a kindness that seemed to radiate from the soles of her feet, and a delicate elegance I immediately loved. They were both much younger than I and yet they had been in the movie business far longer. They were seasoned pros and had spent weeks on set together. They held on to each other, giggling, making private jokes as the crew set up the first shot of the first day in my first movie for the Mouse.

Surrounding me were men, mostly men, mostly white, and, I assumed, mostly cisgender. They huddled in bunches behind a tree off to the left and off to the far right on another arm of the gravel pathway, wearing suits and shiny shoes. Groups of them gathered with three or four younger men, holding coffee cups and pads of paper, all nodding in agreement and writing furiously.

Someone behind another bush yelled, "Action." I stood, Alex and Katherine behind me, still giggling and most likely speaking dialogue from the scene we were supposed to be doing. I stood frozen in abject terror.

I was the only one.

As far as I could see, and as far as I knew, I probably wasn't the only one, but I was the only one who was out in the open. I was the only one. I tried my best to move and speak lines and walk down the pathway past that camera and that group of men in those blue striped suits, and I was certain they were taking notes about me. "His name is too long. His wig is too blond. His clothes don't fit right. He's not very funny. He sounds like a man. Isn't he supposed to be a woman now? Did he have a sex change? His name is really Scott, you know. It's not Alexandra. What a fag!"

"Alex, you have a line here," came a whisper from behind me.

I turned around.

"What?" I asked, the sun glaring in my eyes.

"Sorry. That was weird. Sorry about that, but I think you skipped a line. You say something about the party later."

Katherine's face lit up. She was gentle, and her voice moved through me. She took my hand, she looked me in the eyes, and the sound of her soothed me.

"Sorry. Fuck, I have a line. I have lines in this thing, don't I?" I laughed loudly.

She laughed back. Alex cocked her head and smiled at me.

"I hate lines," Katherine murmured, moving closer.

She stopped for a moment. The director yelled "Cut" and things began to move and the world began to shift and rumbling voices commandeered the gravel, and Katherine stood firm in front of me. I was the only one there and the only one everyone could see, and I began to weep.

"There's a red piece of tape over by the door. Do you see it?" she asked, keeping her gaze fixed on mine.

I turned my head, saw the tape on the ground, and nodded.

"That's your mark. So, you're going to say your lines and then when you take out your keys, your toes will stop right on that piece of tape. Do you see?"

I nodded.

She released my hand, and the world slowed and the gravel stopped heaving and my feet moved again. She breathed in deep and made a small sound as she inhaled and raised her eyebrows, and I did the same.

"Better?" she asked.

"Yeah."

The cameras moved in closer, and more people gathered in toward me. I stood in my blond wig and practiced a little of my Southern accent. Off in the corner, behind a small bush of yellow flowers less than

half a person high, a human crouched, a pair of silver-framed glasses pinned to the collar of their shirt. Their small, half-open eyes darted back and forth, and they saw me clearly and I saw them, and they stood a little taller. They smiled and ran their hand through the part in their black, black cropped hair. I waved timidly, ignoring the voices that tried to bulldoze their way between us, and they waved back. We smiled. I unclenched my fists.

I was not the only one.

And yet, I absolutely was.

~

"Are you in for one take?"

Robin leaned against the gold-painted railing that stretched endlessly toward the massive stage built for the big party that Donna was throwing herself. Surrounded by at least fifty or sixty extras, all in 1980s attire, Robin had been a touchstone since the first day of my LA audition for *Romy*. Her calm demeanor and her ability to put me at ease with very few words was uncanny. I had worked with many directors before her, but none who were able to communicate so clearly to me what she needed in a scene and what was required to tell a story. Robin used *The Wizard of Oz* as her template. Romy and Michele find a pair of red ruby shoes in the trash. These iconic shoes function as a portal to the Technicolor world of music and emotional freedom. Their dream is to become Paula Abdul's back-up dancers, eventually play Vegas with the Diva, and travel the US in style. And Donna was to be their magical Trans, a role that would haunt me for many years afterward.

I saw myself as Dorothy Gale from Kansas.

They did not.

Robin looked around for a moment, scoping out the extras huddled in groups—chatting, excited to be on set, and teased, sprayed, and

painted with green eye shadow in an exaggerated approximation of our style in the 1980s.

"Do you think we can get this in the can?" she repeated in her sedate and peaceful tone over the babble from the center of the ballroom.

I lied. I lied a lot.

I had no idea what I was doing or what anything was called, and without Katherine to guide me and occasionally physically turn me to point in the right direction, I was utterly lost. So, I did what I did best—I lied.

"Absolutely," I answered, puffing on my cigarette.

I wasn't sure what "the can" was, but whatever it was, I assumed I could get it in there before anyone else. My agent in Chicago and I had sat down and signed hundreds of papers in the contract for this gig, and he explained to me, "Daaaaahling . . . you're going to be exceedingly wealthy."

Chrisanne's eyes lit up from across the table.

"You'll be able to buy a fleet of fainting couches," he added.

So I naturally assumed that this movie, premiering on Disney, was a mere formality, and within weeks, Chrisanne and I would move out to Hollywood and I'd begin my new career in television on a hit show, playing Donna, the Magical Blond Trans Lady, and buying yacht after yacht.

Still puffing madly, I said to Robin, "You know, I think this is the first time, by the way."

"The first time for what?"

"I think this is the first time a Transgender actor has played a Transgender character on television."

"Oh."

"Um, yeah. I think . . . I think we're making history, Robin."

"Huh."

She smiled, drank the rest of her water, and turned to the actors milling about on all sides of the ballroom.

"Okay, everyone. We're going to try this. Is Paula here?"

Paula Abdul sauntered out of the dark, flanked by admirers, and slid into place beneath a fabulous spotlight at the foot of the stairs. I didn't have a spotlight. Katherine didn't have a spotlight. I wondered how one got a spotlight. Surely, I'd have one once we went into production and if not then, most definitely after our third or fourth successful Emmy Award–winning season.

As the days rolled on, the more I experienced, and the more I began to understand. I was certain of my success as the very first Transgender actor, and was much more concerned with making history than I was with helping to tell the story. I lied both to myself and to others on set. I was oppressed by the massive empty hole created by the invisibility of our community, not only in Hollywood, but more specifically on set. Although the plague had been reduced to a fashion statement in LA, whittled down from a global panic to a red-ribboned ceremonial cult, the Transgender community was still stuffed in the darkest part of an already impenetrable jail. It was in the smallest details, the almost imperceptible gestures on set, that I was occasionally reminded of how unimportant I was. How unimportant, how unnecessary, and how easily I could be replaced.

I was sitting on an apple box, off camera, speaking to Katherine and Alex during a scene we had outside the police station, after our release from "jail lite." I sat so the camera could catch the light in a certain way while the two actresses spoke to me. At one point, I paused, trying something new. A new take, a new intention, just experimenting. As I did, the cameraman jabbed me in the back with a closed fist, almost knocking me off the box. My lines flew out of me like a hiccup. He had punched me hard below my right kidney and knocked the breath out of me. We finished the take. I stood and walked over to my chair

in the shade of a large, blossoming tree. I wept into my hands silently, so as not to ruin my costume. Complain to whom? Speak to whom? Ask whom for help? I was the only one. There was nobody else. I had nobody to share this with, and so I soldiered on. I didn't want to break apart. I didn't want to lose the gig. Both Chrisanne and I had worked too long and too hard to give up our Emmys and our yachts for one small punch from one tall white guy in a tool belt.

Besides, it hadn't hurt that badly.

~

The thing about Disney is that everything is mouse shaped: the door-knobs, the pencils, the tops of chairs, and the bottoms of toilets. Mouse ears, mouse feet, and whiskers on things that really shouldn't have whiskers. I was standing by the craft-services table, and I had to pee. I took a swig of OJ from the table, set the cup next to the coffeepot, and a tall man with a scruffy beard walked by. "Hey! Don't do that! Don't all you people have the AIDS? Don't leave your disease on the fucking table."

His puffy pink hand grabbed the plastic cup, and he dumped the contents between my breasts and onto my blue disco dress. I looked down. Now I was going to have to change. Back to wardrobe. I had to get back to wardrobe because we were definitely going to do another take. As he walked away, I thought I should tell the wardrobe people because calling me diseased was . . . well. But . . . that's all right. He didn't really know what he was saying. It's not even as if he knew my name. And so, when they asked me what happened, I did what I do.

I lied.

"I was careless. I spilled the juice. It was an accident."

In the back of the lot was a practice room where we were sent to learn Paula Abdul's world-famous choreography for her massive global hit "Straight Up" . . . as she was apt to remind us time after time after

time. I hadn't danced in years, and certainly not in a white puffy-sleeved dress and black pumps. I was in my forties and suffering from a lifelong knee problem, but I wanted to get this right. I stood with the group of actors, all of us wanting to do well, to get the choreography fast and be the best. We sighed if we missed a beat and gave high fives when we spun in the right direction. We laughed, we sweated, and we spun. A lot. There's a lot of spinning in Paula's choreography.

As I was taking a break, standing off to the side, an over-the-hill dancer with too much rouge, whom we dubbed "I Danced with Bob Fosse," walked up to me with a glass of red fruit juice in his hand. He and his friend, who tagged along close behind him, were smirking and walking slowly enough to not be suspicious but deliberate enough to ignite my instincts. I'd seen this walk before. I'd seen these men before. I'd been on this particular playground.

"I'm not going to learn this dance if I have to be sandwiched between you and *him*," I-Danced-with-Bob-Fosse said, his ringed finger shaking under my nose. Two or three actors turned toward us, and his friend with the black ponytail and the too-big shoes laughed out loud.

I turned to him, my head snapping as if it had been held on by a rubber band.

"Listen . . . I'm going to say this once and then I'm going to act it out for you . . ." I began inching toward him, my neck red with rage. "If you ever shake that bony finger at me again, I'll break it off and shove it up your ass. Do you understand?"

I took my towel off the banister, dabbed my neck sweat, and walked to the other side of the room. Two or three people applauded, but I felt no victory. There was no reason to celebrate. I had no one to dance with. There was no hand-holding, or high-fiving, or congratulatory finger snapping from girlfriends or spiritual sisters. There was no one there but me. I looked around at the fifty or so actors in the practice room. Katherine sat in her chair off to the side, knitting quietly. Robin

was discussing the shot with three or four men holding clipboards with whistles around their necks. I stood in silence by the wall.

I made the movie in that white costume and lied to everyone I met. I wanted to go home. I didn't want to do this anymore.

~

About a month or so later, fame was still foremost in my mind, and I knew I wasn't going to find it in Chicago. Although there had been little for me in Hollywood, at least there was novelty. I had no answers, but I certainly wasn't going to find any hiding in my house, doing the same play over and over, or singing at the same clubs every month.

It was time to head back.

This time, though, I was going to make damn sure I was dressed for the occasion. I was going to search for my tribe. I was going to figure out how to apply what I'd learned. I was going to collect other compatible humans and find the fame I truly believed I wanted. I wasn't going to stay silent. This time, if I didn't like the way a scene was going, I would conjure up some of my inner magic, and rewrite it.

Kick my heels. Demand help.

This time those damn shoes better work.

TWENTY-NINE

The Hand over My Head

I was sitting on the edge of her bed. I loved making the extra bed for her. I don't know why. I think perhaps it was because since Mimi died I didn't have any chores to do for any mother. So when we visited my mother-in-law, who by now had been a parent to me longer than my own parents, doing things for her always made me happy: cleaning her sink, vacuuming her house, dusting the knickknacks, of which Jan had millions, or buying sweaters, doing some laundry . . . or just helping her pick things up at the store.

Chrisanne's mother, like Mimi, was fastidious. Cleaning was never really cleaning; it was my chance to do something for her. It calmed me and put a smile on both our faces.

"I put the forks in like this . . . aaand then I put the spoons in like this," she'd say in her best upper-class Southern tone, "and then, if you want, but only if you want, I put the kniiives in like this."

Only if I want. Uh-huh.

It took me about a decade before I would call Jan "Mom." Now, it would feel weird if I didn't. I think there was residual guilt. Mimi wouldn't like it. Mimi might get jealous. Mimi wanted me all to herself,

although to be honest, that was never true. Mimi wanted Bobby all to herself. Never me.

Mom and I were sitting on the edge of her freshly made bed. Chrisanne was in the front room napping, and her dad was in his computer room, computing. Mom was going through pictures, telling me about this one and pointing out that one.

"Oh, and here . . . look at Chrissy's hair! Wasn't it adorable?"

"Um . . . well, she looks a little like Lucy from *Peanuts*."

"She does not," she giggled, nose in the air. "She looks adorable. Look at that dress. Those cute shoes. I remember those shooooes. I bought those shoes for her birthday pah-ty and my goodness, she looked so cute in them. She doesn't like shoes anymore, does she?"

"She likes shoes. What do you mean?"

"Then why does she dress like she's always ready to rake the leaves out front?"

I laughed.

"Maybe she's always ready to rake the leaves out front."

We laughed together.

She shuffled through more pictures, telling me about the parties she went to, the beaux she had had, a few secrets shared only between her and me, and at times, I would cry a little. Chrisanne's mother was open and had talks and let people into her family. Mimi tried. I believe she tried, but it never really happened. To be honest, I never saw Mimi all that happy.

"What are you gonna do, sweetheart?" Mom asked, getting more and more Southern.

"What do you mean?"

"I mean, you made this movie . . . and now what?"

I had no idea. I wasn't a planner; I had married the planner. That wasn't my job.

I sat in total silence. I had failed. I was a failure. The movie hadn't panned out. We didn't make a fortune. I didn't get a yacht. Chrisanne was unhappy, and I wasn't making much money, and even though the virus was becoming contained and I was no longer defined by my HIV, I really didn't know who I was. I was truly bored in Chicago and wanted to get the hell out, but I was absolutely terrified. Down to the core of who I was—terrified. I stared into space.

I really was a failure.

Mom picked up a picture and held it to the light.

"You know who this is? This is my aunt. This is Aunt Reba. She was married to a man named Hayden. And one day, they were driving down the mountain. There was Reba in the passenger seat and Hayden in the driver's seat, and their newborn baby settin' on Reba's lap. And all of a sudden, they began to pass unduh-neath these large rock formations. Well, they hang very low and they tilt on their sides, and they can be very, very dangerous. Now, mind you, they were very young at this tiiime. In their twenties, maybe. Young, young parents and fearful. As we all can be. And there they were, driving unduh-neath these tilted rocks, holdin' onta thah little un, and out of nowhere, Aunt Reba begins to put her hand over the baby's head. Holdin' her hand right over . . . her head as they drove unduh-neath those tilted rocks. And Hayden says, 'What are you doin' there, Reba?' and he's smiling and laughin'. And Reba, serious . . . well, she says, 'I am protectin' the baby.'"

I turned toward Mom, who held a faded black-and-white pocket-sized photograph of Reba and Hayden, standing proudly in front of a long car, posed and smiling, holding a baby wrapped in a blanket, and all of them squinting in the morning sun. Smiling. Happy. Ready for the adventure.

"You're protected too, you know."

It shook me.

I didn't quite hear that . . .

I looked at her again, but she was gone. She was already halfway out the door, still clutching the white shoe box and moving into the hall.

I was sitting in my rented apartment. The sun shot through the large window that overlooked the living room. It was a one-bedroom in a seminice neighborhood in North Hollywood, over what everyone in LA called "The Hill." Every time I told people where I was living, they'd roll their eyes, throw their hands up in the air, and screech, "My God! You mean, Over the Hill!"

Chrisanne was still living in Chicago, and I was here. In Hollywood. Not working. We had given ourselves one year and agreed that if I couldn't find some kind of career, I'd come back home . . . nothing lost . . .

And there I was, weeping into the air—sitting on the floor trying to start my day . . . and weeping. And I fell apart. I curled up and I crumbled. Then softly and tenderly I heard my maternal voices telling me to get back up:

"Don't die giving up. This isn't how it ends."

"You're protected."

Finally, I had stopped searching for fame. I didn't want to be famous. I wasn't dwelling on an interior monologue about money, or connections, or parties, or functions with famous people. This time I wanted an entirely new map. There's a moment in *The Wizard of Oz* when Dorothy comes upon a fork in the road. The bricks go off in four different directions. Same color, same design, no hints. And there, in the middle of a cornfield, is the Scarecrow. He's high up on a pole, and he points. He begins to speak, she's shocked and frightened, and, standing on the four-way intersection of yellow bricks, she wonders if in fact he spoke at all. He then attempts to tell her that some people find it necessary to go both ways, and he points—

In both directions.

Guidance.

Instinct.

Divine Protection.

I lay down and put my head on a warm spot of carpet where the sun had been. I looked around the apartment. I crumbled like a graham cracker. I was done.

I longed to emancipate myself from my shame, but I needed protection.

I got on the phone and called Chrisanne.

"Honey?" I wept, barely able to form words. "You have to come . . . you have to be . . . I need you here . . . you have to come down here."

"Are you okay? Sweetie? You sound weird. Are you okay? I thought we decided on a year. It's only been six months."

I took a breath from the pit of my belly. I felt Reba's hand over my head, and I saw Mimi smile and walk against the wind.

"I need you here. We're moving. Come home," I cried piteously.

And then, I smiled. And in that moment, as I lay on the ground holding the phone, hearing Chrisanne's voice and seeing the light stream in against the walls, my feet tingled, and if I closed my eyes really tight, I could see myself taking both roads.

And just then, someone put their hand over my head, and I was happier than I'd been in a long, long time.

THIRTY

I Knew It

I knew it when I sat down to watch the Oscars. It was in the early 2000s, and two very famous women walked out onstage flaunting their fancy red ribbons. The pins sparkled and had tiny gold tips. I remember thinking, "Boy, those ribbons look really good with those outfits."

I knew it when the camera began to pan across the audience, and everyone was smiling and there were lots of teeth. Everyone's teeth looked so beautiful, I remember. My teeth were cracked and uneven and two in the back were gone, and my life revolved around visits to the dentist. One dentist told me it was a combination of the AIDS and my drug abuse. Also, genetics. And sugar. I ate lots of sugar. In tablespoons, sometimes on the kitchen floor in drag. The teeth on those Hollywood people glistened as the camera glossed over them. And even when they didn't win, they'd smile and clap, and their bodies would rise up off their seats a bit, and you could see those smiles glowing and radiating from the screen. Those were million-dollar smiles.

I saw a face, as the camera passed over the audience. It was a face in the crowd, and his cheeks were sunken, there was no smile, and I

couldn't see his teeth very well. The makeup they had applied to the boy in the audience, who didn't smile, was not very effective. I could still see the dark, deep-set circles under his eyes and that gaunt look we all started to get right before the end.

I was on the cocktail now. The HIV cocktail that Larry hated most of all. More than anything, he warned me against this, his fist raised and his voice pitched high and shrill. "Goddammit, Alex! What the fuck! A bunch of drugs all taken together when no one really knows what the hell any of these things are actually going to do to you?"

"They're saving my life."

"Bullshit. They're making the pharmaceutical fuckers rich."

I took three pills every night, and if I didn't eat something while I took them, there was a pain in my stomach that tore a hole through me. Bread. Pudding. A chocolate shake. Anything doughy or thick.

That gaunt face in that overdressed Hollywood crowd looked halfway gone—as if he was simultaneously with us, and yet he wasn't. The camera kept panning: person after person, smile after smile, and it would pick up a red ribbon, and then not. And then three or four, and then not. And some people would saunter to the podium and talk about how we needed more drugs, and more information and more dialogue, and more help, but most people would rush up and thank their agents.

I knew then.

I knew it, but I never really thought about it. Because how can you know? Living in a war zone, you don't think about the "after it's over" part. You dream about it, and you wish, and you hope, and you cross your fingers, and you bury your friends, and you throw up in your bed, and you slice your wrists, but you don't really think what it'll be like after it's over—or whether there will be an "afterward." That's not part of wartime. Wartime is marching in lines with huge signs written in the red blood of the millions who gave their lives so that you could stand up proud. It's chanting into bullhorns and punching someone in the

face with your closed fist because you are sick and tired of being called a faggot with tits. We were still dying, but now that straight men were dead, AIDS had become everyone's fashionable disease.

I remember when it wasn't.

I knew it would happen, but it felt like it happened in a flash.

~

Dear Pootie,

I don't know what to do, really. I feel so good and yet my insides are torn up. I mean, my health is great. My tests constantly come back freakishly good, so I know these new drugs are working, but I have so many friends who can't take them, or can't afford them, or refuse to take them, and they're still sick, and the government still isn't making these damn things easier to buy. The Clintons hear us. I know that. But, as you say, "Then where the fuck are they when we bury our family?"

I miss you,

Alex

~

The plague was no longer perceived to be a catastrophe, and once the straight community decides there is no longer a problem, the rest of the world acquiesces. The red ribbons, the symbol of our fight against death, had become trivialized. I lived to be a witness to a time I had only dreamed of, and once it happened, I hated it.

Have you ever thought of something and have it actually come true, and then realize after it comes true that it was, in fact, a terrible idea and you're now totally fucked?

Our struggle, our suffering, our deaths had become a fashion accessory.

Trans Hollywood
Terrible Fucking Trouble . . .

My ass vibrated.

I took my phone out of my back pocket and read the text from Honey.

The world has changed, she wrote.

Actually, what she wrote was The weld has changed, but since I knew she wasn't a welder, I just put two and two . . .

I texted back: What's up? New Suzanne Somers special?

Look at Time magazine.

I stopped. It was near the end of the day, and I was on my way home from an audition. Another gorgeous California day, and another audition for another Trans character in another show *not* about Trans people. I googled *Time* magazine, and there on the cover was this gorgeous human in a tight navy-blue cocktail dress, walking toward us with a look of complete serenity on her face. An African American actress who looked very familiar, but I couldn't quite place where I'd seen her before.

I read the title: "The Transgender Tipping Point."

It was 2014. I stopped walking, feeling a little lightheaded. I'd never seen anything like this before and had never dreamed I would live long enough to see anything like this ever. The actress was Laverne Cox. And Honey was right:

The weld had changed.

I arrived in Hollywood and shot my first TV show, *Karen Sisco,* where I played a Trans woman who murders her husband and eventually lands in jail. I had very little experience playing Trans humans, so getting to play them was exciting for me. I liked it. It felt free and powerful.

For about a minute and a half.

I remember being on the set of *Karen* and someone walked up behind me as I was standing there in handcuffs and said, "Bet this isn't the first time, huh?"

He was large and round and white and cis . . . and stupid. He laughed as he passed me and slapped me on the back as if we were watching a sporting event in his man cave. And strangely, and even more horrifyingly, I laughed too. Loudly. In fact, I made it a point to laugh so loudly that I actually checked to see if people were looking at me laughing.

~

We were sitting at dinner, just the two of us. I had ordered the spaghetti and he ordered the lasagna. We were chatting and laughing, and he was so kind and funny and had a long history in the theater. He came from the theater. He understood what it meant to make art, to compile histories of other humans and put them together in a story. He was smart and witty and reminded me of Ray Walston in *My Favorite Martian*—the way his eyes shone from the inside out, the roundness of his head, and the way his ears seemed to perk up when he'd dish about the many celebs he'd met during all his years in the business. He asked me questions, and I asked him questions, and it felt right from the first minute we sat down together.

His name was Billy Miller, and he was about to become my first and (to this date) only personal manager.

Almost immediately, Billy became part of our family and part of our daily lives. I had no idea what a manager did really, aside from the fact that he had to be the "meeny." Greg Orson, the casting director in Hollywood for *Romy*, was not only unbelievably attentive and kind to me, but he also helped me find representation. He had given me three names. I sat in the car, put them out on the passenger seat, and counted, "Eeny, meeny . . ."

And that was it. Billy Miller. Meeny. Done.

We decided working together would be interesting, and if nothing else, funny as hell.

"My goal is to get you to a place where your history isn't going to make any difference," he explained, munching on his salad.

"Really?" I asked, wide-eyed, my face full of spaghetti sauce.

"I don't think it's necessary. You're a damn good actress. Besides . . . you're Alexandra Billings!"

The way he said my name always made it sound as if Liza Minnelli was about to pop out of a cake in front of us. I threw my head back and laughed, and then as I bent down for another big gulp of that fabulous spaghetti, I felt a breeze blow through the front of my mouth. I twirled my tongue over my teeth and felt a gap where a tooth should be. Before I arranged this meeting with this man I wanted so desperately to impress, I had gone to the dentist to try to fix some of my broken teeth. The dentist had given me a cap to cover my front tooth, which had now come loose and was floating around in my dinner.

You haven't lived until you've tried to casually fish out your front tooth from a pile of pasta and red meat sauce.

We sealed the deal, and Billy and I were set. Things were beginning to look good.

~

Auditioning is a lot like dying. I know this because I almost died once. I get very hot, and my face gets very red, and I can't breathe very well, and I feel sick to my stomach, and I keep having to fart, and I lose my appetite, and I hallucinate sometimes. It never gets better, and the terror never goes away. Walking into a room where Mary Pickford and Charlie Chaplin and Greta Garbo sparkled, with the Hollywood sign floating in the background, was almost too much for me. There were many times I'd walk in, get blinded by the glare of the sun beaming in through massive picture windows overlooking Los Angeles, and be confronted by a row of usually white men, usually dressed in three-piece suits and fancy shoes. I'd put my head down and squint. Consequently, there were many times I couldn't see very well and would end up bumping into tables or desks. Auditions never really went very well for me.

And occasionally I would indeed fart.

During those first few years, I was sent out for Trans characters, and in those days, the Trans characters were all in what I like to call Terrible Fucking Trouble.

"Alex, can you try it again, but this time, I want you to really breathe. Like, have a lot of trouble breathing," the director explained quietly, his hand on my shoulder.

"Oh . . . wasn't I having a lot of trouble breathing? I thought I was. I'm sorry. I'll have much more trouble breathing this time."

I was hooked up to an IV, propped up in bed, my hair straggly and flopping in my eyes, and having a terrible time breathing—a skill I obviously needed to work on. The makeshift hospital was filled with extras, some corralled in the waiting room for hours while they filmed our scene, relighting this and readjusting that. I was filming an episode of *ER* called "Skin" where I played Ms. Mitchell, a Trans woman in Terrible Fucking Trouble. The director, whose nails were painted three different colors, came over to me and was very kind and helpful.

"Do you need something? You okay over here?" he asked gently.

I had never watched the show and so I wasn't certain who anyone was. I had never seen *ER*. As a Hollywood wannabe, I was a total failure.

An adorable twelve-year-old with a lip brush and a small black case came over to me . . .

"Here ya go, Alex. Let's deshine you."

She patted me a few times with a large puff and blotted some clear lip gloss on me.

"Are we going to roll?" I asked.

"We are."

"Get those lashes out of your box, girl. Let's do it."

"I don't think we . . . I mean, aren't you supposed to be seriously ill?"

"I'm seriously ill. Not dead. Put on the damn lashes," I commanded.

I was a Trans woman who came into the ER, and the attending physician, after examining me, decides I'm pregnant because he doesn't know I'm Trans and tells another doctor about his diagnosis, and she then tells him I'm Trans—and then I have to make a choice between taking my hormones or dying because I'm Trans. So, I choose death because I'm Trans and in Terrible Fucking Trouble.

With lashes.

"I have something," Billy said excitedly.

"Yay!"

"It's pretty great."

"Do I die?"

"You do. But you have a really fabulous monologue."

"SOLD!"

My first day on the set of *Grey's Anatomy* was nerve-wracking. It was 2006, the very height of the show's popularity. I wanted to do this well. I had had a number of TV experiences by now, so getting into the makeup chair, ordering food, asking for things I needed, and watching my trailers increase in size, were all things I was getting used to but really could not get over. Every time I drove on the lot, a feeling of

impending death would wash over me. I simply could not believe I was working in television and could be on a lot where Lucy had worked, or where *Gone with the Wind* was filmed, or could walk right by a stage where Bette Davis had once sailed up the stairs to her brilliant demise in *Dark Victory*.

I was leaning against the couch, my robe half open and my gray sweats and fuzzy slippers showing. This time I got to look just a little bit better than in previous hospital death scenes. And the lashes stayed. I was a Trans woman married to a cis woman who was taking me to the hospital for the sex confirmation surgery—but we find out my hormones were giving me Terrible Fucking Trouble, so I had to make a choice. And I did—and then I died.

Lashed, dammit!

However, in the middle of all this was a truly beautiful monologue. It was sensitive and spoke about the love I had for my wife and the agony I had put her through. It was filled with guilt and loss and grief and celebration, and I completely understood it. I worked hard on the script. It was almost a page long, which in television, unless you're Meryl, simply doesn't happen. I was honored and very excited. It was one of the first big pieces of text I would tackle on television, and although I was dying, before I left the planet this time, I got to speak my heart.

"Alex," the writer murmured slowly, peering over my shoulder as I reclined on the couch. "We have to cut the speech."

I looked up at him.

"Oh." My heart broke in two. "That's okay. We have to do what's best for the story. It's okay."

It wasn't at all.

"I'm really, really sorry," he sighed.

And I believed him. He really, really was. His hand was shaking.

"I'll put it in somehow," I said, almost defiantly.

"You're amazing. Thank you," he muttered, as he left with his head bowed low.

I convinced myself that in one line, when asked about my wife and I answer with an "I do," the entire monologue could be expressed. The deep subtext isn't noticeable, and it doesn't make any difference to anyone but me, but that's how I got through it. I said nothing, and just kept going.

~

"Are you familiar with *Curb Your Enthusiasm*?" Billy asked, with an extra measure of excitement.

"Well, I know it's super popular, and I know it exists, but I've never seen it."

"Do you ever watch TV, Alex?"

"Yes, I watch TV. I watch *I Love Lucy* and *Bewitched* and *The Carol Burnett Show* . . ."

"Do you ever watch TV from this damn century, Alex?"

"Don't start with me."

"You just go down there and improvise with Larry David, and that's it. This is great for you."

Although we were getting auditions for non-Transgender roles, they never seemed to work out. I believe the intensity of the fear they ignited in me was the primary cause of my lack of success, but to be honest, I didn't win many roles in the theater in Chicago either. The longer I worked, and the more people I knew, the more projects I was invited to. Very rarely did I actually get something for which I auditioned. So, I just chalked the rejections up to the nature of the business. Billy kept his word and tirelessly sent me out. Bit by bit, I was forming relationships with Hollywood people who were gracious and funny and witty and wanted to shake things up, who were trying to create space for us and

open new lines of dialogue. There were many who were trying to break through, but the ceiling that is the Hollywood white patriarchy is thick and very high. I simply wasn't that tall.

Sitting in the waiting room, I couldn't remember ever being around that many other Trans actresses. Usually when I went out, I was the only one. I crossed over to the oblong table set precariously in the center of the room to select one of the slips of paper, each with some lines printed on it. We had been instructed to grab one slip, and it would be the text for our surprise improvisation with Larry. I picked my paper and sat down, squeezed between two other performers, and read:

"You are a Trans woman at a restaurant. The line for the ladies' room is exceedingly long, and you really have to pee. You decide to make a quick entrance into the men's room. Larry and you have a conversation at the urinal."

My usual feelings of panic and oncoming death were now drowned out by my rage at the insulting insensitivity.

A conversation at the urinal? They've got to be kidding. If they think for one second they're going to film me standing upright with my dick in my hand while Larry walks around and mumbles like Woody Allen, they had another thing coming. Visions of Felicity Huffman danced in my head.

I got up, and for the first time since I arrived in Hollywood, I had reached a point of no return. I wanted to say something. I wanted to stop this and say something. As I made my way toward the audition room, up the stairs behind me, like an unexpected hurricane, rose Candis Cayne. We had been connected by Trans Sisterhood for many years, but we had never officially met. Her best friend was Mimi Marks, who had worked at the Baton years after me, and I remembered Mimi when she was a tiny little Trans girl sitting on the edge of Ginger Spice's bed and talking to the two of us about hormones and how to get them. Candis was long and golden. She always reminded me of a gorgeous

deer. Her hair was thick and fell over her like a blanket. She was funny and had a lethal glare. Her eyes were wide open, and no matter how many heads she turned—and she turned them all—I always knew that she knew exactly what she was doing. She had made Hollywood history by becoming the very first Trans performer to get cast as a regular character on the TV series *Dirty Sexy Money*. She had won the coveted Miss Continental Pageant years before and had been in and out of Hollywood since 1995. We had simply never run into one another.

Until now.

"Girl," I said in a hushed voice.

"Girl!" she answered back, hushed as well.

We embraced. It was really good to see her. I didn't know Candis, but at least I knew of her and she knew of me, and I could speak to her about how I was feeling. I handed her the slip of paper.

"This is the audition," I stated coldly.

She read. Her face fell. She looked at me in wonder.

"Shit. I'm not doing this," she declared flatly.

"Uh . . . you're not?" I was shaken. To the bone.

"No. I'm not. This isn't funny, girl."

"It's not. I know."

I don't remember who suggested it. It might have occurred to us simultaneously, but we realized that we could simply leave. So . . . we walked down the stairs to call our respective managers. I told Billy what was happening and told him I was leaving. With Candis.

"Okay. I get it. I really do. And if you want to leave, you should. But just know that someone is going to do that role. Someone's going to do it, Alex."

He was right. If we left the audition entirely, they'd simply cast one of the other actors upstairs and not think twice about it. They would never have known that we were there.

"Candis," I said, as she put her phone down from the same conversation with her agent. "I have an idea. Instead of leaving, which I'm still definitely all for . . . why don't we go in there and try to explain to them why this is a dangerous idea? I mean, if they never hear from us, they'll never figure it out."

"Fuck. Yeah, girl. You're absolutely right. Okay." She flashed that million-dollar smile. "Let's go."

We marched back upstairs, signed in, put our slips of paper back where we found them, and waited with the rest of our Trans Family.

"Candis Cayne?" came a voice from the half-open door.

She smiled at me and patted my hand.

"Here we go," she breathed. She was in the room for no more than ten minutes, and when she came out, she looked renewed—as if she had had a great backrub.

"How'd it go?" I asked.

"They were really receptive. I mean . . . odd, but receptive."

"Alexandra Billings?" the same woman called from the same half-open door.

"Jesus," I muttered directly at her.

I walked into a large, open room toward a long, white table with four or five men sitting behind it, and standing in the center of the room was Larry David. He was much taller than I thought he would be. Usually in Hollywood, it's the other way around.

"Hi," he said jovially.

"Hi, Larry. I want to thank you very much for seeing me. I appreciate this. I have to admit, I've never seen your show, so already I'm batting zero, but that's not really the issue. I need to say a few things, if you don't mind."

He looked stunned, not shocked, as I assume he had just been lectured by Ms. Cayne and was consequently prepared for part two.

"Sure, please," he answered.

"This actually isn't for you," I said to the four men behind the desk, who didn't seem to be paying much attention. "This is for you, Larry. Let me tell you why this isn't funny. This isn't funny because what you're doing is perpetuating a stereotype that Trans women are an idea rather than a protected class of people. By having a scene with a Trans woman standing up and peeing, you reduce us to the lowest common denominator—our genitals . . . and that is not who we are. That is who you think we are. This promotes the dangerous notion that because we might be dudes in dresses that the men who love us need to do it in secret, because people like you might think that they are fags. This in turn might cause them to think twice about us, and fearing public shaming and humiliation might make them want to come after us and, oh . . . I don't know . . . shoot us in the head, or push us off a building, or do what happened to a girlfriend of mine in the late eighties—chop her into tiny pieces, stuff her in a suitcase, and throw her remains off a bridge. And I could forgive all that. I might be able to look past your blatant Transphobia and the intentional cruelty of using us as your personal punch line if your bit were funny. But it isn't funny, because it isn't true. I began my transition in 1980, and I've waited in a million lines with a million other women, and never once did I jump ship so I could stand up next to some dude in a three-piece suit and pee into an oblong, ceramic minislide. I never had to go quite that badly. I hate to sound like Uta Hagen here, but . . . comedy comes from the truth. And this is not only unfunny, it's a goddamn lie. Thank you, Mr. David, for being so kind and allowing me to speak, and have a great rest of your season."

As I walked out the door, I heard from the back of me, "I guess this show really isn't for you, is it?"

It was Larry. I stopped and turned around. "This isn't for anyone, Mr. David."

Before I left the room, I looked hard at Larry's face. He wasn't angry. He was shaken a little, but something seemed to have happened

to him. He was nodding at me. I may have imagined it—that happens to me sometimes—but I truly believe Larry David heard me.

I learned later that year that the episode had been scrapped. I don't know if that was true, or even whether Larry and his pack of boys had anything to do with the cancellation if it were true, but I remember hearing it and feeling a huge intake of breath. I wasn't sure what was happening, but there was a changing of the guard, and it felt bizarre and strange. I wasn't ready for it, and I didn't understand it. I may have sounded off in that room, but I still didn't feel that I had found what I wanted to say. I said things, and they were true, but they weren't specific. Not yet, anyway, for me.

But the ground beneath me was moving. And I felt it.

I began working more, and the more I worked in Hollywood, the more I noticed the same Terrible Fucking Trouble paradigm. Over and over. I cannot say I wasn't still thrilled to be on set, or that the Hollywood world around me had lost its magic. There were times I was so happy that I'd have to stop for a moment and close my eyes and remember where I'd come from. I was just an ex-hooker from Inglewood. None of this should be true. My life was a constant battle between the miraculous humans I met on set, who were caring and kind and loving and funny to the point of pants peeing, and the ignorant ones, who simply had little to no information and little desire to understand who we were as a people. We were brand new. Hollywood had almost no tradition of Trans people. We are varied and multicultural and gender variant and come from all over the world, carrying histories that deserve to be honored, not ridiculed. This had to be taught, and it had to be learned.

More and more as the twenty-first century progressed, we began showing up. More of us emerged from the theater we'd been making, and from the classes we'd been taking, and we tried to break through that ceiling, but it takes more than an army. It takes a revolution.

I was cast in a show in which I played a Transgender therapist, and after a really well-written speech about kindness and our Trans history and how mental health plays a huge part in our spiritual life, the director came up to me between takes and said to me very quietly, using gestures and twirling his neck like a broken whirlybird, "That was great, Alex. Just great. This time, though, could you do it a little more . . . drag queeny?"

I received the same note when I had my very first Broadway audition for the musical *Priscilla: Queen of the Desert*. The man with a long brown sweater tied around his waist watched my monologue about the bus and the humans in it, and how I loved them all and didn't want to see them go, and at the end, he decided it just wasn't "queeny" enough.

And to my horror, in both cases, I did exactly what they asked. I twirled my head. I snapped my fingers, and I added an occasional "Miss Thing" to the text. It wasn't that I couldn't queen out, or that I was ashamed of my vernacular or where I had learned it. I wasn't. But those directorial moments didn't feel like notes, they felt like appropriations. And it turned my stomach. And as much as I was that ball of righteousness and fancy speeches in front of Larry David, when I got on a set and the possibilities of a successful career and fame were proffered, I was a coward. I did what they told me to do. I was ruled by ego rather than principle, and I knew it.

"I have a thing," Billy said over the phone. "Now . . . before you say anything, just listen. It's an audition to play the Transgender daughter who's visiting her dying mother in the hospital . . ."

"Jesus freaking . . . !"

"What did I just say about saying anything? Didn't I just say don't say anything? Now wait. Listen . . . your mother is played by Lynn Fucking Redgrave."

"I'll do it."

The show was called *Nurses*, and it was a pilot for CBS, and the reason you never heard of it is because it was a pilot for CBS and there

it stayed. But the role was wonderful, and Lynn and I had a terrific scene together. As she lies dying in her hospital bed, she tells me I have humiliated her. I tell her that it isn't about blame, and she responds that she's had enough of my life, and I tell her I've had enough of hers. It was not a scene I had to act. The director was patient and between takes actually gave me notes that sparked emotional truth and allowed me to evoke something besides being in Terrible Fucking Trouble.

"Ms. Redgrave, I need to tell you something."

Her face was ravaged and torn, and most of her hair had fallen out. She was lying in her bed, weak and barely able to move. She was still in "the thing," but we hadn't really spoken to each other except to say our lines from the text.

"I am honored to stand next to you and say words. That's all," I whispered. "I just want to be a good scene partner and not stand here and poop on myself. That's all. Keep breathing."

She let out a massive laugh, her blue, blue eyes flashing and the sound echoing throughout the set. She sat up a bit, still smiling, took my hand, and in that glorious English drawl stated, "Jesus, you're terrific, love. Really. You really are terrific."

There was something wrong with my sight line. The camera was set up, and the way I was looking down at Lynn caused my eyes to cross. I know this about my eyes, which is why I am careful about where I look when the cameras roll, but back then, this was all news to me.

"Alex," the director, in his white T-shirt and rolled-up jeans, explained, "we have a sight-line problem. So, George is gonna act as your sight line. I'm so sorry. But . . . you're going to have to do this scene to his fist."

George made a fist below the lens of the camera as it sat next to Lynn's bed pointing straight at me. I was to tell my dying mother how unforgiving and unkind she was, and how much I resented her—to George's fist. I'd never acted with a fist before. Assholes, yes. Fists, no.

"Fine. Great. Love it," I responded quickly, filled with enormous poopy pants of fear.

Lynn came back from her break, the prosthetics of her illness still visible, her bald cap, her lined makeup, and her tubes dragging behind her, while the great youth and vigor of her spirit allowed her to all but skip toward me.

"I can do this, George," she declared, a little like Mary Poppins.

George turned to her.

"Wait," she said, setting her hot coffee on the table across the room. She then proceeded to climb underneath the camera and squeeze herself around the tiny black lens like a warm pretzel, head reaching her knees and arms plastered against her sides. She looked like a basted duck.

"Are you okay?" I asked, shocked and a little frightened for her.

"I'm great. Speak to me here. Let's go," she said, her neck twisted and bent toward the mattress.

The scene happened with Lynn replacing George's fist.

This is what you do for others. This is what it looks like when it's not about being famous or wanting fame or searching for fame. This is what egoless art looks like. This is how you're of service to the story instead of in service to yourself. You twist yourself up for the human in front of you so that the tale can be told to the best of everyone's ability. This is what it looked like.

One day, between takes, Lynn and I ate lunch together. I told her about Mimi and Dad and music and teaching and Viewpoints and Steppenwolf and Hollywood and being Transgender and auditioning and my sadness and my cowardice. And she told me about art and swimming and the beach and her sister and her loves and men and the need for affection and men and we talked and ate, and as we were about to go back on set, I asked one last thing. "Hey. I need to ask you something. I hope this doesn't make you mad . . . but I've been dying

to ask you this for two days. Um . . . can you and I sing a little bit of 'Georgy Girl' together?"

Her eyes got wide, and she dropped her sandwich. She turned very slowly to me, and as slowly as she could, she murmured, "How . . . dare . . . you . . . take . . . so . . . fucking . . . LONG TO FINALLY ASK ME THIS!"

And that day, under this beautiful green tree that sat alone in the middle of a pretend world, I held on to Georgy Girl, and she held on to me, and we sang about what it was like to trip down the streets of the city and smile . . .

A few years later, when Lynn herself passed, I went out onto my balcony and held my hand to my heart. I looked up into the universe and shook my fist, vowing to try to care more for others than I did for myself.

~

"I have a thing, but I'm already guessing it's no . . . but I'm going to ask you about it to see if you want to do it anyway. Just audition for it. It's actually written for an African American Transgender woman, but they might change their minds. It's a new show for Netflix. But . . . you'd be in jail."

"No, Billy. I don't think so . . . and listen . . . here's the thing. I think I'm done."

"Done?" he asked, his voice rising a little.

"Yeah. I'm not playing any more Trans people in hospitals, or visiting hospitals, or leaving hospitals, or getting sick in hospitals. I'm not playing any more Trans people in peril, and I'm not playing any more hookers or drug addicts or homeless people."

"I never sent you out to audition as a Trans homeless person . . ."

"I know that, I'm making a dramatic point. I'm just not doing it anymore. Any of it. No more Trans in Terrible Fucking Trouble. I'm done."

He agreed. Wholeheartedly.

I didn't work for almost three years after that.

The show I refused to audition for was *Orange Is the New Black.* I learned much later what a gift the series was, in that the world was blessed with Laverne Cox, who became not only a great actress, but the first Trans artist in the history of our business to be Emmy nominated and actually win. The "weld" had indeed changed, and thanks to her and her wit and intelligence and her revolutionary spirit, the ceiling we fought so hard to break was slowly cracking.

I was tired of being in Terrible Fucking Trouble and was tired of playing victims—both in my art and in my life.

I wanted freedom.

Terrible Fucking Freedom.

G#D T@LKS

XXX

Did you hear that?

Me

Huh? What? No. Oh no. You're going to tell me I missed something again, aren't you?

XXX

You didn't miss anything. It's going to happen again, but I want you to really listen this time.

Me

I'm trying. But I feel something falling away from me, and it feels scary and worries me. I feel like I'm losing something very dear to me, and so I feel unfocused and can't pay attention, but at the same time, it feels new and thrilling and I know it's causing me to fly into something unknown, and I hate it and I love it. But I need to pay attention more, I guess. You whisper a lot.

XXX
(Barely audible) Hey.

Me
What?

XXX
Did you hear that?

THIRTY-ONE

When the Student Is Ready
The Scarecrow

It was my teeth again. One in the back had chipped off completely, and there was a gap between the ones on the upper right. As I walked into the office, the man behind the desk looked up at me.

"Do you have an appointment?" he asked with a soft, almost Crawford-like whisper.

"I do. Alexandra Billings."

He checked.

"Yes. There you are. Right there. Have a seat and Dr. Rappaport will be right with you."

Sometimes when you meet them, they say very little. They hide, sometimes—like the special present at a holiday dinner you're not supposed to know about or open. And sometimes they sit behind a desk and check your name off . . . you really just never know.

Mitchell was diminutive and yet wiry. There was a constant flow of energy going through him. I could feel it when I walked in. His eyes were bright and awake, and he spoke quickly in short spurts—like a car running out of gas. His life was open and wild. He chased love

and sex and beauty and loss, and he reveled in art. His voice was brisk and lively. There were always gestures. If he was saying "good night" or "come here," there was a gesture. They weren't theatrical, in the sense that they were insincere. They lived deep within him. He was a misplaced vaudevillian. And so was I. And our comedy duo duplicated the madcap humor developed between Honey and me. It felt familial, even when he had three fingers down my throat as he assisted Dr. Rappaport in checking my back molars.

The next time we met was on a float during the Chicago Pride Parade. We sat on the back of the flying tissue-paper structure, and we laughed. The parade went on and the crowd got drunker and drunker, and Mitchell and I laughed so hard and for so long, and the noise grew distant and faint. He'd point and tell me a Chicago story, and I'd point and tell him that's where I first got laid, and he'd point, speaking in fragments and gesturing and turning my shoulders and forcing me to wave. And finally, we stood shoulder to shoulder imitating Kate Hepburn speaking utter filth, and I knew I had found another piece of me. That's how it happens sometimes. They start out sneaky and hidden behind a whisper, and then when they see you and you're there and you're really present, they hand you their heart.

Mitchell came with us, Chrisanne and me. I was getting ready to leave for California for the first time by myself, to test-drive the world, and he moved in and helped with rent and with my wife. He was part of who we are and who we were.

We'd laugh together, and impersonate together, and be in plays together, and Mitchell's turn as Polonius in the Jeff Richmond/Michael Thomas smash *Hamlet: The Musical* was one for the books. He had always thought of himself as an actor first, but I always knew he was a musical-theater performer.

"That's who you actually are. That's your great gift," I reminded him backstage one night.

"But I can't sing a fucking note," he argued.

"Who can? Just sing the truth, don't worry about the notes. I'm sure I never do."

I was teaching a lot. I was teaching for the Steppenwolf and I was teaching in Chicago, and as the nineties drew to a close, I began teaching in universities: the University of Chicago, the Theatre School at DePaul University, Illinois State University, and Howard University. Over and over I walked into rooms and pretended to know what I was doing, and as I worked, as we explored together, I began to believe in myself. And when I didn't, Mitchell's voice would resound in my head, "Think about this, do that, and dream big. That's what you do best, but let's talk about why you're doing what you're doing with these young actors.

Although the universities were beginning to ask for me, and things had begun to change as I found my voice in the room, I continued to seek for me. Nothing. The AIDS plague was still blazing hot. Now that it was infecting the straight community, we were an easy target—as usual, the fags were to blame. And where was I? Where did the Transgender in the room, attempting to teach acting, fit in? I still couldn't find myself, not on any campus, not in any classroom, not walking down any hallway.

So, I did what I have always done: I lied.

Teaching was never a side job. It wasn't something I did to pay the rent. It wasn't something I had decided or even felt as though I had picked. I always believed that teaching chose me. Ever since Tina threw me into the mix, I was slowly becoming a far better dreamer.

But now, I needed to add something more. I knew there was that nasty fork in the yellow brick road, and I had to decide. But maybe the Scarecrow was right. Maybe it wasn't impossible. Maybe I could indeed go "both ways." Maybe.

I didn't know. I wasn't sure. I needed to think.

The Lion

I heard her from across the campus. Off in the distance, there was a woman, wrapped in gray and black, sexy like Hayworth and stalwart like Mansfield. Her hips swayed and her step traveled. She covered space. I could feel it. Thump, thump, thump went the ground. I stopped walking and held on to my friend Sarah, who was taking me around and pointing out things: "There's the library, there's the restaurant where we all hang out, there's everyone's favorite tree, and over there, let me . . ." The woman pulled up. We stopped, and she joined a gathering of three or four others and began gesturing. Her hand pointed, here, there, this thing, that thing, those groups over there—direct and specific. There wasn't a wasted moment. She breathed deep, showing her open spirit, and her long, thick, gray hair tousling in and out of her face, but never directly. Never in her line of vision. Nothing would dare blur that. I don't think her hair had the nerve. She was rooted. The earth and the woman shook in the same tempo, and the humans next to her had a respect and allegiance I hadn't seen since the days at Harbor College with my dad. But above the power and sheer force of nature, there exploded gales of laughter. A thick, throaty, and massive laugh that began far and away from her and landed in her belly. And the others laughed, and they bent over and held on to each other, and they clapped without applause, and they smiled at her and occasionally shook a naughty finger. I knew instantly how frightening and how intoxicating she would be.

"Oh look! There's Joanne! We've talked about you, Alex, so let's go meet her," Sarah trilled happily, moving toward the giggling clump of humans.

I dragged my feet and approached her.

There she stood. Still holding court, still directing, still shining and rooted in the ground. The chair of the Theatre Arts Department at California State University in Long Beach.

Auntie Mame with an edge.

She stared at me. Hard.

I stared back.

"Joanne Gordon, this is Alexandra Billings." Sarah introduced us gracefully, her hand still clutching mine.

"Well," she said in an accent I couldn't quite place, "I've heard so much about you. Sarah's told me quite a bit. I'm excited about the semester." She sounded like Mary Fucking Poppins. But there wasn't an air. There wasn't that distance that flowed through most English accents. When Joanne said "fuck," which she and I both said a lot, she meant it. It was never an accident. "Fuck" she said, and "fuck" she meant. "We'll schedule a time to meet."

"I . . . yes," I stammered.

She scared the hell out of me.

She turned back to the group, all three cis men, all three professors.

"And so the woman says, 'That's not a dildo, that's my husband.'"

They roared.

She said her goodbyes, turned to me before entering the building through the giant glass doors of the Theatre Arts Department, and said pointedly, "Make an appointment. And don't be late. I hate late people."

And as she rode off into the sunset, she began singing "Late People" to the tune of Stephen Sondheim's and Jule Styne's "Some People."

"Laaaate peeeople can fuck right offff!" sounding much more like Judi Dench than Julie Andrews.

And then she disappeared into the sunlight of the massive mirrored structure looming over my head.

I walked around the campus after letting go of Sarah's hand. I said goodbye and thanked her. We had known each other since our Chicago

theater days, and if everything worked out, I'd be joining her on campus soon. In this very building. In this theater building on this campus where I was to be a student for a master's degree in theater pedagogy. I was going to learn how to teach.

Who the fuck did I think I was, anyway?

I walked toward the trees on the massive, grassy landscape peppered with beautiful bushes and freshly cut grass. I walked down a path. I didn't know where I was going or where I had parked, so I walked. Think, Alex. Think. It was 2011. I was on a college campus, and I was Transgender, and I was married to this other piece of me, and I had told Billy I was done. And everyone spoke to me. Everyone's voices descended on me, like a deck of cards thrown up in the air and then randomly collected. Honey, and Eric, and Mitchell and . . .

"You can do this. I can't wait to come to your graduation," Honey reassured me over the phone.

And Chrisanne whispered to me at night while we lay in bed, "I'm so proud of you, honey."

I'm so proud of you.

And I heard Mimi. I saw her face and her smile and the drink in her hand and the ice cubes that clink-clinked when she spoke, and then she told me she loved me. And I heard a bellow from Dad. A big, broad, loud, bellow from my dad: "You've been teaching since you were seven. I threw you in before Tina did. I knew you could do this!" And I heard Mitchell's reminder to use my brain and investigate its possibilities. I stopped and looked up. I was constantly instructing my students to go out into the universe and do something they'd never done before. I wanted them to explore and live in the question, to consider what was next and not drown in the worries about getting the correct result. And so now, I had to do the same. I wasn't a failure as an actor. I wasn't choosing this because I couldn't do the other. *This* was choosing *me*. It had always called me, but finally I was trying my hardest to listen.

"And don't be late. I hate late people."

I have repeatedly told my students, "You say in the room the loudest what you need to hear the most." What I had been teaching my students was how brave, how courageous, and how truly fearless they were. I guess it was time to find out whether I could be just as brave.

"That was great, Alex. Do it again. Again. Right now. Stand over there. And do it," Joanne instructed. Short, quick, Judi Dench sentences.

She became my director and my teacher. She cajoled me, schooled me, lifted me up, praised me, held me, threw me into the den of lions, and then every once in a while when I'd be in my office, down the hall and around the corner from hers, she'd come singing "Everything's Coming Up Roses" and the two of us would link arms and kickline down the center of the corridor—parting our students, who made way open mouthed and cheering. But most of all, she reminded me of what I had forgotten—what I thought I knew and what I thought was real and ingrained but turned out to have been forgotten and ignored.

She had the courage to tell me the truth. And I really hated it.

"Stand. Right there," she directed. I stood in front of her desk as she leaned back in her chair, her arms folded and her head cocked, just a bit. I was reading a monologue for a play she was putting together about the marriage between Charles Bukowski's painful and deeply moving poetry and Stephen Sondheim's story songs that told the history of the brokenhearted and triumphant. The songs were fine. I had those. I could sing those. I never knew why, but singing released something in me. It was when I had to speak that I clammed up—when I had to stand naked, in front of other humans, and be utterly honest. No music, no fanfare, no lush overtures, just my spirit and my reflection. That's usually when it all fell apart.

So, there I stood, in the center of Joanne's office, her door closed, which was rare, just the two of us. In a private rehearsal. I was mortified. I spoke. Words fell out. I forced tears. My voice trembled and I

attempted to shake. I pushed and pushed and acted, and everything I had been telling my students to do, I did the exact opposite. Everything I knew up to that point, the stage work and camerawork and auditions, came flooding back in a huge pile of bullshit. Joanne's ears all but bled.

"Stop it," she commanded, her tone deep and severe. "You don't have to do that, Alex."

"Do what?" I asked, knowing exactly what I was doing.

"Act. Stop acting. You don't have to act this piece. I gave you this piece because this is where you are. This is what you're going through. You know this. We both do."

I started to shatter.

"Now. Think of Chrisanne. The loss of her. See her and stop pretending to shake," she repeated. She leaned farther back, her Judi Dench voice giving way to Vanessa Redgrave: anger turning into compassionate care.

I saw my wife as I stood in the office on the grounds of the university, and I was back at home, and there was my wife preparing to leave me. And she should have . . . she should leave because there was, in fact, this terrible secret I was carrying around. Still. Now. Standing there. In this office. And it ate at me and tore at me, and I knew if I ever told her, she'd leave me. So, I imagined I told her, and there she was packing, her face scarred and red and scratched from lack of sleep. And I stood in that office, and I was completely present in the manifestation.

I spoke. And I fell apart. And I got my shit together and stood there looking at Joanne, who was smiling like the Cheshire cat.

No one had ever told me to stop acting before.

"Do it just like that. I hate bullshit. You know that," she scolded, index finger pointed.

But the fearlessness that poured from the inside of her seemed far away from me. It lived in her and she accessed it when the department needed more money, when the kids wanted to put on extra late-night

shows on the theater building's roof, when the budget didn't balance, when the dean said no, when her students backed away from their own pain and grief. She relied on it and called on it. But I couldn't find it in me. And although I knew what I had survived, I never dreamed that kind of courage could live in me. Because, although I was led by this divine force, and I was beginning to trust it, I also believed that I had tripped and fallen through most of my life, surviving by sheer luck and the grace of other human beings who were kind enough to catch me. No courage. No courage at all.

But that day in that office, a small crack broke through the side of me. A pinch of an idea.

What if Joanne was right? What if I could stop acting? Could I believe I was in love and actually be in love? Everything would be different, wouldn't it?

My gut churned as I felt myself skipping forward toward a newness I never knew existed. I had to think. And I had to keep going. No matter what.

The Tin Man

Being in grad school when you're over fifty years old is a lot like going up a steep, icy hill on broken roller skates. It's exhausting and always feels futile.

My cohorts were all seasoned professionals who'd been working in the business for decades. The amount of acting and directing and writing experience between them was staggering. We fought and dragged each other through late nights of studying and cramming. We put on shows together and put on shows with undergraduates. We highlighted and read and debated together.

And then there was the teaching.

I had never been to college. I saw that world through the lens of my father's career, following him from show to show. But my dad had had a $4.5 million music building named after him, and he had been the musical director of every musical Harbor College staged during his tenure there. So, his presence entered a room before he did. As a fifty-three-year-old Trans student, on a new campus where I saw very few out Trans folk, and certainly none my age, I was utterly lost.

What's a syllabus? What's a roster? A rubric? Then there were the numbers of the classes: teaching the 214s and the 316s while the 113s and the 480s hike the ball to the . . . 324s! There was paperwork and grades and instructions and sheets of paper to fill out that had nothing to do with the papers you filled out yesterday. It was day-to-day newness with no time to think, because after your class with the 113s you had to read all seven thousand pages on acting written by Stanislavski, and Hagen, and Shurtleff, and Meisner and . . . and . . . and then remember to study the script all night for the tech you were going into that weekend.

And then, I walked into class.

And I could breathe.

This I knew. Although every single one of my cohort had graduated from college, I was by far the most experienced teacher in the group. I had no degree, but by the time I got to CSU, I had been teaching for over twenty years, and when I walked into the classroom and saw those university-educated humans all staring at me in wonder and in readiness, the fear that had engulfed me disintegrated.

He stood like a giant oak. His face was bright and caring, and a light emanated from his chest. He was huge. Tall. Not lanky, but towering and very aware of his size. I could see he tried desperately to allow others in. His eyes were deep, electric blue, and when he spoke, the sound vibrated from the top of his head. It rumbled. He was gentle. He

was compassionate and patient and emotional and easily dissolved into floods of tears. A large, lumbering, white man with that much physical power can be overwhelming, and for me, terrifying. I hardly ever had a problem with men of color—not really. Most all my problems are with white men.

Hugh O'Gorman was the head of acting in our department, and he and Joanne Gordon had a relationship much like Davis and Crawford. There was bickering and the tossing of attitude, and a bit of sleight of hand and an occasional bad dinner, but in the middle of it was a truly fascinating and deeply connected respect and admiration. He felt the program should be one thing, and she felt it should be another. Their conflicting ideas inspired us, led to many heated discussions, and enabled us to explore in independent directions. And in the end, the cohort and I took no sides and played no games; we were too exhausted to care—all we wanted was rest and pizza.

"You're not stupid," Joanne declared, leaning into my face during one of her Shakespeare classes.

"I'm not?"

"No. Stupid people are not curious," she reminded me. "Stupid people don't ah-sk questions. Stupid people know this much and then stop. You do not do that."

"I don't?" My heart started to hurt.

"You ah-sk. You are curious. You're an autodidact."

She saw my face.

"You are self-taught," she explained, moving even closer so I would receive this in my skeleton. "And that . . . makes you smart. And that . . . makes you brave."

It did?

After the class, I stood in the hallway, and when everyone had gone into their respective offices, I fell down and clutched my chest and wept. I wept for a very, very, very long time.

"You're going to be teaching the 113s. They're amazing and they're going to love you," Hugh announced.

"You have to remind me about the numbers, Hugh. You know I don't do numbers."

"113-ers. These are the non-majors. These are sports guys and math people and new freshmen coming on campus who want to take a theater class because they want to make friends."

"Hugh. I can't do that. I can't . . . you can't put me in that class. I teach professional actors. I have for over twenty years. I don't know how to do this. I'm not a babysitter."

My ego was running amok, along with my fear.

"They're gonna love you. Teach from here. You know how to do that."

He touched his heart and he smiled. Whatever ridiculous argument I offered wasn't going to work, and at nine the next morning I was headed to my very first class to confront a gaggle of humans, most of whom didn't really want to be there in the first place.

I actually prayed outside the door. I said the Serenity Prayer. Three full times. There were over fifty people in the room, yelling and slouching in their chairs, and on their computers and phones, and chewing gum and sleeping on the floor, and hiding in the corner. So . . . I prayed outside the door.

And then, I walked in to meet the class.

There I stood. A fifty-two-year-old brown Transgender Woman—someone most of these people assumed did not exist, like a unicorn. Many of the students came from countries where they kill people like me—burn us, throw us off buildings. Many of those young people came from right here in the good old US of A, where they do exactly the same thing, only here they take you out to dinner and fuck you first. They stared at me. Their eyes looked me up and down. Most knew. Some, I could tell, did not. But even if they didn't know I was Trans, they knew

something was different. I'd lived in this body for over half a century; I knew those looks.

And there they were. My bullies. All the evil witches and the spells, all the talking trees and false wizards—they were collected right there in that space, in that room, on that sunny California campus. Over there was the football guy who slapped my face with a closed fist as he rounded the corner of the gym. That's the popular girl with her popular friends who pointed and laughed at me while I stood doused in toilet water between classes. And there, in the far, far corner, was Scott. He wanted to disappear under the desk. I could see him. His brown hair combed perfectly, and his shape straight and courteous. He had a pad and a pencil ready as he sat at his desk with his knee tapping furiously. He wanted to be introduced. I knew Scott over there. We saw each other, and he smiled, and I smiled, and he nodded, and I put my backpack down and gazed at the fifty-two pairs of eyes staring at me through their histories of prejudice and acceptance. None of the explanations of who we were as a community prepared me, the Transgender brown teacher standing in front of them, how to tell them who I was. The moment was Instagram worthy.

And so I began.

"Hello, Angels."

And, feeling my confidence kick in, I continued.

"I have no idea what we're going to do, but I know whatever it is, we're going to move through it with kindness, grace, and compassion for each other. I'm not going to treat you as if you don't know how to act. I couldn't care less if you know how to act or if you even want to. It's not really what I teach, anyway. I'm going to treat you the way I'd like you to treat me, and hopefully, before we leave the room, we can all do a little better job out there in the universe. So, we can take everything we've learned in here, and give it away to the stranger we've yet to meet. And that's art . . . I think."

I began to move through the work, and they began to get up and be with each other. I used some of the gifts given to me by Mitchell, Hugh, and Joanne, and some I'd stolen from the other teachers in my life. We laughed, we came apart, and we came back together. We went outside to sit under trees, and we improvised short scenes with passing humans who were simply trying to get to class. I began to understand that art isn't about winning awards. I explored the notion that art is a gift we all have and realized that everyone's story is worth telling. Art is not just for the shiny people in the front row.

I was done. I was done. I hadn't worked in the business for almost two years, and I was fine with that. Hollywood seemed ridiculous to me. I didn't long for any of it.

At the end of that semester, I encountered a bullish boy named Rick, who had a shaved head and refrigerator body. He played football and he wrestled, and one of his solo projects was about the emotional absence and loss of his father. He confessed that he had never been held, and an empty, soul-shaking wail erupted at the end of his auto-drama. He sat on a rocking chair, painted red with indelible marker, begging for forgiveness.

"Alex?" he said in his thick Brooklyn accent.

"Yes, Angel?"

"This was . . . you're the only Trans person I ever met, and you just . . ."

"You don't have to do this, Angel. It's fine. Your work was incredible."

"I never met a Trans person. This Fucking Rocked It, Dude."

I was just about to address the "Dude" part when he threw his entire self into my body and held me there. He shook a little as he wept and tried to hide his face from the rest of the class, who gathered to form a circle around us. And in that circle were the popular girls, wiping their eyes, and Rick's buddies holding their hearts, and there

was Scott, who finally came to us and told us about his boyfriend and the love he'd been hiding. And I realized that the courageous steps forward and the cracking of our collective heart spaces were not caused by me at all.

They were there all the time.

All we had to do—was accept what was true.

When I moved the rainbow tassel over to the side of my square mortarboard, I saw my wife, and both her parents, my uncle Bill and my aunt Linda. Off to the side I saw Dad. And next to him—was Mimi. Standing in the sun, looking out at a vast sea of people, all cheering and calling for their children, I realized I had a family. Chosen and blood. Spiritual and emotional. I walked to the edge of the stage, and as I turned to get my picture taken, the flash of light ignited a fury and a flood.

I had graduated with a master's degree, and I felt something large in me shift. I had really wanted another direction. I had wanted to help create something. I had tried to be well known, but now I needed to get well. I wanted to stay in this place of uncertainty, hold fast to the moment, and capture forever my feeling of ambivalence as I held up my degree and looked for my family. This was the new road. This had to be the way toward the thing I was looking for.

Off in the distance was a chip of green—a slight sparkle of emerald gleaming. I knew I needed to gather my chosen family, because I was beginning to understand I wasn't going to move forward on this road alone. I gathered all my courage, and all my love, and tried my hardest to think about the best way to take that first step . . .

I turned away from the flash of the photographer and, rubbing my eyes in the heat of a new sun, saw Chrisanne's face off to the side . . . only feet from me. Her eyes were wet, and her arms were open.

"You're a teacher!" she screamed at the top of her voice.

After that, the fork in the yellow brick road was no longer useful. I was tired of indecision. I no longer wanted to choose both ways. So, I gathered my family, I picked up my feet, and I knew exactly where to head.

This time, I was going that way.

THIRTY-TWO

In the Deep End

I t's like a warm bath. It's like one of those baths you'd take after being out in the hot sun all day, in the garden, pulling things out of the ground and getting clumps of dirt stuck to your elbows and knees. There's dust covering you, and you can almost feel the heaviness in your caked lungs pulling you downward. It's like wearing a sleeveless wool sweater in the heat as you pull up this weed and that weed, and you look up and see miles and miles of endless weeds, and there simply isn't enough in you to continue pulling. It's exhausting and hot and sticky, and you feel ill. There's dirt and muck in your throat and on your body as you crawl toward your house, far off in the distance. And when you finally reach your door, it's locked. You have to go around back, and the sun is still red hot, and you bend closer to the earth and finally see a crack in the screen of the small window into the kitchen. So, you squeeze through the crack and stumble onto the kitchen floor. You crawl on your belly to the bathroom, where the tile is cool, and the tub is cool, and the small breeze that's coming through the half-open window is cool. And you turn on the warm water. You get undressed and you lie, clean and at peace, feeling nothing and everything and

dreaming of a weedless yard. You sink deep into the water as it washes away the clumps of shit you've collected on you throughout the day.

That's what heroin feels like.

I'm not really sure how I ended up standing half naked on my fifth-floor balcony begging God to push me off. Had you looked at my life, you'd never have guessed how desperate I felt. Had you seen what I was doing, what I was accomplishing, who my friends were, both famous and not, you never could have imagined my terror. I had chosen both ways.

"Where are you off to?"

"I have a premiere and then a party at Fancy Place, Inc. Then I'm meeting La La and New New."

"Their new films are masterpieces."

"They're very excited about them, yes. I'm hoping, though, that we can create more Trans-inclusive content. Hollywood needs to take note."

"Is Chrisanne going?"

"Oh yeah! Of course she is. Our marriage is perfect."

"What about your teaching?"

"Amazing. It's amazing. I'm well on the way to becoming a member of the full-time faculty at California State University. I'll be the first Trans person ever to get hired in the theater department."

"Wow. You're a role model and a scholar."

"Thanks."

"You seem really happy. Are you happy?"

"Great chatting with you. Have a beautiful day."

The wind caressed me as I stood there. Off in the distance I could see a steeple. It pushed upward like the top of a wedding cake. I stood on the railing of our balcony, barefoot. It was 2:00 a.m., and the streets were silent, except for a few trees knocking together as the breeze moved them back and forth. Down that road was the night, stretched out and

peppered with streetlights shining small pools on the black asphalt. To my left, I could see the park and the homeless man and the skateboarder and the empty swing set next to the deserted parking lot. I looked down and there was the shrub that had recently been planted in front of our complex, right next to the tree. When I jumped, I didn't want to land in the bushes. I wanted to land on the ground. I didn't want the shrubbery to break my fall. I had to aim for the ground.

"They say those who can't, teach."

"And I say, those who *can, do*. And those who *should, teach*."

Scott met Chrisanne. It was Scott, not me, with whom she fell in love. She'd never met me. She didn't know me. I lay in that bed the night after our wedding, covered in shingles, and as she lay sleeping beside me, I knew she had no idea who I was. She'd married a ghost. Scott was here, and Scott was present, but Scott was a deadly and constant reminder of who I used to be, and I hated him for it. Chrisanne's love, affection, and patience in trying to help me through a portal of understanding only made me angrier. And then her increasing frustration that I wasn't listening lit the fire that had been building in me since the beginning. So, I'd scream and rage and yell and throw things and stop listening because when I listened all I heard was "No!"

I wanted the filth washed off, but I couldn't seem to find the goddamn window.

Drink. Snort. Inhale. Inject. Repeat.

It was easier when I was high. And it's been that way since I took my first drink at twelve years old. It's just easier. It's prettier and more vivid and funnier and more electric and exciting. It was 1989 when I first came into a recovery room and my life got clearer than I ever really wanted. I looked at things and I worked at sobriety. I tried honesty, and I tried real love, and I tried honest sex, and I tried true friendships, and I tried to do all the things that my natural gut warned me against. I wasn't built this way. I was a liar, and a thief, and a whore, and a quick-change

artist, and a clown, and . . . a boy in a dress. I wasn't all the things that those people in those rooms kept telling me I was. And so, I ran even when I was pretending to stay. Occasionally, I'd believe them. I'd listen and try to learn, and try to go home and be married, and be Alex, and be present. But then I'd let it go. It wasn't nearly as exciting as that crawl toward the bath.

In the late nineties, I threw my back out. I slipped in Chicago during one of the many ice storms, landed on my back, went to the doctor, and the doctor gave me pills. I had taken meth and crack cocaine and booze, but I'd never popped a pill. You had to have a prescription, and I felt certain that whatever they could do for me, I could get the equivalent on the street. I always knew where to go. But this time, after years of sobriety, I really thought I had it. It was in me. I didn't need to maintain my guard. I knew the principles of recovery, all my friends were sober, and my wife was sober. I loved the sober life, and if you looked at my life, if you stepped back, it shone—it sparkled and stretched out like a red carpet.

I got home after shooting a pilot, sometime around 2013, and the pain was almost too much. I got in touch with a friend in recovery who was one of my great guides and asked what to do.

"As long as you stick to the prescribed dose, you're okay, Alex."

I read the side of the bottle.

"Take one or two pills every six hours for pain."

I took one.

I sat on the couch and the warm water began to fill my soul. I floated. My hands went numb and my feet tingled, and I closed my eyes and I lay in the water that held me so gently. And I was serene. They talked about serenity in the meetings I was going to, but it wasn't like this. And as I closed my eyes, it felt familiar. It felt cool and then warm and then cool again and I remembered. So, I took another pill.

And I just kept feeling warmer. And I just kept getting better.

"You seem happier. Are you happy?"

"I'm more than happy, really. I feel rejuvenated, and even though we have a long way to go for acceptance of my Trans brothers and sisters here in Hollywood, I know they'll make room. Because we've always been here, ya know? It's not like we suddenly appeared in the seventies because everyone was doing too much cocaine. So, now we must create real change. Really make ourselves visible and viable. That's going to be the new revolution."

Bullshit. Bullshit. I was mouthing my activism but I certainly wasn't acting on it . . . and all I wanted was more pills. Bullshit.

"Look up, Angels!" I'd yell as some of my students crossed the grassy path on the CSULB campus.

They'd smile and put their hands to their hearts. I'd feel about in my right front pocket for the three small lumps. There they were. It's almost 2:30 p.m.—almost time. I could feel the weight begin, and once that weight began, my world would sink into a shattered mess. I'd shake and itch, and my shoulder would pop and my back wrench, and I'd begin to tear at people and knock them down. Those moments when I ran out of pills and Chrisanne would want to remind me about the dishwasher or the closet or the towel folding were intolerable. "Jesus! Fuck! Can you please! My God! It's just fucking towels!" I would rage.

But then apologies would soothe her, and I would take a breath, blame her a little, allow her guilt to smother mine, and then all I had to do was hang on until the next time I could see one of my two doctors. There was the Beverly Hills doctor and there was the clinic doctor, and all that was required was that I be present in the room with them at different times, at least once a month. I'd get my ninety-pill Vicodin prescriptions, fill them at different pharmacies around town, and be fine.

I was now consuming ten to twelve pills a day.

I'd go home. Where'd I hide that last stash? Oh, that's right, that bottle is in the second bathroom, and there's another one that's half full

in the bedroom underneath the books by my side of the bed. I'll have to move that in case Chrisanne decides to look over there. And we'd talk, and we'd make love, and we'd argue, and my temper would flare, and I'd pop two or three. I'd go to school the next day and make it through my first two classes and teach and tell my students to look up and reach out and believe in their own power and to surrender and release, all the while making sure no one heard the jiggle of the half-full bottle in my bag. Walk to the restroom, teach another class, pop, pop, pop, pop . . .

More water. These taste awful.

My mind would spin, and I'd speak without punctuation, but what was joyful was joyful a hundred times over—although it actually wasn't joy at all. I'd take too many and throw up in the sink between classes. I knew I was wasting pills, and that I only had so many left until the next appointment, so I'd dig through my own vomit, wash off two or three pills, and swallow them again.

I have to stop. I can't keep doing this. I'm not even high anymore. I have to get back to my meetings, and I have to stop lying to my wife, and I have to get sober. I'm going to die. I'm going to die. I know this feeling. I'm going to die.

And I'd stop. And at night I'd shake and vomit and weep, and my legs would snap off and break in two, and my back would ache as if a car were parked on top of me. I'd crack open. Wide. I have to stop. I'm going to die if I don't stop. And the next day I'd get another prescription and sit in another meeting and talk about the many, many years I had been sober. And the constipation would come. And the cramps and the anal tearing, and the rivers of blood and then more pills, and then more hiding, more lying, and more classes and students to see, and back and forth and back and forth, and then one night, without warning, I walked out onto the porch of our fifth-floor condo, and on a gorgeous California night around 2:00 a.m., I stood on the railing.

"Please. Please," I said, closing my eyes. I just wanted it to end. All of it.

"Help," I said . . . to the world at large.

And the breeze kept blowing and I closed my eyes tighter, and as I stood, teetering as if on a balance beam, I wobbled backward. My foot tripped a bit and I caught myself as I stepped down. I thought Chrisanne had tugged my shirt, but that's not where I felt it. I had felt a push in my chest, like a brief pause and then a gentle nudge. I lost my balance just enough to catch myself, coming down on both feet. I opened my eyes. The steeple in the distance bounced a little moonlight off its tip. My eyes were opened. I was still high, but . . . my eyes were open.

The next day I called in sick to school, and I lay in my wife's lap. I shattered for almost twenty straight minutes. The momentous shame that rolled through me seemed to burst out of my chest. It felt like a heart attack, so I held my heart. It might escape from my chest if I didn't hold on to it tightly.

"What, sweetie? What is it? Tell me what it is," she pleaded, holding my head with both her hands.

"I've been relapsing for a while now. And . . . I can't seem to stop. And last night I almost jumped."

Nothing.

The day poured into our living room as I wept and heaved and began to shake. And she held on to me and put her head on top of mine and rocked me very gently. And the judgment and the fear of losing her, and the admonishment I expected, never happened. She just held me. She told me we would get through this. She fixed me food. I threw up and I shook, and I had sweats and I slept on and off, and my back cracked and my insides shriveled up, and shit came flying out of me for hours, and she waited and she poured water and applesauce and *I Love Lucy* into me like vitamins.

And through all the years, through all the things I had put her through, in that moment—and I don't know that I ever knew it before, really knew it—but in that moment of care, I felt a joining. It made a sound. It had nothing to do with love. This was bigger. Larger. Farther. And I knew. That's the moment I knew. No matter what. This was where Home was all along. I only had to open my fucking eyes.

At the end of Dorothy's journey to Oz, she has been pummeled and wrecked and ravaged by the witch and her monkeys and the dark castles and the red shoes. So much had happened to her that by the time the Wizard floats out of sight, she is left naked and stranded in a strange land with her three friends and her magic guide. It is only then that she realizes she has nothing left but her freedom.

The Scarecrow asks Dorothy what she has learned. "If I ever go looking for my heart's desire again, I won't look any further than my own backyard. Because if it isn't there, I never really lost it to begin with!"

THIRTY-THREE

The Eccentric

"And remember, my sentimental friend, that a heart is not measured by how much you love, but by how much you are loved by others."

—*The Wizard of Oz*

Hey, sweetie. What's your definition of the word 'eccentric'?"

"Oh. Out of the ordinary. Someone who bucks the system, writes their own rules. Someone who doesn't conform."

I shifted on the couch.

"Hey, sweetie."

"Yes?"

"Do you think I'm eccentric?"

Silence.

I had no idea how to be married.

But the more awake and sober I became, the more introspective and alive I began to feel. I wanted to be a better wife. The lying and hiding and pretending were exhausting. I wanted to be married. Really, honestly,

truly married. But none of it made much sense to me. I wanted a formula and a set of rules, yet if one was presented to me, I raged.

I needed to find out what was at the center of it. Of love. Of addiction. Of gender. Of sex. Of art. I started to explore the present and examine the past. And standing before me was this human whom I had loved since 1976, and who, in spite of the massive betrayals and lies I heaped upon us both, was still sitting across from me on the couch. Still in love. Still here. Still reading. Still promising to love, honor, protect, and cuddle.

Still.

~

I loved Dr. Dan Webber. He was almost twenty years younger than Chrisanne and me, had wavy brown hair, and always stood attentively, as if he were fascinated by absolutely everything we were saying. He spoke like a shampoo commercial. He was gentle, and his speech pattern was unemphatic. Everything mattered, but everything had exactly the same weight. Tempered. Do this. Take these. Lie down. Lather. Rinse. Repeat.

"Your tests look great," he said in his dulcet monotone, half smiling.

His office was gorgeous. It overlooked Beverly Hills Drive and was bathed in light. It was always great to visit Dr. Webber. By now my HIV was manageable, and aside from a few bowel issues and occasionally two numb feet, my particular virus was under control. Occasionally, it would spike, but generally it lay way down, and I'd forget. I would forget I could die if I missed one dose of the meds Larry had hated so vehemently. I'd forget, because sometimes my bowels would be fine, and my feet wouldn't disappear, and the thrush that splashed my tongue and the sides of my cheeks, making everything taste like months-old cottage cheese, would go away, as if they had never been there. And no more shingles for the longest time. Then, without warning, it would burst out of me like that alien thing out of John Hurt's chest cavity.

"There's . . . I have to say something but I'm . . . I'm not really supposed to say anything, Alex, so . . ."

He was stammering. This was like watching a perfectly wound watch bust a spring.

I began to get very nervous.

"Okay, Dan, what the hell? What is it?" I asked, leaning against the table.

"Well, it's about Chrisanne. You know she came in a while ago because of that balance problem she's been having."

I smiled. We affectionately referred to her wobbly nature as "little earthquakes." But they had begun to get progressively worse, and so we got her some tests. Getting my wife to the doctor is a lot like getting a tiger to become a vegetarian.

"She has a small mass on the lower right side of her brain. It's called an acoustic neuroma, and we're going to have to do more tests to find out how to remove it."

The room sat. I could feel a weight. It got heavy on my chest. My eyes welled up and some tears fell, and my hands started to tremble. I began to hear something falling away, as if I were being chipped at, and piece by piece, small blocks of me fell to the floor. Thud. Crash.

"Is she going to die?"

I couldn't get my hand to slow down. I picked at the long, white paper that ran across the blue table and saw my first gentle AIDS specialist, Ross, and his familiar eyes stared back at me. I recalled Ross' smile and his soft voice and his black mustache and how he affirmed that I would live and that he would do anything he could to make sure that happened. And I remembered Mimi's stone face as she lay down, eyes closed and lips tight. All the color drained from her face as I told her to go, because I just couldn't bear her living in that useless flesh cocoon as it aged and got warped by time and illness.

"Chrisanne has a brain tumor. Is that right?"

He put his hand on my knee.

"It's an acoustic neuroma, and it's most likely benign." He took my face in his hands.

And Ginger's eyes fluttered. I blinked twice and saw her smile. That final smile as she faded off the planet, and my cheeks became wet.

"It's a brain tumor. Say it, Dan. Say it's a brain tumor and you really don't know if she's going to live or die."

The room stopped pressing down on me. There was Dan's breath and calm.

"Yes. She has a brain tumor."

"Is she going to die?"

The sound I made blended into the center of his answer, and although I heard it and it came to me, I didn't hear it and I was furious at him for not saying it.

Eccentric

(Noun)

a person of unconventional and slightly strange views or behavior

I was still working on my master's degree at CSULB, and Chrisanne was my right arm. She typed, rewrote, copied, pasted, debated my theories over and over, and fought for clarity in every single one of my papers. I needed her. I couldn't do this without her. She discussed teaching with me. She became mother, student, professor, bystander, proofreader, judge, and jury.

"This is confusing, sweetie. It doesn't make any sense. These sentences and word usage need serious cleaning up," she'd say, like a stake ramming itself through the heart of my writing.

"It doesn't have to make sense to *you*! It only has to make sense to *me*!" I defended.

"Well, no. This is an academic paper about the effects of pedagogy on what you're calling 'artistic freedom,' so . . . no. It actually has to make sense. Period."

But now she needed healing and focus. In a matter of months, she was going to be surrounded by strangers in white masks and long blue gloves putting sharp silver things into the center of her brain. And then they would cut her open. They're going to place my wife on a table and cut into the side of her head and take something out.

This brain tumor thing could go straight to hell.

My wife then began doing the thing she does. She filled her brain with information, and weaponized her knowledge against this unseen mass. She read everything. She downloaded pictures of the tumor, which made me throw up repeatedly.

"Do you want to see my tumor?"

"I do not want to see your tumor. Stop showing me pictures of your tumor."

"But this is my tumor from a different angle. If you turn it sideways it looks like a sleeping cat!"

My wife is an unbelievable student. I watched as she confronted her life and death with wit and smarts and facts and grace and more courage than I ever thought possible. And one by one, moment by moment, my Watching became Doing. I did stuff. I brought her things. I took her here and there—made sure she wasn't late for this and that. I dusted and polished and held her and rocked her and wept with her and gave her pep talks, and through it all, I knew I was not going to lose her. I knew it. I felt it. And once I held that conviction in my hands, I tried to give it to her. I was doing things. Things for her. And these things filled me with joy, and the joy was brand new.

This is what marriage feels like. Well, for me, anyway. And I began to really like it.

~

Off to the left of me, behind the too-short couch, Dr. Chu, Chrisanne's surgeon, entered. I was holding on tightly to Tom, part of our chosen family. Tom and his spouse, Alan, had guided me through this ordeal with humor and wit and a sense of stability that lived nowhere near me. Chrisanne's imminent death loomed above me like Snoopy on that branch when he gets really, really hungry. And sitting off to the far end of the corner table, in a chair with little support and too many pillows, was Lysa, with a freshly cut bob and a bright glorious spirit. Lysa and I had gone through the CSU program together, and her steadfastness in calming any situation was becoming more and more necessary as the day wore on. Chrisanne's doc was dressed in blue and spattered with small dots of red and dark brown, as if someone had thrown a hot dog at his face and missed. His long, jet-black hair fell over his eyes a little, and he attempted to brush it aside with his forearm. He was a big man, sturdy, square jawed, and a man of very few words. When he explained the surgery months before, his words had come in short spurts of ideas, glued together by my paranoia and panic.

"And then there's this thing that will happen while we do this other thing—so the thing that didn't happen the first time won't fall off. You have to be careful because the thing that usually falls off isn't that thing at all. And we'll make sure to use the bleepator and the megatool. If not, the thing could blow up. And you don't want that, believe you me. That's . . ."

Or something like that . . .

Now he removed his mask. His voice rumbled in his chest, and as small beads of sweat fell from his cheek, he moved in a little closer to me.

He held both hands to his side with his palms up. They were covered in more red and brown goo.

"Alex. The tumor has wrapped itself around a very small part of Chrisanne's gland near the ear. So, we have two choices. I can either go in and try to take the whole thing, which is complicated, but I think it can be done, or I can leave some of it in, and there's a chance it might grow back."

I sat on the couch. No one spoke.

Tom gently scooted closer to me, his wide brown eyes staring straight into my center, letting me know I had this. This was a decision I had and one I could make without any guidance or help. All three of these humans collectively breathed and left me in charge. For the very first time in my life, I was to make this decision and I was to make it alone.

I looked at Dr. Chu's hands and realized it was my wife's blood and some of her brain that was splattered on his gown and was dripping slowly from his right-hand glove.

I didn't think. I didn't wonder. I didn't question. But the person I usually turned to in these situations was lying on a table with her head peeled open, hooked up to a brand-new bleep-a-meter.

"If you take the whole tumor, what are the risks?" I asked pointedly, in a voice I didn't recognize.

"She could lose her sight or her sense of smell, or she could be paralyzed and lose function on the right side of her face."

Think, Alex.

Use your heart.

Be brave.

I looked at my three friends. Tom smiled. Lysa edged a bit closer, and Alan took a breath and nodded.

"Don't do that. I know her, and although she isn't vain at all, I don't want her to wake up and not be able to move something, or really hate what she sees in the mirror. Leave some of it in."

He got up, hooked his mask onto his other ear, and left.

Eccentric

(Adjective)

(of a person or their behavior) unconventional and slightly strange

I felt a hard knock against my chest. I bolted up in bed, my head spinning like a top. The moaning from the other side of me was loud and unfamiliar. It was low and gruff and pulsated through our entire bed. I turned to see Chrisanne holding her bandaged head and wincing in a kind of pain I had never seen before.

"What? Honey? *What is it?*"

She could barely speak.

"My . . . head . . . I can't . . . my head hurts."

I got up, threw on a T-shirt, and woke my mother-in-law, who was sleeping in our spare room. We came back together and there was Chrisanne, rolling back and forth and holding her head as if someone were stomping on it.

"I'm going to get her some pain meds," I announced, gathering my things.

"Didn't she fill that prescription when you all came home from the hospital?" Mom asked.

"I tried to get her to, but you know your daughter."

She smiled.

I was not smiling.

I kissed my wife on the forehead and sped to the local CVS. When I arrived, the twelve-year-old boy behind the counter, shaking and

yawning, asked me for the prescription. I handed it over, trying to keep a lid on my panic and focusing on getting back home.

"This doesn't have a serial number," he said in a very high-pitched, whiny voice.

"I don't know what you mean."

"It needs a serial number or I can't fill it."

"I don't know what you're talking about, but I just left my wife in bed. She had brain surgery three days ago and she's in an enormous amount of pain, so I suggest you fill this thing and fill it fast."

"Ohh, I'm sorry," he whined back at me with his bleached-blond surfer do sticking straight out of his head. "I can't. Sorry. Call your doctor and have him give you a serial number."

"Hand me your phone," I said, my temperature rising.

"Ohh . . . I can't do that. It's against company policy . . ."

"If you don't hand me the phone, I'm going to hold your *face* against company policy."

What it lacked in logic it made up for in tone.

I called Mom, told her she needed to get a serial number.

"She needs a number? A *number*? What is she, a lotto ticket?" she exploded.

Thank God for Mom—for her wit and sense of humor and her mere presence. I was still trying to keep up at school, and as Chrisanne recovered, having Mom in the house was a godsend. We could not have survived without her. And even if we had, we most likely would have writhed around in inches of dust and dirty dishes and stacks of empty McRib containers.

I waited at the CVS, pacing back and forth between the eyelashes and the suppositories.

"Here it iiiiiiiis . . ." he whined from the back of the counter.

"Great. Fill it, please."

"Okay, but, ma'am, it's gonna be another hour because I'm really backed up, and I don't know how much time . . ."

I walked up to the desk and stood within inches of his face. I leaned in and held the back of his head with my hand. And very slowly, and maniacally, so he wouldn't miss a syllable, I began to speak like Vincent Price.

"You listen to me, young man. My wife is in pain, and I've been here for over an hour, which is fifty-nine minutes longer than I intended. I got you your serial number, and I have been waiting patiently while you whined to your manager about how late it was getting, and how sad you were that you were going to miss your Lindsay Lohan marathon. Now . . . *those* are my wife's meds and you're going to fill those meds because if you don't, I'm going to shove your entire head up your ass . . . So, stop your whining and bust out the Vicodin, bitch."

I probably could have achieved the same effect without the hands-on threat of violence, and most assuredly the Lindsay Lohan reference went right over his head. However, I was at the beginning stages of digesting this whole responsibility-and-service-to-others thing, so I gave myself a little leeway.

Her meds were ready ten minutes later.

Mom and I sat in the living room. In the distance, Chrisanne's small snores wafted down the hallway.

"You know, honey, you're doing a great job. You know that, don't ya?" she murmured, smiling.

"We wouldn't have survived this without you, Mom. I mean that."

She sat up.

"Yes, you would have. Don't make an excuse. You're responsible. You can do all the things you need to do in order to take care of things. You don't need instruction, honey."

She fluffed the pillow behind her, momentarily checking the dust level and then propping herself up. She had been irreplaceable since she arrived. We held on to each other. We watched movies together.

We made sure Chrisanne got her pills, her food, and her walks, and we kept her mind sharp and her spirits up. And every so often, I'd come into the bedroom and there they'd be, Mom in Mimi's rocking chair reading a book as Chrisanne slept. Mom would read, and look up, and read some more, and look up and put her palm on her daughter's leg, and I would stand in the doorway and gaze at what parent and child could look like. And I knew. Even though I was jealous and even though I felt cheated, as I watched in silence and in plain sight, I began to let go of the blame. Mimi did the best she could with what she knew. The Transgender daughter she had was a mystery and a blessing, and the times I chose to remember were those when the lights went out and she knelt beside me, sitting on the edge of my bed and warbling a one-note version of "Feed the Birds." Mom Blankenship read Shakespeare, Mimi Billings sang show tunes. It all began to make sense.

"Ya know, honey. Ya'll are truly blessed to have each other. The way you teach each other."

"I know, Mom."

"Your mom did the only thing she knew how to do."

I nodded.

"With all of the things you've survived, I'm tellin' ya, y'all have an angel the size of Mama Cass sittin' on your shoulders."

I laughed so hard, the sound drowned out the snore.

~

"Joanne?" I asked over the phone, as we chatted about the book I had begun writing about my weird and wonderful life.

"Yes?"

"Do you think I'm eccentric?"

She paused.

"Jesus! That's exactly what Chrisanne did!"

"No. I don't. I don't think you're eccentric at all," Joanne answered swiftly and with great authority. "You have worked so hard and suffered so much to be fully accepted for who you are. You don't need to be eccentric."

There was a small piece of me on the ground—a piece I thought had been chipped off and would never be glued back. I bent down and picked it up. I put it back into the center of my heart space and held it there with my hand. I could do this by myself. For the first time I realized I had the power to make myself whole.

I looked out of our window. It was getting close to dinner. I had a paper due. Chrisanne's bandages needed changing. And the next day I was teaching my 113ers, so I needed time to dream. To manifest.

"Mom? I have to go manifest stuff. Can you fix dinner and I'll change Chrisanne's bandages?"

"Manifest away, honey," she said with a smile.

~

"Sweetie?"

Chrisanne shifted on the couch across from me. She peered over her book.

"I asked Joanne earlier today if she thought I was eccentric."

"What'd she say?"

"She said no."

"I agree."

"What? Well, why didn't you say that the first time I asked you?"

"Sometimes I get scared to tell you . . . I don't want to hurt your feelings."

"You thought I wanted to be eccentric?"

"I think *you* think you want to be different when really, you want to be the same. That's what you've fought for your whole life. Sameness. Inclusion."

Eccentric

Having the axis or support away from the center

Yes. That's right.

Now . . . I had to commit to a total and spiritual search for the center.

~

S/he and Me—*acting with my students*
(Photo by Keith Polakoff)

And teaching seemed to be my center—my anchor. My academic career was flourishing. I was an instructor in the Theatre Arts program, and

the first year after graduating, I was invited to be the commencement speaker at the 2015 graduation of the College of the Arts at CSULB. This honor was highly unusual, as giving the commencement speech is traditionally reserved for the rich and famous. I spoke about being present and not worrying about the consequences, and with planned theatrical aplomb, threw my notes in the air and spoke from the heart. I had arrived in the world of academe. I was certain that the inevitable step of becoming a tenured professor was imminent. But when Joanne Gordon tried to get me hired as a full-time member of the teaching faculty, under a special dispensation as a "minority hire" to a university that was seeking to diversify its faculty, the Big White Cis Man in Power laughed her out of his office.

"Only *you*, Dr. Gordon!" he proclaimed, huffing and panting and wiping his eyes as she stood there fuming. "Only you would think to ask for something so ridiculous! Transgender is not a legitimate category for a minority hire."

I still wasn't there.

This time, however, unbeknownst to him and many other self-important bureaucrats, I was.

And she did it. Joanne did not give up. She made the same request the following year—but this time she was prepared for his mocking laughter with threats of her own. After climbing over a million barriers and exploring a million loopholes, she got me on contract. I finally became the first Trans assistant professor in the history of the CSULB Theatre Arts Department. I now had a "real" career. I was a legitimate certified teacher. I was here, grounded and making my way through it all over again, but this time I wasn't going to let go. I wanted tenure. I wanted to have security so that people like the Big White Cis Man in Power couldn't laugh me out of academia simply because they were too stupid and ignorant to recognize my existence.

"This is great!" Joanne crowed, standing in our shared office. "Now . . . do you know how you can really cinch this tenure thing?"

"There's another loophole? Love it!"

"No, no . . . no loophole. It's simple, dahling," she announced. "Get yourself a TV show."

I stood there waiting for the punch line, but nothing came.

We stared at each other. I was approaching sixty years old. I was brown. I was Transgender, and I desperately wanted to teach. Who was going to hire me to be in a TV show?

I burst out laughing.

Ah well.

Onward.

I embraced her. We chatted, parted, and I walked down the hall. Walk. Walk. Past the professors and students, and off in the distance, the young artists were running under the trees, laughing and rehearsing and figuring it out. And I breathed and I held on.

"And so, I think what we all really want to know is, in spite of all the things you've been through and even, some may say, put yourself through . . . are you finally happy?"

"That's not the point, I don't think. I'm here. That's the point. And my life, as weird and awful and fabulous as it's been so far, is like one incredible, fantastic, long-awaited warm bath. And I'm relaxing in the deep end this time."

A TV show?

That was ridiculous.

THIRTY-FOUR

Transparent
The Beginnings

I hadn't checked Facebook in a while, so I went in and perused the private messages. I didn't usually get that many, but if they went unchecked, they could stack up. And there, under a few names I didn't recognize, was one I did, but hadn't spoken to in almost thirty years.

> Hi Alex. It's Faith Soloway. Remember? Listen, I know we haven't spoken in a whole bunch of decades, probably since Chicago theater days, but I wanted to talk to you about something: My parent is transitioning and as you can well imagine, Joey and I don't know what to do. Nobody in our family really does. And we were wondering if you had any advice or could maybe just help us through this in some way. Sorry for the weird, out of the blue message, but I really didn't know where else to turn, and your Facebook is always so full of advice

and kindness, I thought I'd reach out. I know you're busy and I'm sure you get asked this all the time, so if you can't find the space for it, I completely understand. Thanks for reading this far. I hope you and Chrisanne are well. Love, Faith.

I had reached a place in my life where the days of taking care of cis people and holding their hands or calming their panic or dread when someone in their lives transitioned were over. I was done. I was no longer the Trans in Charge of Party Poopers, Inc. Families mistook my kindness on social media to mean that I was put on the planet to calm the nerves of grieving cis people. Transitioning should be a joyous and momentous event, but in my own family it had been everyone's nightmare—everyone's shame and everyone's public humiliation. And it had all been my fault. I paid for it by comforting others, over and over. I accepted the notion that I wasn't supposed to complain, and I was supposed to make sure I wasn't having too much fun by keeping my joy at a level five. Don't be too loud, and make certain the neighbors don't see me. Draw the shades, passersby might think there's something to celebrate.

No more. I'm on the side of Trans Humans, and if a family is still dealing with sadness and loss and grief over some presumed death, that has absolutely nothing to do with our celebration in the next room. Mourning a transition says much more about the mourner than it ever will about the human who's getting down with their bad true selves. Each transition should be a party. If one receives an invitation and does not wish to attend, please RSVP and leave a present at the door. Vitriol and hurt feelings have nothing to do with me, or the human who has finally found the courage to live truthfully and loudly. A transition is not something they are doing *to you*—it is something they are doing *for them*. I was beginning to find a way to navigate some of this deep

shame of mine and turn it into a powerful reconciliation. I am not my past. I am not who I was. I am who I have always been. Knowing I was born Trans was a freedom I had to grow into. And I wanted other Trans Humans to feel the same emancipation.

"What do you need me to do?" I wrote back.

It turns out their parent was transitioning from a father figure to a mother figure, and because they had lived presenting male for almost seventy years, the family was confused and angry and envious and beside themselves with guilt and shame. To the average family, Trans folk are an anomaly at best, and at worst, we are destroyers of normalcy. We both defy and challenge the American idea of decency. Faith and I spoke intermittently. I even sent her parent a few messages. After a while, it tapered off and I assumed they had gone back to family life and that their newly found "mom" was beginning to find their way. I tried my best to instill pride in Mom and self-reflection in the kids. I am speaking as if this were easy for everyone, and of course it wasn't. I knew it wasn't. No transition is. But my goal was to free Trans people from absorbing and holding on to other people's shame.

I had settled into my life of teaching at CSULB and intermittent auditioning. My future was set. I hoped to work occasionally in Hollywood and onstage, but primarily I would teach. I would retire at CSULB and live my life fully in my classroom with my students and revel in the artistic language we were all creating.

But . . . something's always close by to fuck things up.

~

Hey, Alex. It's Faith again. I just wanted to ask if you were interested in being involved in an idea Joey and I had. We are going to turn our family into a TV show, and we were wondering if you had

379

any interest in maybe auditioning for it, if it ever happens. I know this is weird. Sorry again. Love you. Faith.

TV show. Lord. How many times . . . that's ridic . . . Nobody's going to make a TV show out of . . . oh, Soloways . . . I rolled my eyes, and wrote back, "Absolutely! Let me know when and if! I'll be there."

~

I sat in the overstuffed hallway, keeping to myself and in complete awe of the number of Trans actresses who surrounded me. I felt like Rip Van Winkle waking from that one-hundred-year nap. When did this change? Where had I been? What had happened while I was gone? It was as if while I'd been studying and teaching in academia, a dam had broken, and Trans humans poured out of a hidden crack into the laps of the Hollywood bigwigs.

A glorious tall blond woman sat next to me. Her smile was huge and her demeanor was calm.

"I . . . You here for the audition?"

To be honest, I wasn't completely positive that she was Trans. In fact, there were many women milling around I was uncertain about. Usually when that's true, I say nothing, but here I was thrilled to be around so many of my family.

I hadn't auditioned since I told Billy I was done. This was the first one in almost three years, and because it was for the Soloways, whom I knew, and because I already had a full-time teaching position at CSULB, which I truly loved, and because I graduated not too long ago with a master's degree and was an assistant professor, this particular audition held little weight. It wasn't that it didn't matter. It did. Or that I didn't want to do well. I did. But . . . I wasn't desperate. Our rent didn't

depend on this job. My career wasn't teetering on the edge of anything. The script was wonderful, the part was really well written, and the premise of the show was not only insightful, it seemed universal. But it was being produced by Amazon.

You know . . . the place that sells books.

"I am. I'm so excited. So nervous. Fuck, girl. This is so great, don't you think?" the blond said, breathing heavily and eyes wide.

"Yes. Yeah. Sure. Yes . . . it is exciting and I'm . . . Yes, this is great." I couldn't bring myself to lie about my nervousness, and I didn't want to take any of her joyful excitement away, so I stammered a little and smiled.

One by one we were called into the small room off to the left, and the circle of women got smaller and smaller. A young man with a neat goatee walked up to me, clipboard in hand, and asked if I was ready. He led me down a hallway and into a small room with no windows, decorated with a couch and a chair. On the couch sat Joey and Faith. You could sense the family in them. Their closeness. Their smiles were the same. Faith was lighter in the air. She seemed to be the dreamer— Joey the realist. The script combined Faith's sense of whimsy with Joey's dark humor and biting realism. The Soloways had made a name for themselves in Chicago as edgy theater artists, and as they crept under the radar into Hollywood with this semiautobiographical Transgender story told through the lens of their Jewish heritage and produced by the place that sells books, they seemed to be doubling down on that reputation and then some.

"Alex!" Faith's face lit up. Her smile widened and her hands flailed.

We held each other as Joey stood, and the three of us made a sort of hug sandwich.

Off in the corner, sitting quietly in the one chair in the room, was a man I recognized immediately from almost every TV show I had ever seen. Most notably, and don't ask me why, from the 1970s blockbuster

smash-a-roo farcical bedroom comedy *Three's Company* and its companion piece *The Ropers*. I couldn't believe I was standing in the room with this icon. It was then I began to want to throw up.

"Hi," he said, flashing that toothy smile.

"This is Jeffrey Tambor. Jeffrey, this is Alexandra Billings," Joey said as they and Faith sat back on the couch, intertwined and comfy.

"I've heard a lot about you," Jeffrey said, lying through his teeth.

"You did not."

"You're right, I was trying to make you feel better. Did it work?" he asked, leaning forward.

"It just made me want to poop."

"I've been pooping since you walked in."

"Was it because of me?"

"At my age, I poop when I can, not when it's convenient."

We both guffawed.

And from that moment on, Jeffrey and I batted one-liners across the table at one another, finding each other mutually hilarious. We fit together perfectly from the first mention of poop, and it was clear before we read one word of the text that our chemistry wasn't something you could fabricate. It wasn't something on the page. It was something divine and powerful, and when one feels this kind of synergy, when you're in the middle of it, it is both shocking and beautiful.

Jeffrey and I had been around long enough to understand this and realize how precious it was. He possessed an outright ease in his acting, and his ability to joke his way out of any situation was unmatched. He had large hands and long legs and seemed to lumber his way along the planet. He wasn't without grace, but there was a definite, deliberate concentration to his footwork. This step here, then that step there, then one more step over here. He planned and he thought and he analyzed and yet, the most miraculous and mind-numbing thing I witnessed was his apparently effortless transformation into Maura Pfefferman.

"Are you both ready? Because we could just write this stuff down and put it in the show . . . or we could actually do the script," Joey interrupted, laughing.

"Is that a threat or a promise?" Jeffrey shot back.

I picked up my pages and stood back from him, still smiling, still in the joy and silliness of our repartee. His shape moved to the left, just a touch. He sat up. It wasn't stiff or rigid or uncomfortable. His spine simply seemed to lengthen, and his head reached upward. He held the script between his fingers, and his eyes lowered a bit. Then he gestured, his hand moving as if he were fanning his face over a slow-boiling pot. His voice remained the same; there was no artificial adjustment, no fake register. He simply spoke. Because Maura was finding out who she was, so was Jeffrey, and his voice reflected this exploration. It came from a place of truth and curiosity—trying something on. Not a replacement, but a redesign. His Maura expressed a newness that was balanced with a profound sense of personal history.

And at that moment, I was looking straight through Jeffrey and into the soul of Maura.

I had never, in all the years I had been in the theater, experienced anything like this. He wasn't putting on a character, he was releasing a truth. Something in him knew this human, and that was enough to manifest the experience of a person in some kind of transition. It was remarkable. I couldn't speak.

"Stop acting, Alex. You don't have to do that." Joanne's words twisted around me.

I spoke to Maura, which was different from speaking to Jeffrey. I answered her. I helped her. I tried to not push or make something happen. I was with her and I was beside her and I loved her. I loved her because I knew her. I had known her for years and years. I wasn't speaking to someone while they held on to their prosthetic genitals, or spoke in a phony upper register, or gesticulated while they poured tea

and whispered in a bad Marilyn Monroe accent into the ear of their female lover. I was with Maura. It was simple. And . . . it felt like home.

I missed Honey. I missed her and I missed Ginger and Leslie and Daphne, and I missed Chili and Kelly. And there sat Maura—reminding me. Holding me. Loving me and keeping me safe. I had forgotten I was auditioning, and quite frankly, I no longer cared.

I got the role.

"Now if you got a TV show, tenure would be in the bag."

I remembered Joanne smiling as she waved her Glinda wand over my unsuspecting head. She walked out of my office, and I remember walking across the hall to the restroom and seeing my reflection in the mirror above the sink. Fifty-two years old. Brown. Weird eyes and built like ET—square, with sharp corners. Like a Chiclet. Trans. HIV positive. And really, only peripherally interested in getting shoved around Hollywood again, shuffling from hospital to hospital, all the while struggling to get famous when getting famous seemed like a waste of time. A TV show? That was ridiculous. I wanted to teach. I loved teaching. I wanted to be with my students and study more, and practice more, and learn more, and be in the classroom with them more. Getting cast on a TV show was absolutely ridiculous.

Until it happened.

~

Driving through the gates of Paramount studios is surreal, but driving through the gates of Paramount studios when you actually work there is something else entirely. The very first morning I showed up for work, I waved at the human in the booth, with his blue shirt and white striped name tag, and crowed, "Hawkeye! Hello!" and drove off into the pretend painted sunset that loomed over the lot.

When I looked back, he was waving and smiling, either out of recognition of the Norma Desmond quote, or out of pity because I was completely nuts.

When I was hired initially, I was not a regular cast member. I was a guest star, which basically meant less money and less time in the central story. The show was never intended to be about the Trans people in it—the show was always about the Pfeffermans. It was a story about a Jewish family and their navigation through life's transitions. It just so happened that the patriarch was slowly moving toward becoming the matriarch. As the Transgender life was never at the heart of the story, there was never a need to put me in the middle. Part of me knew that, and of course, the other part of me did not.

When *Transparent* premiered in 2014, casting Jeffrey was not a major stumbling block. Television was still a barren wasteland when it came to Trans leads, and so the fact that the story was being told at all was revolutionary. All of us understood why Jeffrey got this role—we understood and accepted it. In fact, I celebrated it. I reveled in his freakish ability to find Maura and reveal this Trans human in a way that was always about her humanity, her wit, her insecurity, and her powerful movement forward into her own identity. The stories were fantastic, but the gift of Maura Pfefferman would not have been fully realized without the gift of Jeffrey Tambor. I knew that from the very first poop joke.

~

I sat in the big, comfy chair amidst my character, Davina's, things. I was in her house, among her throw pillows and her talismans, her perfumes, and her large, overstuffed couch. I had walked around the set and put my hands on pieces of art and clothing. In TV land you have very little time to do much of anything. There are people rushing around, handing people things, dressing people, combing hair, fixing

lights, straightening plants, and placing tea bags and pen caps in very specific places. But there was something different here. People weren't running. No one was out of breath, and no one was sweating. People were breathing deeply and laughing.

I had met the cast a week or so prior at the table read, where everyone gathers around a large table and reads the words of the script for the very first time. Jeffrey and I had chatted for a few minutes. Joey, Faith, and I hugged, looked around, and kept pinching each other that this was actually happening. It was one of the biggest and most genuine hugs I'd received in years. Amy Landecker came flying around the corner and held me close, whispering and half weeping with joy.

"I can't believe this! I can't believe it!" she murmured, holding on tight and breathing into my neck.

My breath released, and I allowed myself to be held. Really held.

Amy was playing Sarah Pfefferman, the daughter of Maura/Mort. Sarah was a neurotic, misunderstood, beautifully tragic, hilarious mess of a mother. Amy's deft and magical portrayal of this particular sister was a mirror for me, and one of the great dark comic characters that the writers and Joey had created. I was shaking and riddled with fear and self-doubt that first day, and Amy's recognition of me was the first time since I'd arrived in Hollywood that I actually felt seen.

"God, I'm glad you're here," I breathed.

"Same. Same."

We held on to each other, I took a million and six pictures that I immediately posted to every social media account I had, and we continued to hug and weep.

"Do you believe this? I can't believe this!" she mouthed.

"No. I cannot believe this. It's insane and I'm still not sure why they cast me. I keep waiting for Joey to call and tell me they made a mistake."

"They're not going to do that, Alex. They're lucky to have you."

They were? They were?

"I don't know what to do with that, Amy."

"You don't have to do shit with it. I'm just so freaking happy you're here!"

~

Joey walked on set, and most everyone turned. I stood up from my comfy chair and faced them. They had a small set of earphones around their neck, and they were dressed a little like Annie Hall—a collared shirt, baggy jeans, and mussed hair. Their face was glowing. They were diminutive in physical size, but the rest of them took up the entire soundstage.

"Good morning, everyone."

Everyone smiled, said good morning, and stood waiting with eager anticipation. I'd never been on a set where there was so much time to be filled. I kept thinking the "hurry the fuck up, dammit" was right around the corner. But it never came.

"We're gonna shoot this thing, and it's gonna be great. I have a feeling it's gonna go great . . . so . . . good morning, Alex."

"Hey, Joey. Good morning."

"You okay? Do you need anything?" they asked softly.

"Uh . . . nope. No. No. I need nothing. I don't need a thing, not a darn thing."

If I need something, I'll probably get fired. It's the needy ones that get fired first.

As Joey spoke, their tone filled the space, and as riddled with fear and self-doubt as I was, something soothing came over me, and I sat back down in my big, comfy chair and listened as they spoke about the day, what it was going to look like, how it might feel, and they explained that the script was merely a foundation. We did not need to feel constrained by it. It was our blueprint, but not our gospel. We were

all finding our way through it together and it was brand new. There was no other television show that had a Trans character as the lead. It simply didn't exist. So . . . we made stuff up.

I looked around. There were Trans faces, nonbinary faces, cis faces, and feminine/masculine/both faces, and all of us were joined together on the soundstage. I kept looking around, face after face, and the endless histories and constant stories from otherized tribal ancestors spoke loudly as we prepared ourselves to make our little TV show for the place that sells books. I had never dreamed I'd be around this many Trans people. I had never dreamed we'd be creating something together and that we'd tell it through the lens of the Pfefferman folk. I had never dreamed that I'd be lucky enough, at fifty-two years old, after walking the streets and living behind dumpsters, getting thrown in jail and marrying my best friend, waging war against the white, male machine, almost dying and begging God to push me off my balcony, that I'd be lucky enough to bear witness to this. I felt as if I had finally reached Oz.

Transparent—*series finale billboard in Times Square*

I was there, cuddled in a blanket I had found in Davina's bedroom—curled up in a comfy chair.

"And remember, everyone, before we start, usually on a set you hear we have to hurry up, we have to get this finished, let's go, let's go, let's go . . . but think of this . . . this is *Transparent*." Joey moved closer to us, people surrounding them, holding on, clutching and breathing together . . . "This is the story of family—chosen and blood. And instead of reminding everyone here that there's not enough time, or that we're running out of money, or that we're losing the light, let's play it like this: there's more than enough time, we have more than enough money, and *you* are the light."

We all looked at each other, and in that moment, I felt every young Trans person in that circle. We had never heard anything like that before. No one had given us permission like that. This was a first, and we all wanted to see each other's faces while we remembered it.

Joey stood in the center of us.

"Okay. Let's go."

~

I tried this and I tried that, with visions of me at Club Victoria, in my Capezios and leg warmers, leaning back in my chair waiting to be doused by a bucket of stale water. And I watched Maura walk around my house talking about her family and her transition and her loss and her love for her wife and her children. I thought how neurotic these kids were and that Maura really needed me. I knew that. As I sat in that chair, I knew she needed me, and I knew I needed to stake my claim to the central part of this story. Maura was alone in her Transness, and just as I had needed my community in order to be found, so did she. The script was a starting place and at times we spoke exactly what was written, but Joey also let us discover what was true in the moment.

Spontaneity and honest responsiveness were what I was teaching, so my work became my joy as I shifted from what I was saying in the classroom as a teacher to being on the set as an actor. Some things worked, and some things crashed and burned, but it was all thrilling and honest and free.

~

Maura sat at my dressing table trying on sunglasses and necklaces when Joey asked for a little something else.

"Alex . . . I wonder if you could fill this moment here. Just fill it with something," they whispered to me between takes.

I sat in the chair, and I manifested an image of Ginger. Her eyes and her smile and her hands and the way she hiccupped a little when she laughed too hard. And I felt her, and I remembered her, and I could hear her voice. It had been so long since I heard her, the sound of her made me jump as I sat in the chair and listened to Maura. And then I paid attention to Maura. I received her, and instead of pitying her, I needed her to hold me—to be with me and to see me clearly. I also needed her to get her goddamn hands off my favorite pair of sunglasses!

"You know, it's going to be all right, girl. You know that, don't you? You're doing the best you can," I stammered. Joey smiled, and they moved on to the next setup.

Jeffrey remained in the chair as he let go of Maura. His shape changed, his legs took up more space, his hands fell to his side, and his head drooped a little. As they prepared for the next shot, Jeffrey and I chatted about teaching—what it was like to be in front of students and how we felt about acting. I told him about CSULB, and he told me about *Three's Company* . . . because I asked . . . and as we spoke, one of the hair crew came by with a brush in her hand. She stood in front of Jeffrey and asked if she could fix the back of the Maura wig.

"Jesus CHRIST, could you get the hell out of my way? What the . . . c'mon! Move! Can someone get her out of my *fucking way*!" he bellowed at the top of his voice. With no warning and out of nowhere came this part of him that shot through the soul of everyone on set. People kept moving. People kept hanging things and pushing things and straightening up, as if absolutely nothing had happened.

I sat. Paralyzed. I couldn't move. Images flashed before my eyes.

Bobby and Donny and the many men who had wanted to fuck me until I screamed "No," and then they had wanted to hit me. Big, sharp blades slicing into my skin and peeling it off, layer by layer and screeching like bare knuckles on a chalkboard. "Bitch. Pig. Fucker. Stupid whore." There was blood everywhere. I was fileted and left panting and gasping among the beatings and the rapes. Whoosh. Boom. Whoosh. Whoosh. Jeffrey's voice paralyzed my insides. I stared at him, and I said nothing. The woman with the brush smiled and left—she snuck off the fake porch, and the hive of activity continued.

"You know my daughter is graduating soon, and I think she's smarter than the whole family put together," he said with a gleam, turning to me and putting his hand out.

"Well. She might be. I don't know. You'll have to take that up with her. Depends on where she's studying," I burbled back.

"She's at Yale."

"Then yes, she's smarter than the whole family, Jeffrey."

My head rattled. I moved my little finger just to make sure all of me wasn't dead.

Hours later, as I readied myself to go home, I sat in my trailer and began taking off my third costume of the day and breathed a sigh of relief. I made it. I made it through an entire day. I had many more scheduled, but I made it and no one died. Almost no one. For me, that counted as a success. The explosion did not reoccur that day. Probably just a fluke. Something that happened because he was tired. That's right.

That's it—he was tired and overworked. He was on edge and nervous. Actors. Honestly. I sat on the edge of the couch and remembered where I was, in the middle of Paramount studios and helping, in whatever way I could, to tell this story. I very intentionally chose to stay in gratitude.

Maybe I should have said something. Come to her aid. Spoken to Joey. Reached out to the other Trans folk. If I was intimidated, were they frightened too? But it wasn't my place. I wasn't the star—I was not a regular, and these people were grown-ups. Don't pretend you know everything, Alex. That's your ego. You have a problem with your ego. Work on this. Stay out of it. Stop playing God. It wasn't my place . . . and this gig. I didn't want to lose it; I loved this gig. I loved these humans, and he was probably just really tired.

The next time I worked was a week or two later. I drove past Hawkeye, and this time as I drove off, I heard from behind me, in a faint but measured tone, "Great to see you again, Miss Desmond!"

I parked in my usual spot, bounced into the makeup trailer, greeted the few cast members there, hung on tightly to Amy, as was our morning ritual, and sat myself down in the chair. Seven a.m. is an ungodly time for me, so idle chitchat was always difficult, but I did my best. They sat me next to Jeffrey, but this morning his chair was empty. He wasn't called until later in the day.

"Hey, Laura. Where's the hair girl?" I asked, eyes half open.

Laura was one of the many humans with a clipboard who came in and out of the trailer trying to keep us all on schedule.

"Oh. She's gone. She'll be back soon. How's everyone doing on time here?"

People nodded and made the okay sign . . .

She's gone? She was only here about a week. Where'd she go?

I never saw the girl with the hairbrush again. She never did come back. I wondered what had happened to her and I wondered where she had gone. But I said nothing. As I stood outside the trailer in my

makeup robe, Jeffrey's guttural attack echoed in my chest. I saw her face and I remembered her moving out of the lights and off the porch. She seemed to have been erased. This one's gone. Call another one. That was the last anyone saw of her—the girl with the brush. I didn't even take the time to get her name. I did nothing. I said nothing.

I went back to my trailer and got dressed for my scene. It was almost time for Joey to speak to the cast and I didn't want to miss that.

"There's plenty of time, we have all the money in the world, and you are the light . . ."

The Celebrations

I sat in my canary-yellow dress with the long train and the fitted skirt, trying to lie a bit sideways so it wouldn't wrinkle before I got out of the car. Chrisanne, dressed in her sleek black-and-white suit and fabulous new designer sneakers, held my hand, and occasionally we'd smile and kiss each other. Climbing out of a limo holding the hand of your wife of over twenty years and walking onto a red carpet when you're inches away from Glenn Close or Tom Hanks or Whoopi Goldberg is surreal, and no matter how many times it happened, I never got used to it.

"Did you get to speak to Julia?"

"I didn't get a chance . . . I was buffet-ing with Cher when I bumped into Viola on the way to Charo who was cocktailing with Johnny who was smiling at Elton who was dressed like Cher!"

"That's a weird party."

These amazing moments in these glamorous rooms with these insanely gifted artists would happen, and Chrisanne and I would sit and applaud and watch Jeffrey and Joey collect awards, and we'd eat fabulous food, and people would snap pictures, and I just couldn't stop

seeing Scott—Scott on the edge of his bed with a pad and a pencil getting ready to keep score, his eyes wide, and Mimi right next to him. They'd battle about who was going to take home the gold. They'd eat and laugh and pick apart performances, and Scott got better and better at being specific.

"He's really good," he'd say.

"But why? What exactly makes him good?" she'd ask.

"Well . . . he's funny," he'd answer.

"But what exactly does that mean? I mean, is he funnier than Lucy?" she'd challenge sternly.

"No one's funnier than Lucy," he'd snap back.

"So why doesn't she constantly win? Why doesn't she always win if no one is funnier? There has to be something else going on. Doesn't there?" she'd press.

And he'd think and eat and sit on the bed and write things down and defend his positions, and awards shows became a time for the two of them to be together—for the two of them to forget why they were so very mad at each other so very often.

I sat, careful of the yellow dress and long train and the red, red salsa, eating and sipping and laughing. I was walking around that first Emmy Awards ceremony in a fabulous gown designed by my pal Megan Knowles, who was a master's student at CSULB. After the ceremony, we stayed up dancing at the *Vogue* party and the *Variety* bash, dishing the dirt with Marcia Clark and watching Lady Gaga.

It was beautiful, and it was like leading a life in my own reflection. I was going through the looking glass, I was arriving in Oz, but as it went on, I became less and less sure about what was real and what was not. What was the dream and what was the ball? Who was Dorothy and where was Oz?

~

"I love it, but I've done it, sweetie, so I'm not going anymore," Chrisanne announced one year after our first Emmy ride.

"You don't want to go to the Emmys anymore?" I was appalled . . . and jealous.

"If you really want me to go, I'll go. But no. I don't want to go."

My wife wanted to be in her PJs watching the cats and reading about Gandhi.

I married this human. This should not have been a surprise.

"I want to do everything once is what I mean. And I've done it . . . once."

So there I sat, after season two was nominated in numerous categories, without my wife, who was usually the famous-person finder. I was rudderless, schmoozing at a table with Jeffrey and Judith, across from Audra and next to Jeff Goldblum, who was chatting with Oprah, who was leaning over some guy's salad, when from the center of the room came a glow—a beam of golden fairy dust that shot up into the sky and rained down gently on all of us.

It was The Streep.

I hadn't seen her on the red carpet, and I didn't see her enter the room. I only saw her appear before us, at the center table in a white gown, hair piled high and beaming. She was smaller than I had imagined and more fabulous than I could bear. She greeted everyone. She stood and shook hands with everyone who came toward her and saw them clearly and smiled and threw her head back and laughed and giggled and leaned in, and every single human who came into her circle, she took in. This wasn't Hollywood bullshit. This was an actor in the middle of her gratitude extending a hand to her pals and her colleagues. My eyes were glued to her, and I vowed I wasn't going to leave until I spoke to her. This might be my only chance. This could all end tomorrow. I turned to Amy.

"There's Meryl Goddamn Streep," I said, panting, barely able to breathe.

She turned to the center table.

"Wow. You know . . . Jeffrey probably knows her. You want me to nudge him and get him to introduce you?"

But I wanted this to be mine.

"No. Thanks, Amy . . . no. I'm gonna do this alone. I'm gonna make this happen."

I'm not sure why I was so determined or what was churning in me to do this.

During one of the commercials, as the lights flickered on, I pushed my dessert over to the side, excused myself from the table, and made my way through the crush of famous people who were heading toward the queen. My heart beat every four or five minutes, and I slushed through the crowd as the time ticked by. I was living the Viewpoints. I sideswiped Glenn and elbowed aside Jeff Bridges, threw a slow right hook to Jason Bateman, and mowed over either a slew of Culkins or the Olsen twins . . .

And there, standing in her white gown draped over her left shoulder, was Streep, smiling gently and speaking to some woman in a hat. I stood, a bundle of half-injured celebrities behind me, and palmed my phone.

They spoke. Streep smiled. She focused on the woman in the hat, stayed with her, and I felt time going by. The commercial breaks only last a few minutes. This was it. I was standing in the receiving line, and I wasn't about to miss my opportunity.

The woman with the hat left. I walked up to Meryl.

"Hi. You're Meryl Streep. My God. Meryl . . . well . . . I just want to tell you how much I admire your work and how special you are to me, and I just want you to know I think your ability to speak clearly and honestly about the human experience is a miracle. I just want to thank you and tell you that."

I could barely breathe.

"I love your show," she said in that famous half-eyed whisper.

"Huh?"

"It's wonderful. I love your work. And I just want to thank *you* . . . and tell *you* that."

Meryl came a little closer to me and took my hand. She stood with me and held on to me. I cannot tell you how it happened, but she began to tell me a story about a Transgender teacher she had met many years ago, when the danger was real. She confessed that she wasn't acquainted with many other Trans humans, but that this teacher was one of her guides and one of her heroes. She had taught The Streep all the words to "The Star-Spangled Banner," and Streep had never forgotten them.

"Why 'The Star-Spangled Banner'?" I asked.

"I . . . don't know," she answered slowly. "But it never left me."

A teacher. Her teacher. I remembered class. I saw my students. I imagined the circle.

I asked if I could take a selfie, and I took about four hundred, and we laughed, and as she held on to me one last time, I tried to picture the face of this teacher. I missed my students.

"Thanks," Streep said out of nowhere.

The Streep line was getting longer as the lights began to flash.

I couldn't tell you if we won that night or even why we were there. Meryl and her teacher—that moment shook me. But I can tell you I understood why Chrisanne was left at home with the cats. I needed to do this alone.

The Unexpected Journey

Pootie,

How are things going? How are you feeling? I heard you were back in the hospital for a while. How's the new kidney? The pics of you smiling and writing from

your bed are pretty great, love. But I want to know how you're really doing. I'm not the public.

Also . . . stop telling me how much your organs hate you. That's actually not a thing. Your organs don't have feelings, and even if they did have feelings, since they belong to you, they probably keep all their feelings inside and then randomly take them out on the rest of the world by writing the truth about them all, pissing them off, waking them up, and then creating a revolution that begets a worldwide movement. So, don't start with me. You're going to be around for a long, long fucking time.

Everything's weird. You keep asking me how things are, and the only thing I can say is that everything's far weirder than I ever thought it would be. My life's odd and makes no sense. I filmed an episode of *How to Get Away with Murder*, that show with Viola Davis. She was amazing and so kind and really direct. I'm learning so much working with these artists—watching how they behave with other humans on set. If something isn't right, there isn't any screaming or shouting or throwing of props. Viola was calm and serene. I could see she was pooped, but who wouldn't be? To be on set with another artist who's been marginalized by the white patriarchal machine in Hollywood was just mind-boggling. She cared so deeply about everyone on set.

We were sitting between takes, and Viola and I started to talk about acting. I brought up Steppenwolf . . . I do that when I want to name-drop and I don't have to drop any actual names. Her eyes got big and she asked about Jeff Perry (cuz

everyone loves Jeff Perry . . . which reminds me, the two of you have to meet . . . that matters to me . . .). She said she was genuinely happy I was there, and I actually believed it. I know you think everyone is full of shit, and probably you and Chrisanne are right, but I don't. I don't think that's true, and it's definitely not true of Viola.

We did a scene where I fall apart a bit, and she holds me and takes care of me, and it wasn't going well. I asked her what to do, and she said, "Don't try so hard. In fact, do one where you don't try at all. Look at me. Confess. Just tell me what you did." It was like the greatest master class I ever had. I don't know if I executed it well or not, but it was like lying in the hands of Uta.

I also did an episode of *Goliath*, Billy Bob Thornton's new gig. I think he's won twenty-five Emmys or something. It's really good. Odd. Funny. Quirky and super dark. All those things you love. I know you abhor most TV things, but I think you'd like this. And here's what I loved most . . . I'm not a murderer. I'm not murdered, and I don't help someone murder anyone. I'm a judge. They actually had it cast, and the actress playing the role wasn't working out. Billy, my manager (someone else you need to meet . . . cuz he matters as well . . .), called and said, "They want you for this judge role on *Goliath*. Billy Bob knows your work and asked for you." And I got all excited and my ego got a big burst of energy and I thought I was really something for a minute and a half, and then he said, "Because she wasn't bitchy enough and they

needed someone bitchy and Billy Bob suggested you. Cuz you're pretty bitchy."

My nasty-ass attitude is finally paying off.

It's about time.

Freaking white-washed, male-infested, hetero-cis-wussie-assed Hollyweird.

But Pootie, there's this other thing that's happening, and I just wanted to write to you about it because I don't know what to do with it. *Transparent* is changing my life. It's opening portals I never knew existed, and it's presenting chances that are really fucking with my brain. It's not that I don't think I'm good enough or that I don't think I deserve things . . . or maybe It's exactly that. Whatever the psychosis, the more sober I get, the more uncomfortable I feel. My skin is starting to hurt. Our show won a Peabody Award, GLAAD honored us, the Human Rights Campaign threw a dinner specifically for me and gave me a shiny thing and actually thanked me. And, although all these things are truly surreal, I don't seem to be able to believe them. I know they're happening because I'm buying the dresses, and Chrisanne and I are flying all over the place, and we're able to take grown-up trips now . . . to Israel and Paris and Rome, and it's because of this thing that's happening. But Larry . . . when the community begins to give back to us, something shifts in me.

I don't know what to do with it.

Just last month the entire cast was invited to the White House.

We all hoped that the Obamas would be out gardening or maybe casually taking the dogs for a walk,

or that he might be signing some new law about Trans people into the books, but no such luck. However, and this is the thing I am really writing about: there is a panel of Trans artists that is the first of its kind to be held under any American presidency in the history of our country, and Joey asked if I would moderate it.

I remember shaking to the bone and thinking I will most likely sit there and pee quietly into a cup. That I won't be able to function. That the moment will be lost and shoved into a drawer and forgotten. I will be a failure. I know I will be a failure. It is other people who are fooled, not me. I don't think I can do this. You see, it's the celebrations I can't seem to get used to. I've gone through all this therapy and counseling and sober living, and I surround myself with humans who are far smarter than I am, and my best friend, Honey, is a constant source of light, and my wife is the most trusted voice I have, and still, there's something moving in me, and it's pushing me farther and farther away from whatever it is I'm supposed to be feeling.

Does our little show deserve this much stuff?

Do I?

I'm sorry I rambled. I wanted to catch you up, and we haven't spoken in I don't know how long. I miss you. I miss hearing you. The world is so different now, isn't it? Do you ever think about that? The amount of sacred dirt we shoveled onto the faces of our friends and family and the many times we stood on street corners screaming over sirens and straight people with red veins popping out of their necks, demanding equality. And you know, for us it's still

happening. And I know you and I go back and forth about this, but it's happening in a way that it isn't happening to the gays. Trans women are under attack. It's 2016 and we're still being murdered and hunted and eradicated from most every conversation. We are here and we are Americans and yet, even now, even as far as we've come, we're still a fetish and we're still a choice. If only I could stop doing all this, most of my problems would go away. I was born a man. Why can't I be a man? We are reaching a breaking point. I can feel it. This isn't a fad—this is a life path and I'll be goddamned if I'm going to bury my community all over again just because some scattered groups of simple-minded, ignorant religious zealots hate my fashion sense. I'm sick and tired of not getting invited to the party. If there's no room at these tables for us, we need to bring our own tables.

Anyway . . . that's what's happening.

My classes are saving my sanity. *Transparent* is shifting too. Things are getting odd, but that's a whole other email. I guess I just need a lift from you. I know philosophy isn't your forte, so I'll just ask a question:

I don't want to moderate this panel. But I do. Does that make me a coward?

I love you. Watch one of my shows, please, I want to know what you think. And stop blaming your organs for shit they didn't do. It's not their fault.

Alex

~

Dear Mrs. P,

No.

It does not make you a coward. It makes you human. Now shut up and go do the thing you were meant to do.

Love,

L

The Unhappy Endings

Trace's spirit was the first thing I noticed. I was sitting in a booth in our pretend bar, and we were filming a scene in which Trace, Maura, and I were talking about dating and being Trans. Trace is from a younger generation than I am, so we had three different representations of Trans life in our pretend world. Her skin shone under the lights, and her great belly laugh filled my heart.

"You know, Alex, it's *The Pfeffermans*. I mean, that's it. That's the show. It's never going to be about the Trans community," Trace would argue over the phone.

"I know. I do know that."

"So, we have to go in there and ask to be represented."

Her warrior-like spirit ignited a fierce calling in me. She was right. And we did. The writers took us in, and heard us, and wrote for us as best they could. But Trace was right—this was not a show about the Trans experience. It was a show about this family. We needed to know and accept this and help tell the story as best we could. So we supported, and the writers gave us room.

And one afternoon we shot the scene where we talked about our Trans vernacular and had a great time going back and forth saying, "Yaaas

queen." There was Maura, dressed in her muumuu, and Trace, just waking up with her mussed hair and her T-shirt and shorty PJs, and me in my robe with my Jerry Lewis hairdo, which I loved. Jeffrey and I were constantly looking for moments when we could sit down. The less we had to move, the more we liked it.

"Can we do this scene by the pool?" he asked randomly.

"It's a dream sequence, Jeffrey. You're asleep," the DP reminded him.

"What's your point?"

At the table as we shot take after take, speaking our "yaaas queens" to each other, for each other, and with each other, we laughed and did it again and again, and drank secret coffees hidden around set. Then Jeffrey patted Trace's backside and made an offhanded remark about my breasts.

I watched. And I said nothing. I did nothing.

~

About four or five years ago, someone sent me a video of a woman playing the piano and singing an original song about hope, delight, and the celebratory newness of life. I was mesmerized. I played it over and over and over, learned the lyrics, and wanted desperately to sing it. I searched for her and found her on social media. She gave her name to us all—"Our Lady J." This classically trained pianist with an ability to heal and lead the way in the Trans revolution became my guide. Our . . . Our Lady J. As a writer on the series, she was part of that tight inner *Transparent* circle, and this blond spiritual human became my friend, my confidante, and my daughter. Her delightful sense of play and her deep musical life force rekindled the joy I had found in the deep recesses of rehearsal and in my dad's ability to dream big. She and I joined together, and when I went in, with Trace leading the way, to ask for Davina's very first nude scene, Lady J was one of the first writers

to say yes. She understood me and Davina because she wrote out of her own experiences as a human with HIV. She wrote from her soul as a Trans woman searching for love.

I was taken care of that day. I was naked, and the crew and the writers and Ray Abruzzo, who played my boyfriend, Sal, all had me in their hearts and in their artistic pockets. Joey and the writers came up with the idea of having Davina naked because she had just finished showering, and she and Sal were alone in their bedroom arguing about sex and love and about their time together, so being naked made sense. It wasn't about my genitals. It was about a relationship and what it is like to be in a particular body at a particular age, living with HIV, and being with a man. Ray's deft ability to feed kindness and a soulful dignity into every moment we fought was everything I needed. And so, lying on the bed naked and turning over felt powerful and perfectly normal.

And I saw Michelle with her needle full of silicone, and I felt my hips plump up and my breasts enlarge and the drops of silicone dribble down my armpits. I saw the ceiling of the motel we had been in, with its lobby filled with young Trans women, all waiting for their illegal foray into a new body and new reflection. I turned over as the camera panned down, and the lumps of my hips and on my ass and through my legs were magnified. And my penis fell to one side, I turned back over again, and Ray climbed on top of me. I threw him off and the scene continued as we tried to repair the relationship we had almost destroyed. Being a Trans woman feeling body shame as I lay naked, while Davina felt body shame as *she* lay naked, was an experience I'll never forget. Art and life fused. There was no distinction. I knew it was possible. I had been teaching it . . . and now, I was living it. And as I turned over and I shoved this Cis man off my naked body, I knew this moment would live on film forever, and my life began to snap and unravel and become exposed to the searing sun of both my past and what lay ahead.

Art. Life.

"Are you okay?" Lady J asked.

"I am. What you wrote was beautiful. Really perfect," I answered.

Zackary Drucker, one of the executive producers and a filmmaker herself, held me together. She was almost twenty years younger than I was and came from a Trans community that believed in change in a way that exuded hope and power. Because of all we had endured, my generation, with a few shining beacons of courage, seemed tainted by time. I loved these younger Trans folks. They were buoyant and angry and smart, and Zackary radiated kindness in a way I truly needed. I specifically asked if she could be on set for this scene, and she readily agreed. With her blond hair pulled back and her direct and peaceful demeanor, she came by after a take, helped cover me up, and held my hand.

"Anything you need, Diva?" she inquired, half smiling.

"I don't. No . . . I love you . . ." I replied almost sleepily.

"I love you. You're doing great. It's going great."

And it *was* going great. Just me and Ray and a few of the crew. The Trans humans on set held me, and I felt them with me, surrounding me, and begging me to speak. But I immersed myself in silence. I needed to believe that I was fine. That it was all going well. And I said nothing.

I stood by and said absolutely nothing.

~

There was the time when the cast was at a screening at a fancy movie theater in Hollywood. There was food and music, and people were drinking and dressed up, and the cast was dispersed throughout the party. Amy over here, Joey and Faith over there, Trace at one end of the room, and Our Lady J at the other. Everyone beaming and shiny and smelling great. I wandered up to Jeffrey. I was without my wife at this particular function, and as I leaned in to say hello amidst the many other humans crowding us and pushing us toward opposing barstools,

he grabbed me and pulled me toward him. It was forceful and it was uncomfortable.

And I said nothing.

~

We sat in the pretend downstairs bedroom. Davina had lost every-thing—her boyfriend, her money, and her job—so Maura gives her the downstairs of her house to stay in for as long as she likes. Davina (and I) were ingratiating ourselves into the Pfefferman family, and conse-quently our stories began to explore more of Trans experience alongside the familial one. Joey and the writers began to evolve, and the longer *Transparent* ran, the deeper into the movement we found ourselves. More and more cisgender actors were coming under fire for playing Transgender characters, and despite the massive silence I had imposed on myself, the larger and louder voice of our community pulsated and expanded. I wanted us to tell our stories. I wanted more Transness, and I wanted more power. I was in a show where this genius of an actor was giving the performance of his career and helping so many Trans Humans simply by speaking up at awards shows and by giving Maura a soul and a depth of character. But for me, time after time, interview after interview, I'd wrestle with my own conscience.

"How do you feel about Jeffrey Tambor playing a Trans character?"

"Well . . . he was cast at a time when Trans people had no repre-sentation. Literally nothing. *Transparent* needed star power, and Jeffrey had it. And thank God. I mean . . . he's won all these awards and shone a light on our community that might never have been acknowledged. I don't know. None of us do," I tried to explain.

And I explained it often.

It wasn't all of what I wanted to say, but . . .

~

There we were in the makeshift basement, surrounded by all my stuff in overflowing boxes, and take after take, Maura and I spoke, and chatted about men, and made jokes, and tried to put Davina's life back into some semblance of order. Then Joey called "Cut" from the back of the set.

"*GODDAMMIT!* WHAT THE HELL! I *CAN'T* FUCKING HEAR YOU, JOEY!" Jeffrey screeched. He walked over to some random boxes and pushed them over. I sat frozen, as I often did. And then I leaned in.

"Jeffrey. Stop!" I hissed under my breath.

It was the only sound I could make.

"Get in here . . . Jesus!" he yelled again.

Joey, arguably one of the most powerful humans in TV at that time, came onto the set and spoke quietly and with great restraint to Jeffrey as he stood in full Maura regalia. Jeffrey's red-hot temper shook the very foundations of the set. My feet tingled, and I wanted to throw up. Joey nodded, Jeffrey took a breath, and they found their way back up the pretend stairs and turned themself into a tight little ball, squeezing between a light and the camera lens.

"Okay . . . action. Let's go again," they called from over my shoulder.

And we did it again.

And that, for me, was it. I was done.

That would be the last time.

~

Joey's attempt to keep Jeffrey happy, or content . . . or at bay, was making me sick. Watching them take time out of their life and seeing them

be a director while policing the world where they were supposed to be a dreamer made me physically ill. Watching Trace's face fall whenever he'd pass, feeling the rumble from several Trans folk on set living in fear that Jeffrey would react in a way that would traumatize them—it all ate at me. I remember one of his assistants, a young man, sitting at a table while Jeffrey and I rehearsed a song we were to sing for a talent show in one of the episodes. His head was bent, and his spine curved. He was very young and had curly brown hair and a delightful appetite. He and I shared an addiction to sugar . . . real sugar, not that orange stuff they pass off as a sweetener for McDonald's tea.

"You okay?" I asked him during a break.

He looked up at me, his eyes watering and heavy. I saw myself clearly. I recognized the feeling.

"He's . . . he's trying to . . . yeah. Fuck. I'm fine," he stammered.

And there was that feeling again. Jeffrey's behavior worsened and grew more dangerous. It would happen on set and during interviews. I believed, and still do believe, both Trace Lysette's and Van Barnes' accounts of what happened to them. Some of the events I witnessed. Other allegations of abuse I believe because I know the two of them, and in a visceral way my gut tells me it was so.

I was worn out. I had been coming home from the last two seasons telling Chrisanne I needed to say something to someone, but I couldn't, and I didn't know why. I wanted out. I simply couldn't watch the star of the show hijack everyone else's life. No TV credit was worth it. I kept imagining the suffering experienced by my Trans family on the many days I wasn't on set. They had to endure his harassment and rage-filled outbursts time after time. The fact that Jeffrey behaved this way dressed as one of the Transgender community's role models was what appalled me most. In Maura, Jeffrey and Joey had created a character who radiated human decency and courage. While clothed in the outer form of this beloved icon, who had redefined a new generation of

Trans representation, this cisgender chauvinistic actor had abused and belittled the members of that community. This seismic chasm between the goodness of the character and the imperious meanness of the actor caused me regularly to vomit in my trailer before I'd head home each night.

This had to stop.

As season four wrapped, I was ready to tell Billy that I wasn't coming back. I had witnessed so much, heard so much, and experienced so much, but to my profound shame, I had continued to say nothing. And slowly, I began to fall apart, to spin out of control. I, too, began to feel nothing. And I was determined not to go through that again.

Once was enough.

Events moved faster than I did, however. Only a few short weeks later, a letter Van Barnes wrote privately on Facebook complaining of harassment at work by an actor was snatched up and plastered all over the internet. She then came forward publicly and named Jeffrey Tambor as the actor. Shortly after this, Trace Lysette came forward with her own allegations. Lawyers were engaged. Various attempts were made to save the show, the character, the Pfefferman world, and Maura herself. All failed. It all blew up. My soul was shredded. Oz, our Utopian world of tolerance and love and acceptance, lay in tatters. The curtain had been pulled aside and the sham revealed.

And I had said nothing.

I had to say goodbye to it all. We all had to. The new revolutionaries needed space—it was their turn. We had to step aside. We had told our stories to the universe of make-believe so that they could resonate more powerfully in the stratosphere of the real.

"The end of something is always the beginning of something else."

THIRTY-FIVE

The Light and Broadway

I was sitting in my hotel, stuffing a burger and fries down my throat like a drunken sailor. The best thing about room service for me, is room service for me. I was on a press tour for *Transparent*, and Amazon had put me up in a swanky hotel with long Celine Dion curtains that billowed when the outside exhaled.

Bored with flipping through the channels to find something to watch on a television set that needed its own zip code, I turned to my trusty laptop. I began to fall headfirst down the YouTube rabbit hole and came upon Elizabeth Taylor and her tireless work for the AIDS community. I watched video after video, tribute after tribute. I was mesmerized by an awards ceremony in the mid to late eighties, with everyone in shoulder pads, red ribbons, and more sparkles than a Liberace waistcoat. The MC, in black tie with perfect hair, was going on and on about how the honoree had all but single-handedly changed the HIV movement. He chronicled how she had brought us together, HIV positive as well as HIV negative, how she had worked endlessly not only for care and compassion for the sick and the dying, but for education of those who still believed this disease had a conscience and a plan.

I'd watched dozens of videos that evening, and I hadn't seen a tribute as touching.

As I sat back, chomping on the last of my burger, the man with the hair said, "So, ladies and gentlemen, please help me welcome the woman of the hour, Ms. Judith Light."

I dropped my sandwich and froze.

Judith walked into a solo spotlight and smiled. Her famous blond mane tousled and coiffed, she stood at this podium speaking about AIDS and how we needed to pay attention, we didn't have time, and how we all deserved a life—not a life half lived and over at twenty-two, but a life with children and friends and lovers and spouses and employment and health care. She spoke about change. She spoke about revolution, and she spoke about peace. This event had taken place at the height of the AIDS pandemic.

I wept. My heart was beating so fast it almost burst out of my chest. I thought about Ginger and Daphne and Gloria and Michael . . . and well, me. I thought about me. I didn't often do a lot of thinking about me and my AIDS, and so I sat there in that fancy hotel with the curtains flailing back and forth, and I thought about having AIDS. Sometimes the sun burned my retinas and I had bowel and breathing problems. These were all the things Larry had said would happen, and they had. I didn't think much about them. But there on my computer screen was the unambiguous reminder that I was sick and had been for decades, and here was a human who gave a shit and actually was doing something about it. I thought about working with this human who had been changing the dialogue ever since I was first diagnosed. I had seen Judith every day for months. We had had dinner, laughed, and talked about kids and husbands and the business. I had known she was a legend, but seeing her there on my laptop, speaking to a generation of queer folk in the middle of their collective last breath, and dreaming of the ones who were yet to listen, was almost too much. I felt foolish. I had no idea of

her close ties with my own life force. I had never realized that while I was hanging on by a thread, sweating and shitting myself, begging for a way out, she had been marching through the streets and using her fame to ignite a revolution. I did not know. I was not aware.

I was asleep while wide-awake.

And then her Light shone on me.

~

We were standing in a circle, the designers, the actors, the producers, the humans from the Manhattan Theatre Club, and our illustrious director, Dan Sullivan. I was surrounded by Tony- and Oscar-winning artists on the very first day of rehearsal for my very first Broadway show, *The Nap*, a comedy written by Richard Bean.

I played a one-armed Transgender mob boss who was trying to collect on a debt from a broken-down pool player, played by the wonderful Ben Schnetzer. My character is discussed for almost three pages prior to my entrance, so when I finally appear, it is dead center, and the action stops cold. In my white pimp suit, with my wooden arm clenched to my chest, I take a long look around the room, slowly, like John Wayne sneaking up behind the bad guy. I circle the gigantic pool table that filled our set and begin to speak.

It wasn't lost on me that I was a Transgender woman in her fifties standing on a Broadway stage portraying a Transgender villain, complete with a Joan Crawford entrance and truly fabulous lighting. I knew what this all meant, and I was very much aware of its significance.

Rehearsals were always filled with such joy and a glorious sense of ensemble. Dan's constant support, when none of us thought we were very good, was the key to this odd little comedy working.

And it worked. Thank God, it worked.

~

I am not a New Yorker. I get into an elevator and I start to shake. I go to a party with more than six people and I have trouble breathing. If there isn't space around me in my own home, a rage descends over me. Simply by walking outside, New York is all these things, and more. If you're born there and it makes sense to you, it's not something you notice. But when you're doing six shows a week, and you must walk down Forty-Second Street every day, the power of the city can smother you.

I loved New York.

And I hated New York.

I was crossing the street. As I moved, I passed a man lying on the ground. He was filthy. His shoes were in tatters, and his coat was so foul that I smelled him long before I saw him. He was motionless. I bent down and saw myself, asleep on the ground, with my gray suitcase for a pillow and my pants wet with urine. The world froze.

I turned to the right and there, flashing red and purple with sparkles, was *Head Over Heels*, the Go-Go's hit musical, and its star, Miss Peppermint. And I turned to the left, and there was the Steppenwolf crew along with Kate Bornstein in Young Jean Lee's dark comedy, *Straight White Men*. And we were all there, middle-aged, and Transgender. And I saw myself moving in and out of alleyways, trading sex for drugs and rummaging through garbage cans. And I breathed and I walked, and I saw Shanté and Ginger coming out of Club Victoria, and I saw Kelly hailing a cab outside the Baton. And I walked to the intersection of Forty-Sixth and Ninth, and I wept.

And I turned to the left and stopped, and I made my way through the crowd, and as I turned one last time, looming over Times Square were Amy and Jay and Kathryn and Gaby and Judith.

And me.

The Pfefferman family together for one final musical hurrah.

We were plastered across a billboard as long as a New York city block, and we were smiling . . . and we were free . . . and our arms were linked, and we were in midstep as we faced the road ahead.

And so my mood fluctuated: up and down, up and down—until opening night.

Joanne, Mom, our dear friend Deidre, and Chrisanne all went across the street to the opening night party at the famous Copacabana and, like a scene in a 1940s movie, waited for the reviews. When they came out, as I walked downstairs from speaking to the press, the look on my wife's face was enough to tell me I wasn't going to be drummed out of Broadway (the accent goes on the last syllable for this reading, please—Broad*WAY*).

"They loved you!" Joanne exclaimed, sitting back in her chair and crossing her arms in pride and an I-Told-You-So happiness.

"I knew it. I just knew it, sweetie," Deidre said, weeping and holding me tight.

"You're a hit! That's what they say, isn't it? You're a hit!" Mom yelled, hugging me.

But it was Chrisanne I was waiting for. As I had always waited, after every single opening night since I was fourteen years old. It was her reaction that mattered. I knew she was happy about the reviews, but I wanted to know how she felt.

She looked over at me, took my hand, held it close, and smiled. Her eyes twinkled. She leaned into me and whispered, "I'm so proud of you."

~

She barged into the rehearsal, hair still wringing wet from the scene where she learned Maura was dead. After the year-long wait to let the

smoke clear and our spirits renew following the very public outing of Jeffrey Tambor's abhorrent behavior on set, we were filming a musical version of our final season of *Transparent*. I was back in the arms of the Soloways and Amazon . . . which was, by now, selling books on the side.

"Can I help?" Judith asked simply.

Joey turned, surprised.

"Don't you want to rest for a minute, since you have another scene coming up?"

Judith shook her head.

We were crammed into a bathroom at the LGBT Center in downtown LA. It was hot and sticky, with little air circulating, and I was on the phone telling Shelly and the Pfefferman children that their Moppa had died, and that I had just found her. It was large, heart-breaking stuff the kind of thing I still wasn't very good at in my actual life but that was becoming a bit more familiar and a little easier to practice in my art.

In swooped Judith, half in costume with her Shelly wig askew.

"I'll go in here, Alex, and be on the phone."

She opened the door to a filthy bathroom stall, squeezed herself behind the cameraman, and sat on the toilet clutching her pretend cell phone. And for a ten-minute phone call, we improvised for almost half an hour.

We needed to tell the story. We *really* needed to tell the story. This is what I had been preaching to my students for all these years. It's not about you. It's about the story.

Judith could have taken the time to practice some self-care, but to Judith, we were all in this thing together. And when someone needed her help, she helped them. Whether they couldn't keep their food down because they were so sick that the act of eating was inconceivable, or they weren't being heard or taken care of by their government, she was there. And when I was the actor stuck in my fear and unable to speak, and the story itself was in danger of not being told, she stepped in.

Judith Light taught me: That's what you do. You don't pretend none of it is happening. You step in.

~

I passed by the house. Every night I would pass by the house, and I would swear I could hear the rumble and feel the ground shake. I would pass by the field where he'd been nailed to the pole. I would pass the poppies and the pail and the shovel and if I looked up, I could see the shimmer of a silver bubble hanging mysteriously in the air—empty and waiting for the magic.

As a rule, I always arrive very early to any theater.

My cavalier attitude to my initial audience with Uta Hagen had taught me a powerful lesson.

"Early is on time. On time is late" was my dad's call-time decree.

There is magic in this place. It's all around us, and even as I pass stage-hands pulling ropes and cleaning up, I'm filled with absolute wonder. I am in awe of the house because everything else is adorned in bright, bold colors, but the house, still lying on its side, is a stark black-and-white.

Soon, there will be a rumbling of voices and a smattering of footsteps as more artists enter the theater, and people will scuffle past me, waving hello and singing, reading, or taking out their ear things and plugging back into the music of our world. And Jamie, my dresser, will be in my dressing room to pour me into my first costume. With a delightful laugh, Jamie will gently shove me out onto the stage at the Gershwin Theatre for my second Broadway show, *Wicked*, where I played the very first openly Trans Madame Morrible, headmistress at Shiz University.

I was finally in Oz, and it was exactly the way I dreamed it would be.

I would come every night and sing the songs, make the magical gesture to conjure up the weather that brings that little girl and her dog into our world, and it made complete sense to me. I was still hanging

on to the edge of my bed at ten years old, holding Mimi's hand and eating peanut-butter-and-jelly sandwiches, waiting for the monkeys so I could sit just a little closer to her. It was just like that. Every night.

I would sit backstage and pull up the small stool that stood near Madame Morrible's fainting couch, and listen as Lindsay Pearce proclaimed her freedom and righteous indignation at being terrorized by the entire Oz community, singing to the top of the universe that she was flying free. She'd literally fly into the air, and every night without fail, I'd shatter. I could hear Scott screaming to get out, to reach up to her and grab her hand and beg to be pulled up there with her on her broomstick. "Just let me fly. Just once, like that."

I was bearing witness to the Ozians and slowly learning their lessons. As Madame, I was the cause of the chaos. I summoned the weather and I praised the distance between Glinda and Elphaba, but I learned that even as a villain, even when I did bad things to good people, no one is all bad. No one is *all* anything. The bullies and the hunters of my spirit and my vessel who had come after me in droves and haunted my nightmares seemed to get just a little smaller. Because you see, I was finally in Oz.

There was the Gold Ball I attended each performance. There was the Scarecrow I saw get ready every night, and as I passed his dressing room, I would tell him, "You're magical, you know."

There was Glinda with her crown and her ball gown and her misunderstanding of goodness. There was Elphaba, whom I got to love every night and be led by her miracle. It was real and it was happening inside and outside of Oz. Walking down the street was still a daily battle. But I had Oz. I was always on my way to Oz.

At the end of each show, I would arrive, having learned about Dorothy and her shoes. I rediscovered what goodness truly meant and learned each night that without forgiveness of both oneself and others, one cannot ever truly fly free. I would stand waiting for my final bow, and on a small screen stuck high above the rolling bench in the darkness

Alex as Madame Morrible in Wicked
(Photo by Joan Marcus)

of the wings was Dan Micciche, our maestro, our conductor, with his baton and his gestures flying up and down, cutting the air. There was music in his fingers, and the atmosphere changed as he rose and fell with each note. And out in the audience I could see Mimi, smiling, waving, getting ready to applaud long and loud for me as I walked out and claimed my space in Oz. And there was Chrisanne on opening night with her ear-to-ear smile. I saw the many souls I carried with me and the many I had yet to meet. I saw all the Trans kids who came backstage to visit me with their parents. And finally, I believed that I wasn't going to be thrown in jail when I walked down the street on my way home from the theater, and accepted that this new generation of queer people was the gift we'd been waiting for. The yellow brick road was opening wider, and there would be more room for all the humans, the bisexuals, the nonbinaries, and the ones who didn't want or need a name at all. We were all coming together with arms linked—skipping.

And I dreamed.

And as the final chords came crashing down, and I stood in this, my second Broadway show, my dad appeared in place of Dan on the tiny TV screen, like the crystal ball in the witch's castle. And he smiled, big and bright. His mighty arms lifted as he held the string section for a moment longer than they could stand, and with a blow powerful enough to shake the walls of the ancient theater, he threw his arms down, landing on a final note that flew swiftly into the heart space of every human in the audience.

And he looked through the TV and saw me clearly. For the very first time in my entire life, my father saw me.

And I saw him.

And my dad smiled at me as the thunderous applause that swelled from beyond Oz ran like a river at our feet—beautiful, kind, compassionate, and powerful. And I saw him and I wept, and I turned and made my entrance for the final curtain.

Every night.

Every show.

Every moment.

That was Oz.

And then, unexpectedly and without warning, darkness descended. People were getting sick. No one knew what it was or where it started. People dropped out of the show, and understudies replaced understudies. I got sick, and Lindsay got sick. People grew weak, and it spread across the world, and people were dying. I saw trucks on the news that were supposed to be for loading ice but were filled with the bodies of the dead. I was right back where it all began.

"You cannot stop. If you do, you die," Larry declared.

You cannot stop. But . . .

Broadway shut down. We all went home.

~

I never knew how any of it happened, this Broadway thing. It was only after I had returned to isolate during the coronavirus pandemic that I heard the story of how I had been cast in *The Nap*. I don't believe I should have been on Broadway at all. I should have died. Many, many times over. But Richard Bean had been stuck. He had written a Transgender role in his play about a pool player and his whacked-out family. He had added a Trans character because he had a real-life Transgender friend and wanted to honor them. But they couldn't find a suitable human to fill the role . . . so they had a meeting.

"Where are we going to find an over-fifty-year-old Transgender actress who can handle drama and comedy?" he had asked, sitting at a table filled with producers of the play and members of the Manhattan Theatre Club ensemble.

"Um . . . I know one," came a voice from the back. "I have her number right here."

It was Judith Light.

And the Light shone on me.

~

As this new plague infects our world, I don't now know what the next moment holds or where my yellow brick road will lead. I do know, however, as long as I try my best to listen to the teachers around me, I'll be led to places I have never been. When the student is ready, the teacher appears.

Once again, I am at the crossroads, wondering where to go next. I hear the Scarecrow say very plainly, "Some people find it pleasant to go both ways."

I believe if I keep exploring all the roads, with a touch of Light and a bunch of hope, I can move on. It may not be where I want to go, but it usually turns out to be the place I *need* to go. I've been searching for the wrong things, deluded by other people's values and my desire to fit in. But I have finally accepted that there is no need to search for Home.

I am already Home.

I have always been.

Alex and Chrisanne on vacation

G#D T@LKS

(A large old-fashioned tape recorder, the kind Scott used to set up in front of his TV to record The Wizard of Oz *in its entirety, is set up. A cassette tape lies next to it. It is unmarked.)*

Alex

I think I've got it.

G*D

Great.

Alex

I used to think it was like being a concierge at a hotel. That whatever I needed or thought I needed, I would call down for. I lived in expectation, you know? Like . . . get me this, bring me that, why aren't you getting me blah, blah, blah . . .

G*D

Uh-huh.

Alex

Now I think you're more like the maintenance crew. The kind that really wants to help. The kind that when you call, you better have at least tried the thing you wanted fixed first. Don't call down and demand stuff. They're busy. They're professionals. They have things to do for everyone in the hotel, and they are not at your beck and call. I used to think that. I used to think you were at my beck and call, and when you weren't, I wanted revenge. So, when I call now, I don't ask for shit to get fixed. I ask for guidance, and I ask to be led by what you want. Because even if I think it's broken, if I look hard at the pieces, there may be a gift in the brokenness. Is that right?

(There is a very, very long silence.)

Alex

I mean . . . is that closer to how it works . . . for me?

(The tape is picked up and placed in the old-fashioned recorder. It begins to turn with a small squeak, and plays Bette Midler's "From a Distance." Really loud.)

(And then God smiles.)

EPILOGUE

Dear Angels,

I am an accidental revolutionary. Everything that has ever happened to me has been one great big oops. I never meant to be on a TV show, and I had no idea I'd end up in the White House. I hadn't a clue what I was doing walking a red carpet for anything, let alone the Emmys, and appearing on Broadway with my huge image on an iconic billboard in Times Square was beyond my wildest dreams. It all happened because I wanted to tell stories.

The very first day we met, you were all sitting in a circle on a hard concrete floor in a rehearsal space at the Steppenwolf Theatre in Chicago. I think there must have been about fifty of you. All with your eyes on me like I knew what I was doing. I remember walking closer to you and thinking, "I can run. If I just turn around, I can run out the door and pretend to be sick, and certainly one of the other company members will take over. I'm an actor. I am not a teacher."

And ever since that day, I have never walked into any other classroom and thought anything different.

When I was so high on opiates that I could barely stand up, you did the work, and we laughed and played and wept together. When my marriage was falling apart, we created and spun around and kicked a few holes in the walls doing our triptychs. When other teachers walked into our room and were agog, mouths open, with absolutely no idea what any of this was as we ran, or walked in straight lines, or mumbled words and shattered into thousands of unrecognizable pieces, we celebrated. I'd walk into room after room and see you all, filled with fear and self-doubt, and within minutes, I'd be standing in the center of you screaming about the universe and its power and your power in it and your role in using that power.

There's something about you. There's some magical synergy that happens to me, and when I'm away from you for too long, I get very sad and there's an emptiness in my heart space. Sometimes, it feels like a mild heart attack. This doesn't happen when I don't act, or don't sing, or don't sashay down red carpets, or don't sit at fancy dinners. I miss you. I can't tell you that every single day is joyful and full of light and I bounce to work on my toes like Cyd Charisse. That would be a lie. But I can tell you that even on the days when my ass is dragging and I really don't want to see your faces waiting for me to continue this creative thing we're all in, once we're there in the opening circle, and we're gesturing and we're breathing and the world begins to spread out and we feel ourselves in

flight, I am released. I am utterly with you. I am present. I am not my past. I am here. And this is largely thanks to you.

And gradually, I have begun to understand what is happening. I am slowly shedding my disbelief in myself. I am no longer convinced that I have absolutely no idea what I am doing. I have begun to see you, and with this understanding a sense of belonging and a sense of ownership is emerging. I may not know everything, but I am beginning to know something.

If I'm completely honest, I began writing this book because I wanted to leave behind a trail of queer history—where we were, what I've lived through, and how it felt. I believed that I was writing to Chrisanne. I wanted it to be personal and true. But somewhere in the middle, when I didn't really know where I was heading, you crept into my consciousness. And I realized that all along, it was for you. I was writing to say thank you. I wanted to tell you things I couldn't tell you in class, so that if the things that happened to me began to happen to you, you'd recognize them. In our core we are the same. The breaking and falling apart and the worrying and the discovering and the exploring and the loving and the regretting and the forgiveness—all these emotions are human. I believe there is a divine sense of being in every single moment. How else could I have survived? Blind luck can only go so far. No one's that lucky. There has to be something else going on. Every day when I walk into class, you remind me that I can survive anything—that there is an inexplicable force at work. As you go through life,

you bring with you a glorious sense of self and the courage to reflect, fall down, and crumble. I have seen you time after time get right back up off the floor and try again. That's divine. That's power.

That's art.

We are the keepers of the human experience, and it is our job to manifest the stories of those who have gone before us. This way, no one ever really disappears. We must tell the stories of those we do not like, do not understand, and who do not like us, so that we can better understand how to live in a world where we can bless our differences and fight for our space. Throughout the years, I know there have been some of you who wouldn't touch me, couldn't come too near me, and were afraid of what I was and how I lived. I've always known that. And yet, you did not flee. Not one of you. So, you see . . . I learned from you. You gave me that gift. For you have always been my greatest teachers.

I need you to go out and do the thing. I need that. I need you to fly fierce and create newness. I don't need you to heal others or explain away your or other people's pain. I only need you to blossom in the brilliance that is your broken, beautiful path toward the telling of our tales. The healing happens after the work is over. And the wonderful thing is, the work is never over.

You taught me that too.

So, thank you, Angels. Thank you for seeing me and allowing me to see you. After all I've been

through, I have felt present in my openness with you, and that continues to heal me.

Rosalind Russell, one of my favorite actors, is rumored to have expressed it best:

"Acting is very simple, really. All you have to do is stand on a stage, in front of everyone, totally naked, and turn around, ve-e-e-ry slowly."

Allow yourself the freedom to revel in the shedding. Be seen. Fully. I am still practicing. And so together, we'll keep rehearsing this hilarious, accidental human experience. Let's just keep making it up . . . everyone else is.

And remember, Angels, that you are made of stardust, and because that is true, anything is possible.

Love,

Alex

2020

SPECIAL THANKS

Here is a group of humans. Some of them are related by genetics; others are related by spirit. All of them are family, and all of them profoundly changed me, and none of them were mentioned enough. I need you to know their names.

Sean Abley

Randy Amantes

Andrew Azzarello

Jacob Blankenship

Jim Blankenship

Kyra Blankenship

Dr. Dan Bowers

Jackie Cannon

Kristina Carlisle

Mike Checuga

Tom Colby

Rachel and Carolyn Collins

Patti Cakes

Jan Billings-Circle

Dana Douglas

Maya Douglas

Erica Duvall

Molly Glynn

The Hartman family

Cole Hartman

Kaden Kearns

Stephanie Kempka

Mike Kight

Karen Klausner

Elizabeth Laidlaw

Jeff Lucas

Joanne Macilraith

Maryanne Mayberry

Eric McCool

Jeff McKluskey

Ezra Michel

Matt Mishkoff

Amy Morton

Linda and Bill Nelson

Ryan, Julia, and Tracey Nelson

Monica Pannell

Sheri Payne

Jonathon Pitts

Nancy Reiff

Joey Ruggiero

Joanne and David Woolley

ABOUT THE AUTHORS

Alexandra Billings is an actor, singer, author, teacher, and activist who has appeared on numerous television shows, including Amazon's Emmy and Golden Globe Award–winning *Transparent*. Billings, who has been acting since 1968, has also performed across the United States in hundreds of plays and musicals. She made her Broadway debut in *The Nap* in 2018 and joined the cast of *Wicked* as Madame Morrible the following year. Every role played by Billings is thought to be a first for an out Transgender human. She is the recipient of countless awards and holds an MFA in acting. Billings has lived with AIDS since 1995, and her LGBTQ and HIV/AIDS activism stretches across the continent and culminated in her moderation of a panel on Transgender rights in America at the White House during the Obama administration. She twice married Chrisanne Blankenship, whom she met in 1976 in high school, where they costarred in *Twelfth Night*. Billings has not touched Shakespeare since then—and vice versa. For more information, visit www.alexandrabillings.com.

Joanne Gordon is an award-winning director whose accolades include five Drama-Logue Awards, a Los Angeles Drama Critics Circle Award, the Polly Warfield Award, and a Women in Theatre Red Carpet Award. Joanne is also an internationally renowned Sondheim scholar who has

directed many Sondheim works worldwide, including the first Chinese-language production of *West Side Story* in Beijing. Other directing highlights include *S/he and Me* (conceived for Alexandra Billings); *Indecent* (named best of the year by both of Saint Louis's major newspapers); *The Goat, or Who Is Sylvia?*; *Disgraced*; *How I Learned to Drive*; *Evita*; and *Next to Normal*. She is the author of *Art Isn't Easy: The Theater of Stephen Sondheim* and *Stephen Sondheim: A Casebook*, and she contributed to *The Oxford Handbook of Sondheim Studies* and the *Sondheim Review*. Gordon is equally well known for her dramatizations of the work of Charles Bukowski. She received her PhD from UCLA.

Praise for *This Time for Me*

"Alexandra Billings's extraordinary memoir moves from nightmarish, traumatic horror to a magical journey toward self-worth and artistic flowering. Alexandra has given us a treasure of a book full of wit, insight, and love."

— Charles Busch, actor, playwright, cabaret entertainer, novelist, and
screenwriter

"Alexandra's warmth, humor, perseverance, and compassion shine through on every page of *This Time for Me*. The arts reflect and shape our world every day, and Alexandra has been at the heart of Hollywood's long-overdue Trans revolution. Alexandra brings you along for her moving and human journey of hope undeterred by hardship, grace in the face of indignity, and the kind of radical love that fosters real change—both for ourselves and our society."

— Delaware state senator Sarah McBride, author of
Tomorrow Will Be Different: Love, Loss, and the Fight for Trans Equality